IMAGES
of America
SLATON

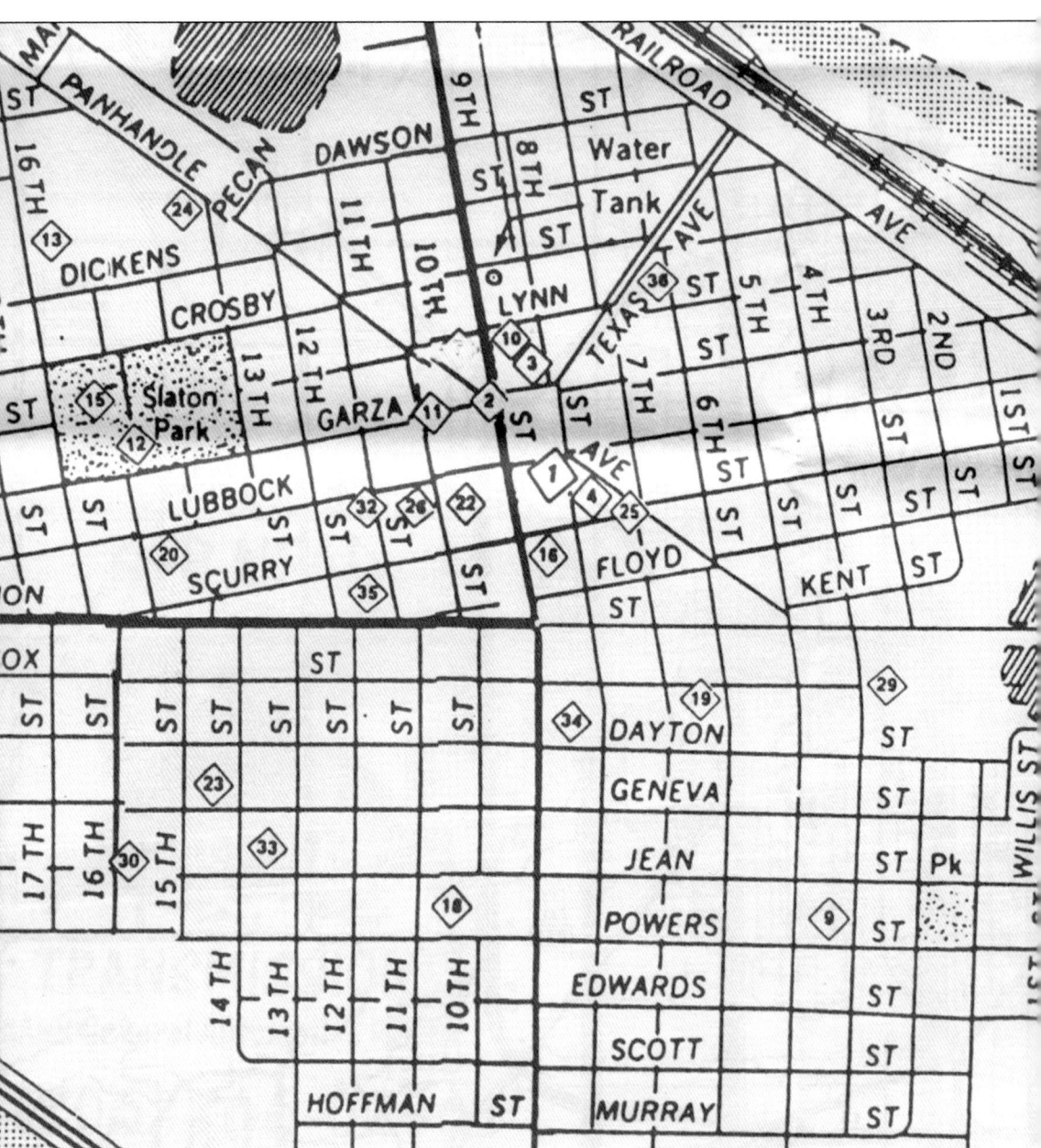

Slaton was laid out in the shape of a wagon wheel—similar to the layout of Washington, DC—based on an idea that came from Atchison, Topeka & Santa Fe Railway chief engineer J.W. Walter, a Chicago native. (Courtesy of Alton Kenney.)

On the Cover: This photograph was taken on June 10, 1955, and shows Slaton's first diesel locomotive sitting in front of the Harvey House. (Courtesy of the Slaton Harvey House and the Slaton Railroad Heritage Association.)

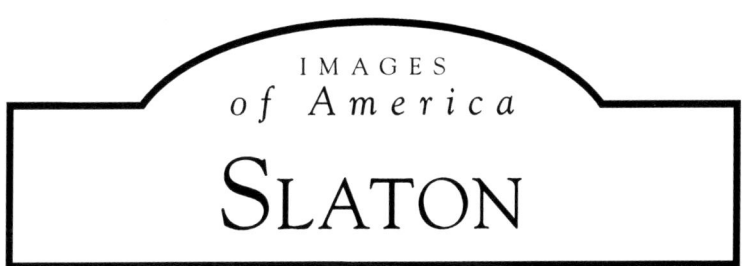

IMAGES
of America
SLATON

Cathy Whitten

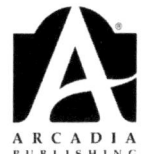

Copyright © 2015 by Cathy Whitten
ISBN 978-1-4671-3351-7

Published by Arcadia Publishing
Charleston, South Carolina

Printed in the United States of America

Library of Congress Control Number: 2015941073

For all general information, please contact Arcadia Publishing:
Telephone 843-853-2070
Fax 843-853-0044
E-mail sales@arcadiapublishing.com
For customer service and orders:
Toll-Free 1-888-313-2665

Visit us on the Internet at www.arcadiapublishing.com

This book is dedicated to those who have worked to preserve the history of Slaton through pictures and stories, as well as the early pioneer families of Slaton and the dreamers who made Slaton a reality.

Contents

Acknowledgments		6
Introduction		7
1.	Slaton and the Santa Fe Railway	9
2.	The Harvey House	29
3.	Boomtown Is Born	41
4.	Memory Lane	71
5.	Celebrating Success	95
6.	A Picture Paints a Thousand Words	105
7.	Slaton, 104 Years Strong	117

ACKNOWLEDGMENTS

I would like to thank the Kenney family, and especially Alton Kenney for the use of his extensive picture collection and his tireless efforts to preserve the history of Slaton. All images presented in this book appear courtesy of Alton Kenney unless otherwise noted.

In addition, thank you to the Harvey House and Slaton Railroad Heritage Association and Jolene Fondy and the Slaton Museum for your help as well as the use of your images. A big thank you to Kevin Stillman of the Texas Department of Transportation (abbreviated throughout the text as "TxDOT") for use of his images as well. Thanks to Don Caldwell, and also to the T.G. Caraway Collection, Crossroads of Music Archive, Southwest Collection/Special Collections Library, Texas Tech University. Thanks to Jeremy Boreing and Junior Vasquez for the pictures from their film, *The Arroyo*.

If it were not for these people, and others who have kept priceless photographs of Slaton's extensive history and the stories that go along with them, this book would not have been possible. The older I get, the more history means to me and fascinates me. I have really enjoyed the journey of discovering and learning more about Slaton while working on this book. I have come to appreciate even more those who came before us and paved the way by accomplishing their dreams—no matter the cost or sacrifice.

I have done my best with the resources I have to capture the history of Slaton through a variety of pictures and words documenting a sensational Santa Fe Railway town. There is no way to include every picture and every person who has made a difference in the history of Slaton, but my hope is that this book will give readers an overview of a great Texas town that has survived and succeeded for over 104 years. As readers flip through the pages of this book, it is my goal to inspire them to feel a sense of nostalgia and come to appreciate history even more.

Whether you are from Slaton or not, this book is for you. It reminds us that each day counts, and that history will continue to live through the pictures, memories, and stories that we can continue to enjoy for generations to come.

Thank you to Arcadia Publishing for giving me the opportunity to tell the story of Slaton, Texas.

Introduction

In the mid-1800s, a pathfinding expedition led by R.B. Marcy of the US Army included a journey through the plains of Texas. Marcy described this land as an ocean of treeless, desolate waste of uninhabitable solitude where no man could permanently live. The area he was referring to included land that would become the railroad and agricultural Texas town named Slaton, located in West Texas on the South Plains of the Llano Estacado, in the southeast corner of Lubbock County. Slaton is considered a suburb of Lubbock, which is only 15 miles away.

The State of Texas first patented the original townsite to Eli Stinson and J.I. Case on September 1, 1879; six years later, they sold it to Western Land and Livestock Company. This transaction began the IOA Ranch, which was sold to J.W. Kokernot and H.L. Kokernot in 1901. The Kokernots have received credit for much of the settlement of Slaton in the first decade of the 20th century.

The Kokernots sold to J.C. Phillips, who then sold to the Atchison, Topeka & Santa Fe Railway (Santa Fe) when Santa Fe sent vice president W.B. Storey Jr. from Chicago to purchase the land for establishing the town; the latter transaction was completed on April 15, 1911.

The land of South Park Addition, an early add-on to the original townsite, had been patented in 1879 to Cunningham H. Huston, the assignee of the Houston, East & West Texas Railway (HE&WT). In 1900, it was transferred to the St. Louis Cattle Company for just $1 per acre, and later became the Hat-H Ranch owned by A.B. Robertson and Winfield Scott. This area became the South Park Addition when Robertson deeded the land to L.A. Wells in 1910.

Slaton owes its existence to the Santa Fe Railway. Thundering from coast to coast, the Santa Fe needed a new division point for servicing trains traveling through Northwest Texas. The official opening date of Slaton, when it became a town, was June 15, 1911. People came by horse and buggy, team and wagon, train, and on foot to purchase plots of land. J.F. Utter of Amarillo was the first conductor to bring passengers by train to Slaton. On that hot summer day, many brought their own lunches and ate under shade they created with wagon sheets or under a mesquite tree. Others ate in the cafe, which was just a boxcar the railroad had provided near where the depot was later located. Prominent railroad officials came from as far as Topeka, Kansas, as well as many who were looking to fulfill their destiny by making Slaton their new home. Many lots of land were sold that day to some of the first citizens of Slaton, which was nicknamed "Tent City" because residents lived in tents while small frame houses and businesses were built. Slaton was named after local rancher and banker O.L. Slaton, who was instrumental in getting the Santa Fe Railway to come through the area.

Santa Fe chief engineer J.W. Walter, from Chicago, designed Slaton in the style of Washington, DC, which was laid out in a wagon-wheel pattern. The streets radiated like the spokes of a wheel from city hall. Streets go outward from each corner of the square into residential and business sections of town. The population grew rapidly, and Slaton eventually serviced four daily northbound and southbound trains between Amarillo and Sweetwater. With the Slaton depot, the town became the center of the largest division in the Atchison, Topeka & Santa Fe Railway. Passenger and freight service became central to the economy.

In 1876, Fred Harvey created the Harvey House chain by partnering with the Santa Fe Railway, which paid $75,000 for the construction of the Harvey House in Slaton. The Harvey House was well known for its food and hospitality, including the hostesses called "Harvey Girls." Some have said that the Harvey Girls helped settle the West with their strong character, education, and good manners. Some came from poor backgrounds but were encouraged to take pride in their appearances while working as Harvey Girls. They were between 18 and 30 years of age and are perhaps the lasting legacy of Fred Harvey. These women were memorialized on film in the 1946 MGM movie *The Harvey Girls*, starring Judy Garland. The Harvey House in Slaton consisted of a library and reading room, card room, offices, living quarters, and 18 bedrooms and toilets. It had electricity and hot and cold water.

As Slaton grew, businesses opened, including a cotton gin and mill, hotels, lumber and hardware companies, banks, and grocery stores. Cotton farming has always been one of the main industries of Slaton; cotton was grown in the area even before the actual town began. In fact, by August 1911, cotton acreage in Slaton was estimated to be 4,000, with a half-bale per acre listed as the expected yield. A year later, the Post City Cotton Mill began production with capital of $50,000—this helped the cotton industry in Slaton.

With the development of railroads and farming, banking also became a big industry at this time. First State Bank opened with officers J.S. Edwards, O.L. Slaton, and J. Foster Scott. Slaton State Bank, originally called The Paul Bank, was opened by the Paul family, who had previously been in the banking business in Amarillo. Both banks collapsed during the Depression in the 1930s. Later, J.S. Edwards opened Citizens State Bank. By the end of 1911, Slaton had its first motion-picture theater and a weekly newspaper, *The Slaton Journal*, later known as *The Slatonite*. W.P. Florence was influential in opening public schools in Slaton, and the first one opened on October 16, 1911, with 50 pupils. At first, school was conducted in the Methodist and Baptist churches. At Florence's school, he was the principal and had one teacher assisting him—Miss Howell, from Tahoka. On March 9, 1912, the public school incorporated as the Slaton Independent School District, which included almost 100 sections of land.

In June 1911, the Methodists became the first denomination to organize in Slaton, followed by the Baptists, Presbyterians, Lutherans, and Roman Catholics. Slaton's social life centered around home and church. The town incorporated on October 26, 1923.

In 1929, the Sisters of Mercy were invited by Rev. T.D. O'Brien to erect a hospital in Slaton. The city donated two blocks, valued at $3,300, plus a cash bonus of $20,000. The four-story Mercy Hospital building was completed in November 1929 for a cost of $125,000. The hospital could accommodate 44 beds and 34 patient rooms. The purpose of the hospital was to offer care, nursing, and relief to the sick and injured and to make no distinction based on race or national origin when providing services.

Slaton, founded in 1911 as a major hub of the Santa Fe Railway, is now 104 years old and still going strong. The people who reside in Slaton exemplify the spirit and character of our great state of Texas and of those who came before us. Some who call Slaton home come from families who were here from the very beginning, and some are here because they chose to make Slaton their home. The story of Slaton is one of success, struggle, prosperity, endurance, and a community that will continue to thrive for centuries to come.

One

SLATON AND THE SANTA FE RAILWAY

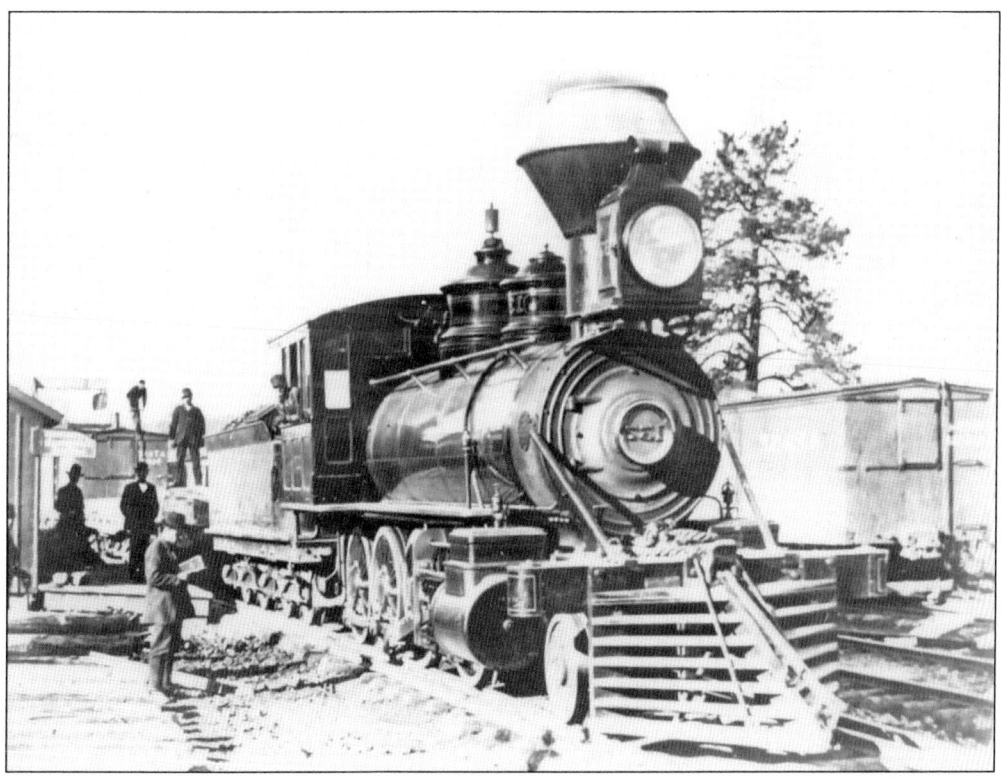

Pictured is a Santa Fe Railway locomotive constructed in 1905. Slaton came to be because of the Santa Fe. The railroad company needed a site to serve as a division point to service trains traveling through northwest Texas. After the Santa Fe purchased the Slaton townsite on April 15, 1911, representatives of the railroad began establishing the town. The future was promising. The Santa Fe brought with it new opportunities, and Slaton became a destination for many people. Builders had trouble keeping pace, and the town filled with land agents. The railroad constructed a two-story reading room for Santa Fe employees next door to the Harvey House. The town thrived on the railroad and agriculture, and Slaton eventually became the largest division in the Santa Fe system.

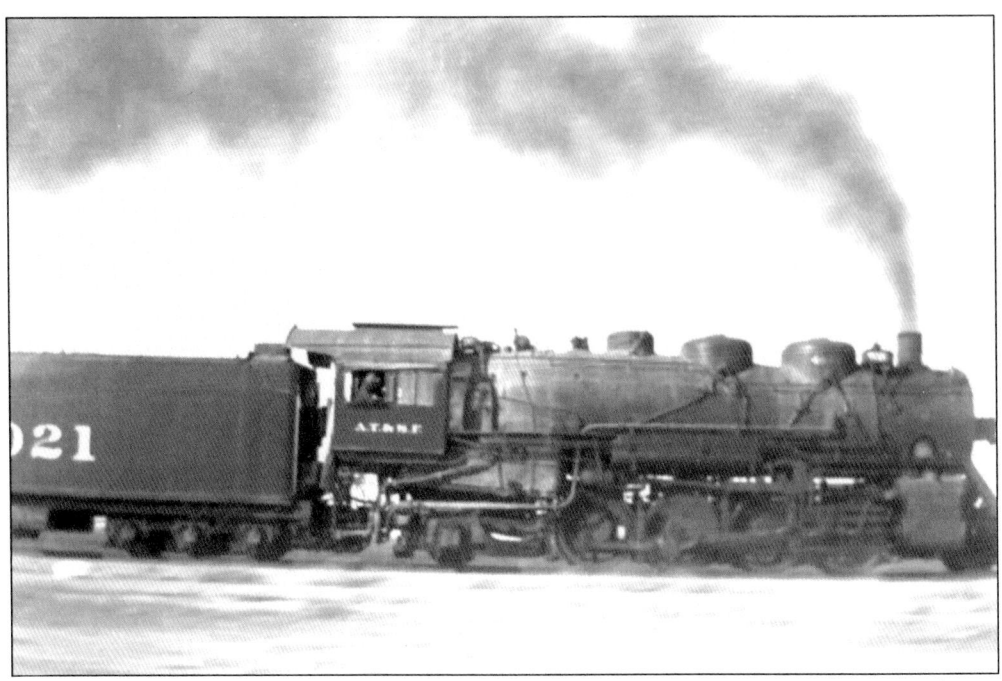

The Santa Fe Railway brought with it an adventure for many who decided to settle in Slaton, one of the flattest areas in the world, where people believed that the land was too barren and desolate for any humans to permanently live. However, Slaton proved to be a great place to call home. The town was named in honor of O.L. Slaton, a rancher and banker who promoted railroad construction. At first, the area was referred to as Tent City, because the new residents lived in tents while houses and buildings were being constructed. Slaton officially "opened" on June 15, 1911, and rapidly grew as Santa Fe employees made their homes here. These pictures may stir up emotional memories of the lonesome sound of the train rolling down the track and the whistle blowing across the West Texas skies as the train takes passengers and freight to their destinations while traveling through Slaton.

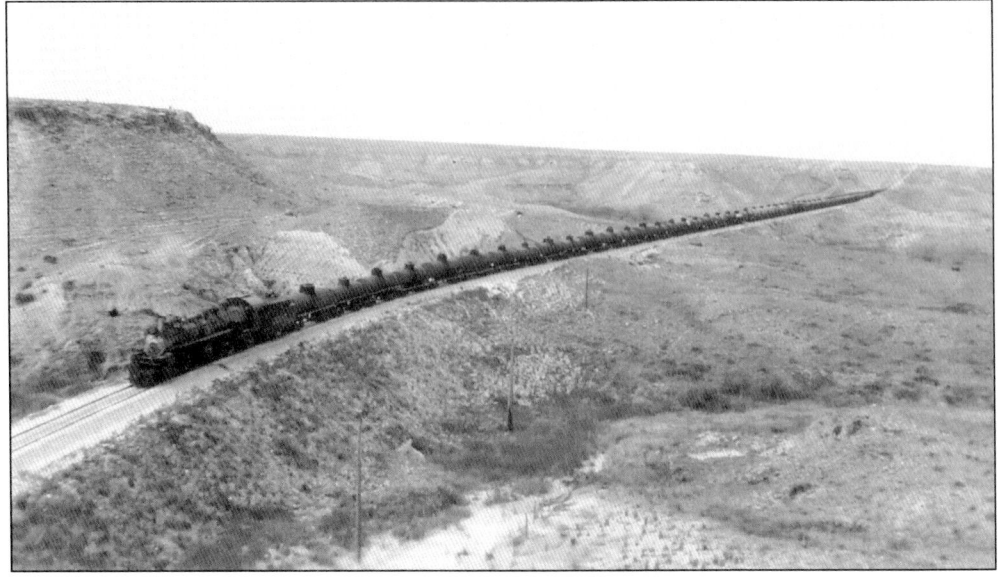

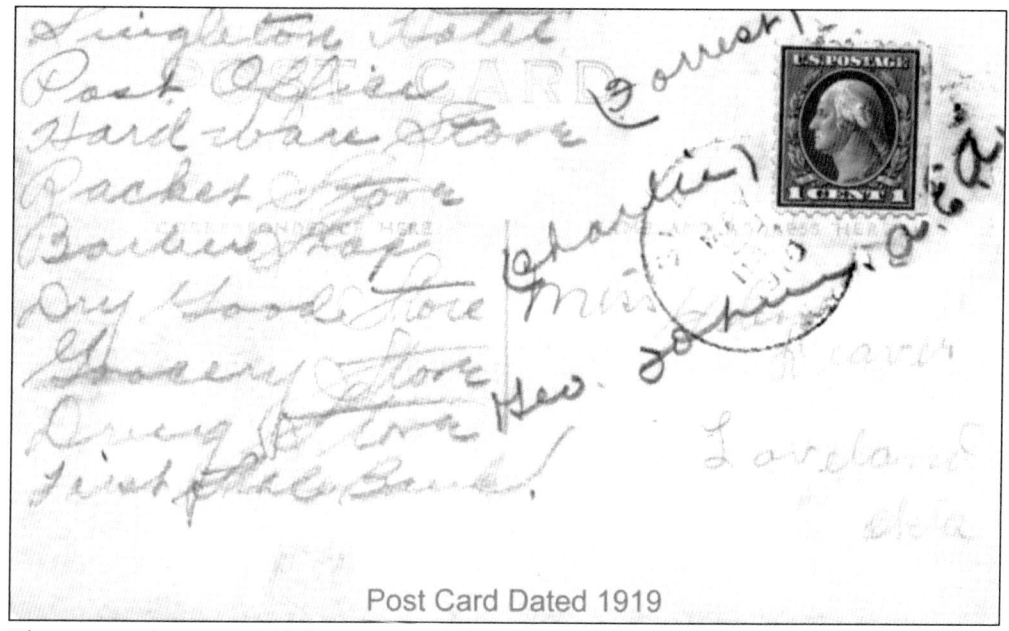

Post Card Dated 1919

This postcard, sent to Oklahoma in 1919, lists some of the businesses in Slaton at the time, including the Singleton Hotel, a post office (note that postage was only 1¢ in 1919), a hardware store, a barbershop, a dry-goods store, a grocery store, a drugstore, and a bank.

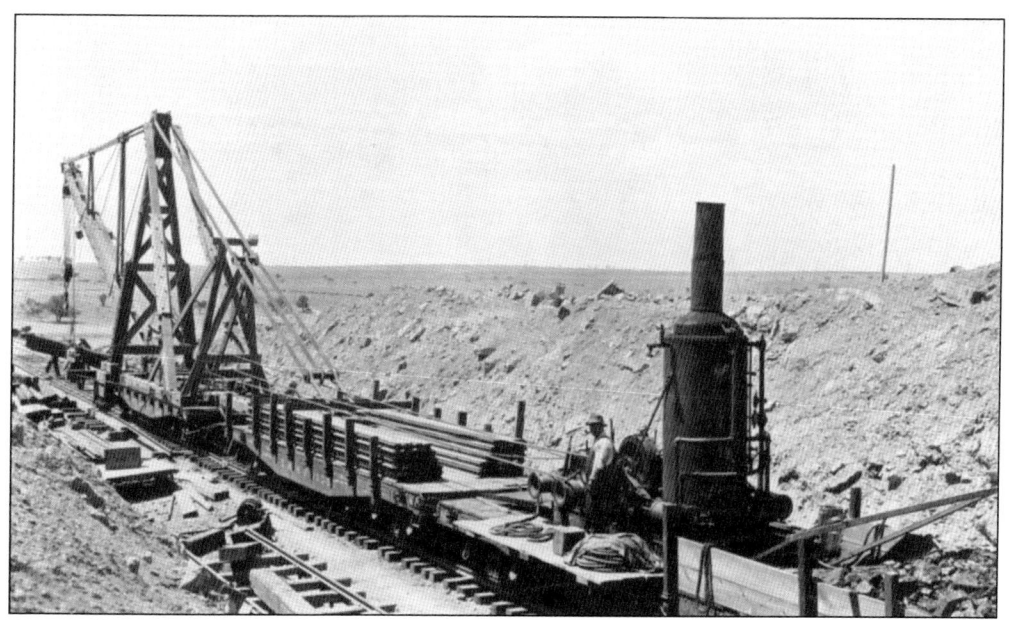

Pictured here is a rail-laying machine built in 1910.

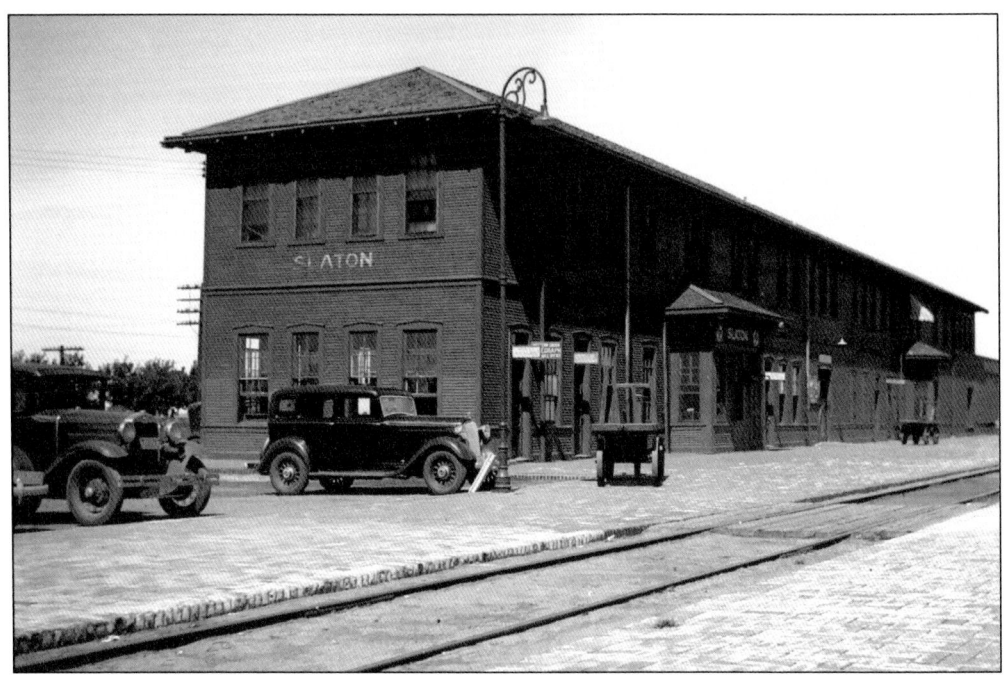

This 1920s image shows the Slaton depot, located near the center of Texas Avenue. In an article published in the *Fort Worth Star-Telegram* in November 1921, R.A. Baldwin stated that Slaton boasted the largest population in Texas for its age; the population at that time was roughly 3,000.

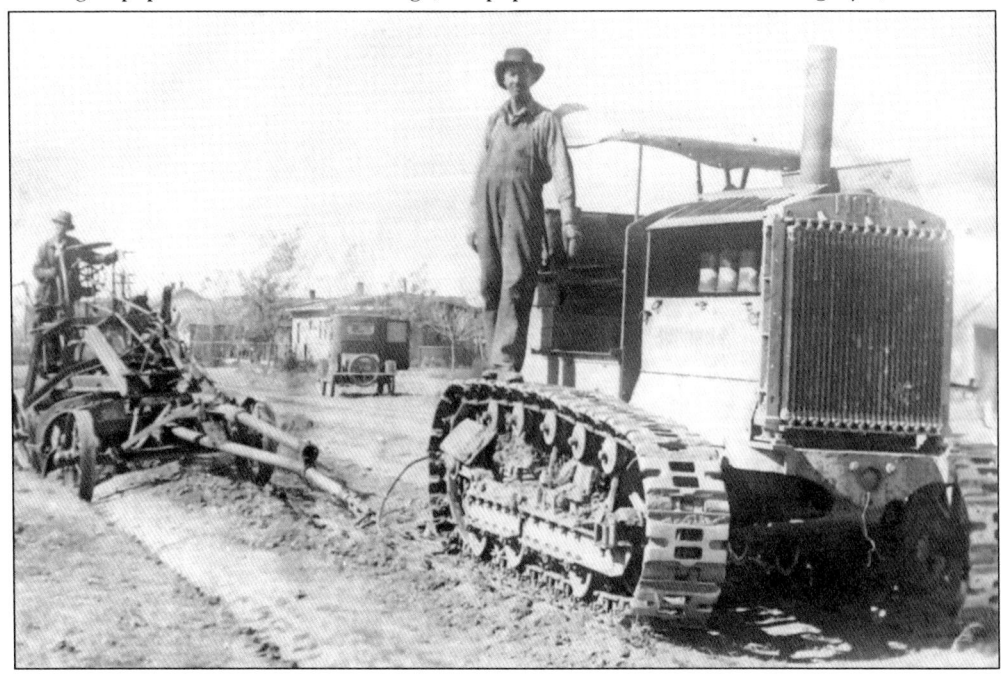

William Edward Kercheval, pictured here, was born on October 24, 1879, in Indiana. He moved to Slaton in 1919 and was employed by the Santa Fe Railway until a strike in 1922. He then worked for Lubbock County, driving a Caterpillar used for road construction, and later worked for the City of Slaton.

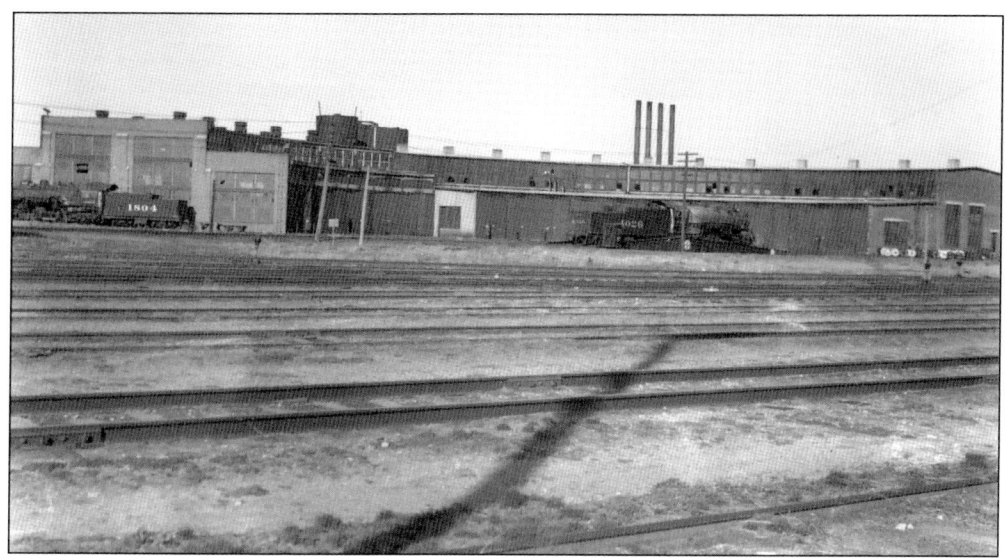
This picture was taken from the northwest side of the Slaton roundhouse in 1912. Roundhouses, used to service locomotives, were large circular or semicircular structures—hence the name.

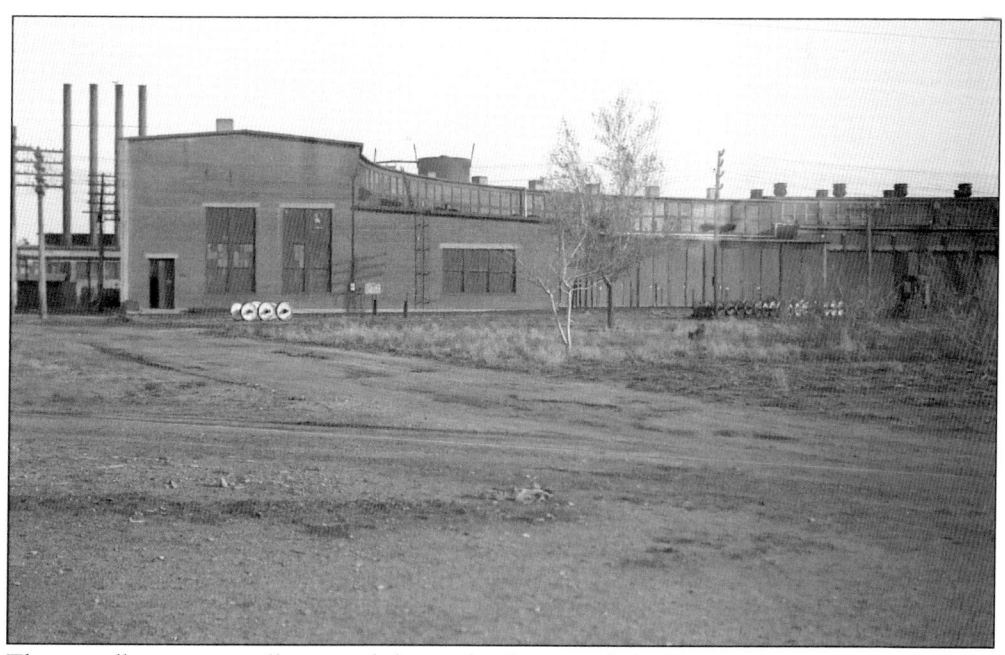
The roundhouse—as well as switch lines, the depot, and the Harvey House—contributed to Slaton becoming the center for area rail transport in the early 20th century.

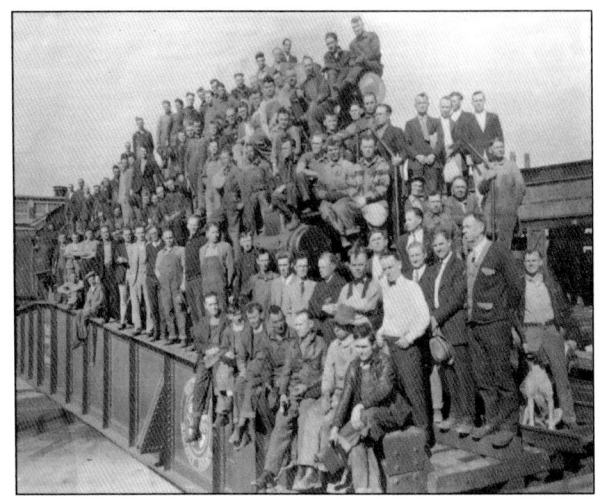

This 1933 photograph shows the Slaton roundhouse crew on turntables. Turntable crews would turn the rolling stock, usually locomotives, back toward the direction from which they came. In the early 20th century, most locomotives could not run for extended periods or as fast in reverse, so turntables were necessary to turn locomotives around for return trips.

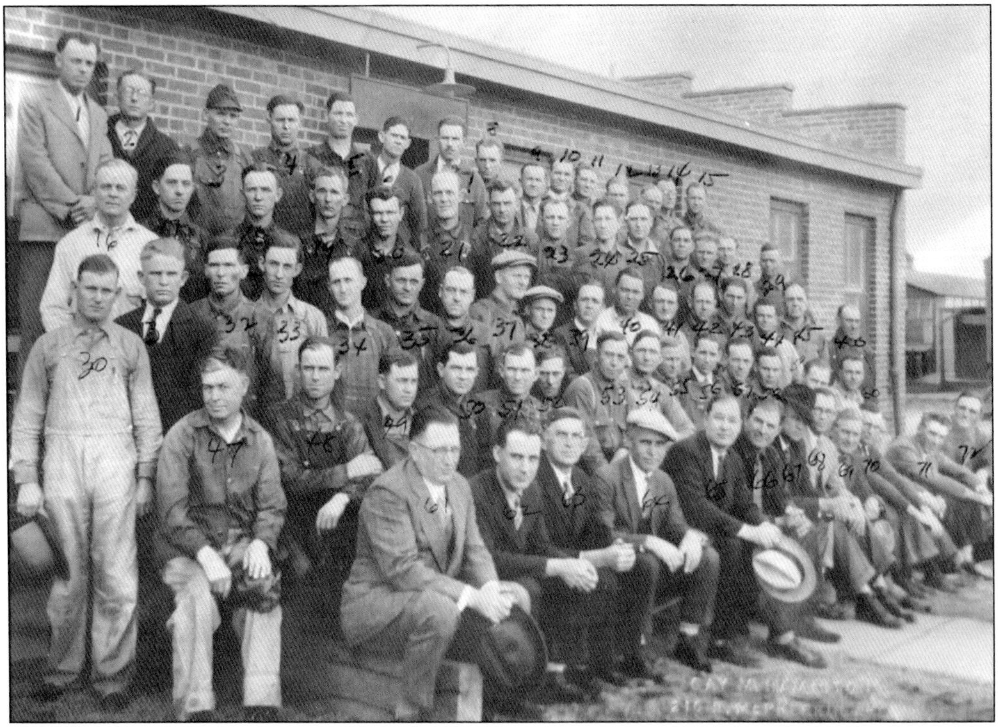

Pictured here are, from left to right, (first row) ? Nicholson, R.B. Bechtel, Joe Lemon, Joe Haynes, unidentified, Ben Cooper, ? Oliver, Harry Tunnel, ? Neihoff, unidentified, L.B. Hagerman, and Woody Tudor; (second row) C.E. Wardes, Leo Wendell, J.E. Fater, Milton Wheatley, Alex Shelton, L.D. Splawn, Carl Cramer, Bob Swafford, Cotton Gerron, ? Robertson, A. Dennis, C.E. Smith, Geo Lauderbauch, and Brownie Clark; (third row) Jim George, ? Fortes, ? White, unidentified, Avery Gregg, Luther Gregory, Fat Turneo, Geo Wilinesmier, unidentified, Howard Pinkey, Roy Ely, unidentified, Geo Culwell, two unidentified, M.A. Grant, and unidentified; (fourth row) Shorty Clark, unidentified, Frank Harvey, A. Morris, ? Halloman, Jo Jenson, Jack Waldrip, J.E. Powers, E.J. Kenney, Bevis Hanna, John Hartsfield, and three unidentified; (fifth row) H.L. Carruth, C.R. Thompson, Mark Willeair, Ernest Robertson, Nick Deavers, Charley Martin, Hugh Bryan, M.L. Taylor, Jess Young, John Nealston, J.F. Baldin, two unidentified, Geo Cooper, and unidentified.

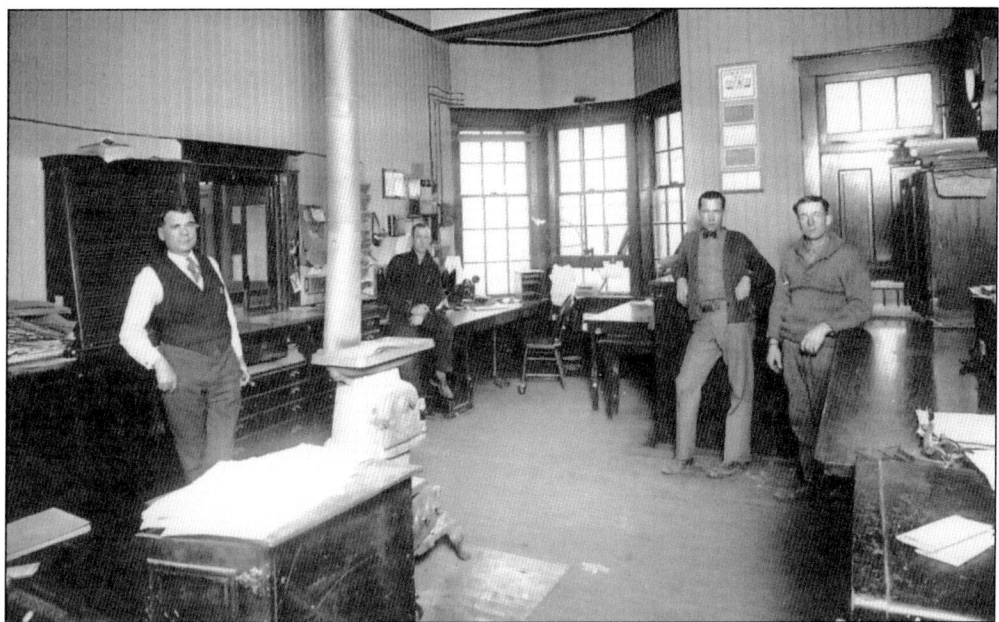

This 1920s photograph shows personnel inside the Santa Fe Railway depot in Slaton. The depot was a central point in Slaton in those days, and the employees who worked there were very important. The depot was the first or last place that most visitors experienced, and in the days of the horse and buggy, it gave many people a means to communicate with the outside world. Trains brought news, merchandise, and mail, and telegrams were dispatched from the depot. The stationmaster took care of everything—selling tickets, handling baggage, and sending telegrams.

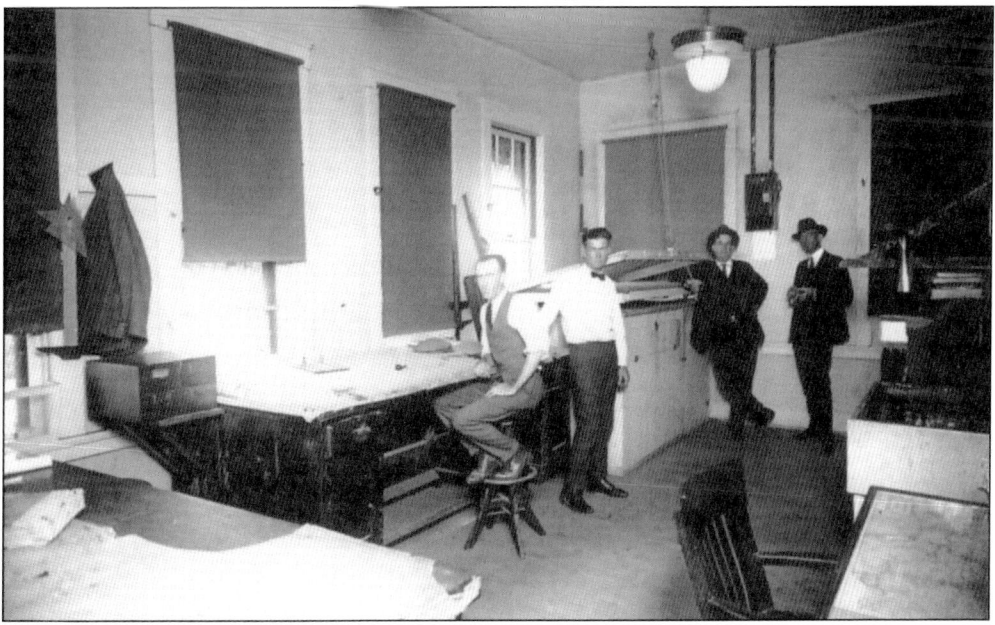

This is another 1920s photograph showing the inside of the Santa Fe depot. The 1920s were a time of growth for Slaton and the Santa Fe; the railway built an addition to the Santa Fe office building, donated three lots to be used for the waterworks system, gave seven lots to public schools for more playgrounds, and even donated 22 acres for the county park built in the west part of town.

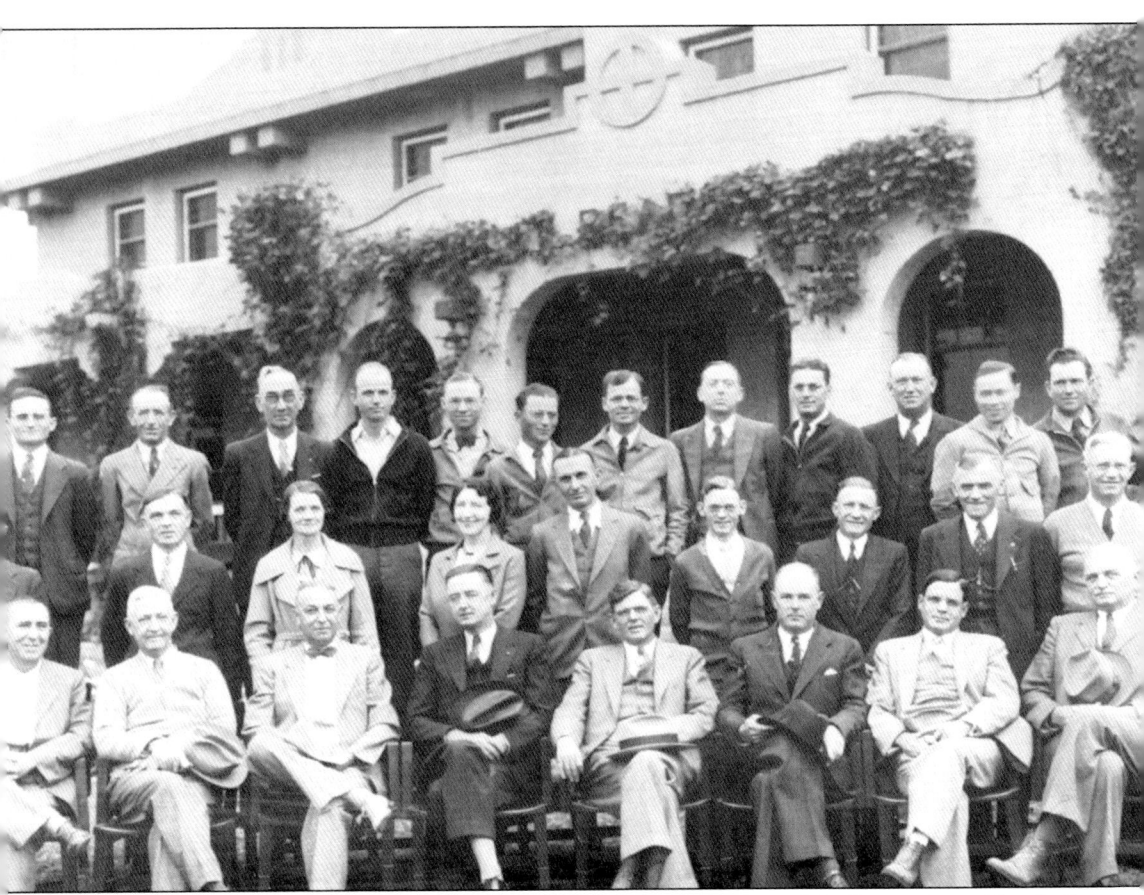

This picture was taken in front of the Santa Fe Reading Room in 1933. Pictured are Claude S. Cravens, superintendent of the Slaton Division of the Panhandle & Santa Fe Railway Company, and his staff. They are, from left to right, (first row) W.O. Bowen, E.K. Keefer, Kirby J. Brown, Floyd A. Baker, Cravens, C.W. Taylor, T.A. Blair, and J.A. Klasner; (second row) C.F. Stanford, Gus Seal, Jessie Prosser, Olive Rooney, B.W. Jones, R.M. Shepard, Claude Young, M.J. Nelson, and John E. Nichols; (third row) O.R. Satterlee, S.A. Peavy, R.A. Swanner, Bill Stotts, Dayton Eckert, Johnny Reynolds, J.W. Bagby, Basil Brady, A.J. Butler, C.L. Tanner, R. Haas, J.B. Huckabee, and Charlie Suite. (Courtesy of the Slaton Museum.)

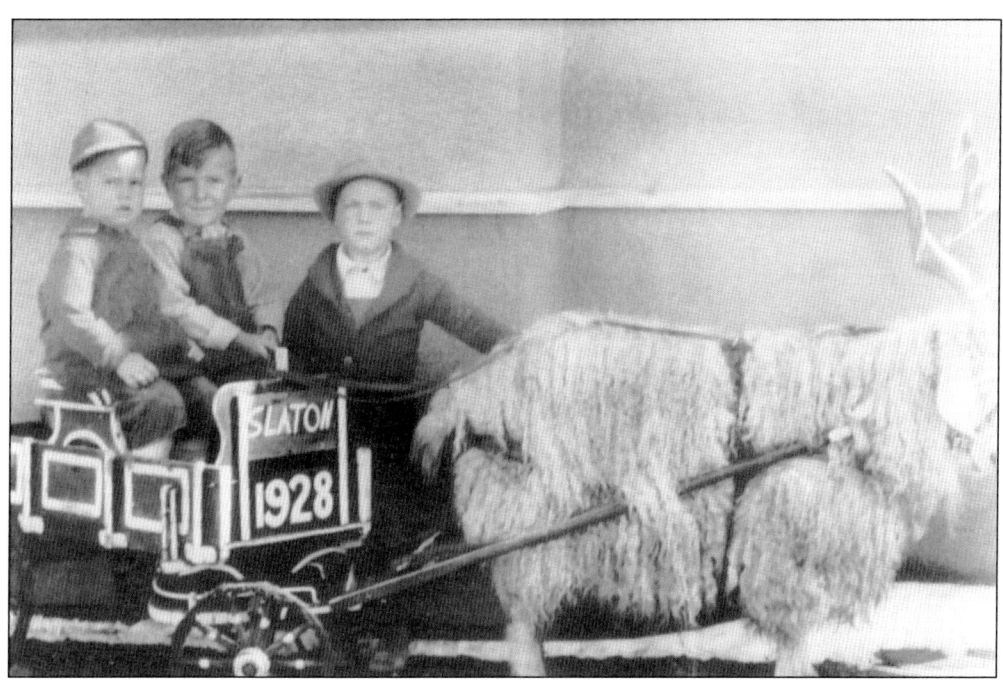
This photograph from 1928 includes Bill Green, Lee Bickerstaff, and an unidentified young man. (Courtesy of Slaton Harvey House and Slaton Railroad Heritage Association.)

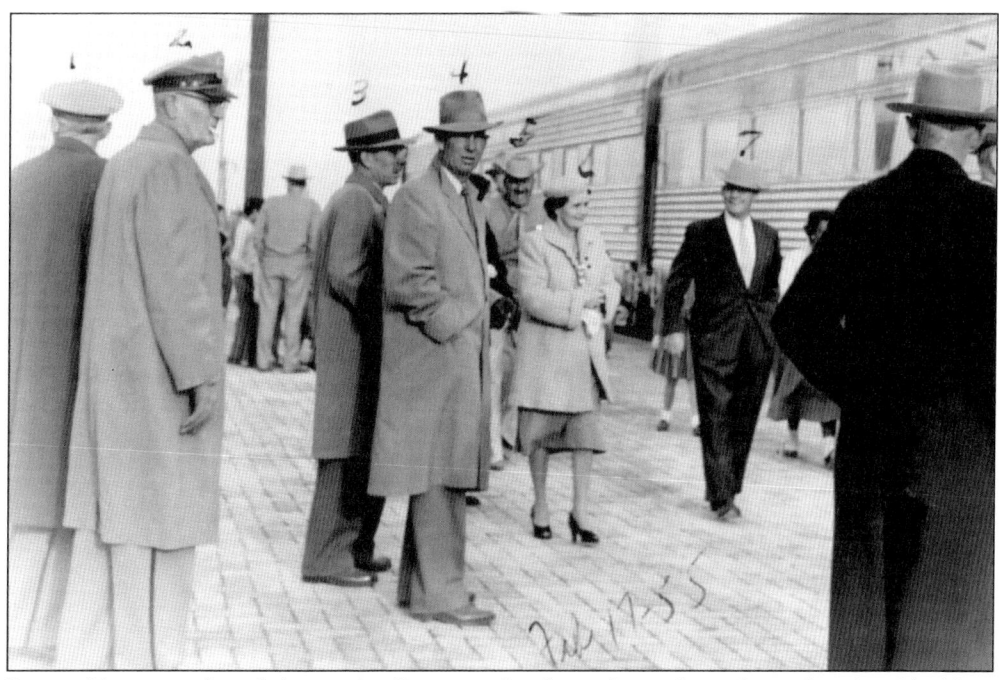
Pictured here are, from left to right (foreground only, with numbers above their heads), Alvin White, E.A. Gentry, ? Gregsby, E.A. Nelson, Charley Yeats, Ethel Young, and C.C. Young.

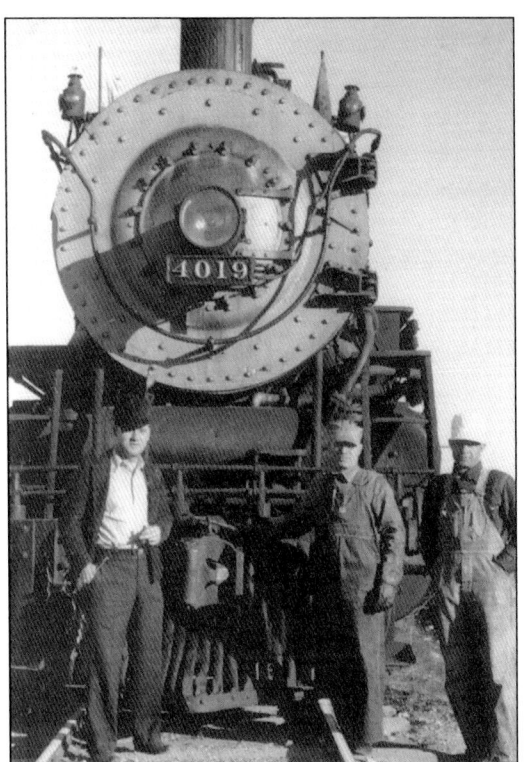

Pictured here in front of Engine No. 4019 are, from left to right, Clarence Heaton, Joe V. Bickerstaff, and an unidentified man. (Courtesy of Slaton Harvey House and Slaton Railroad Heritage Association.)

This 1944 photograph appeared in an issue of *The Santa Fe Magazine* (a publication for Santa Fe Railway employees) and features the Slaton Division personnel, including Olive Rooney, personal record clerk; C.L. Suit, senior clerk; Vivian Williams, file clerk; Christine Myrick, steno clerk to C.D.; Francis Sikes, mail clerk; Eunice McDonald, steno to C.C.; Jessie Prosser, clerk to general foreman and roadmaster; Donna Sanner, stenographer; Joe Wicker, payroll clerk (US Navy); Gus Seel, trainmaster's clerk; John Nichols, transportation clerk; and Norbert F. Young, chief clerk.

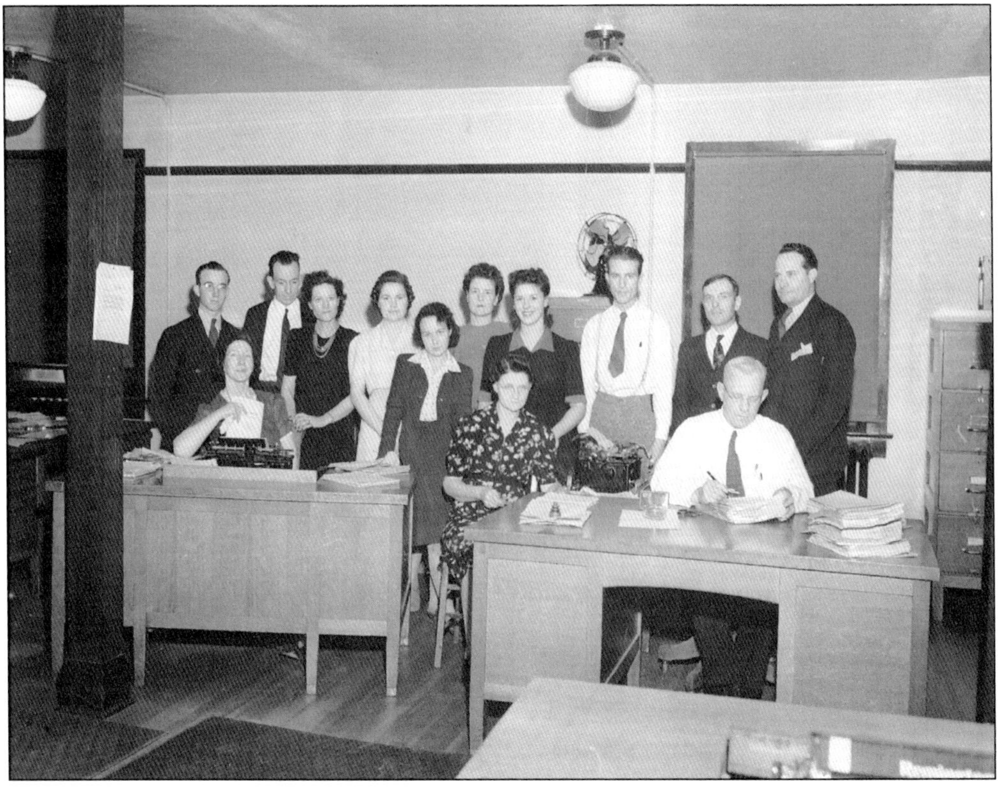

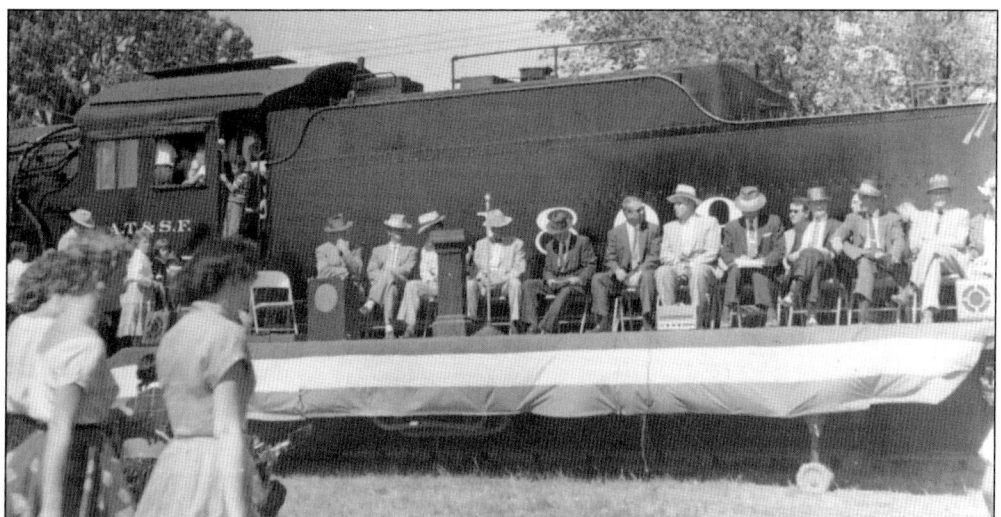

This is the 1955 presentation of the first diesel engine in Slaton. Because of the Santa Fe Railway's long stretches of routes that traveled through places without easy access to water, the railway became one of the first buyers of diesel locomotives for freight service. The Santa Fe was also known for its passenger trains and the eating houses and dining cars operated by Fred Harvey.

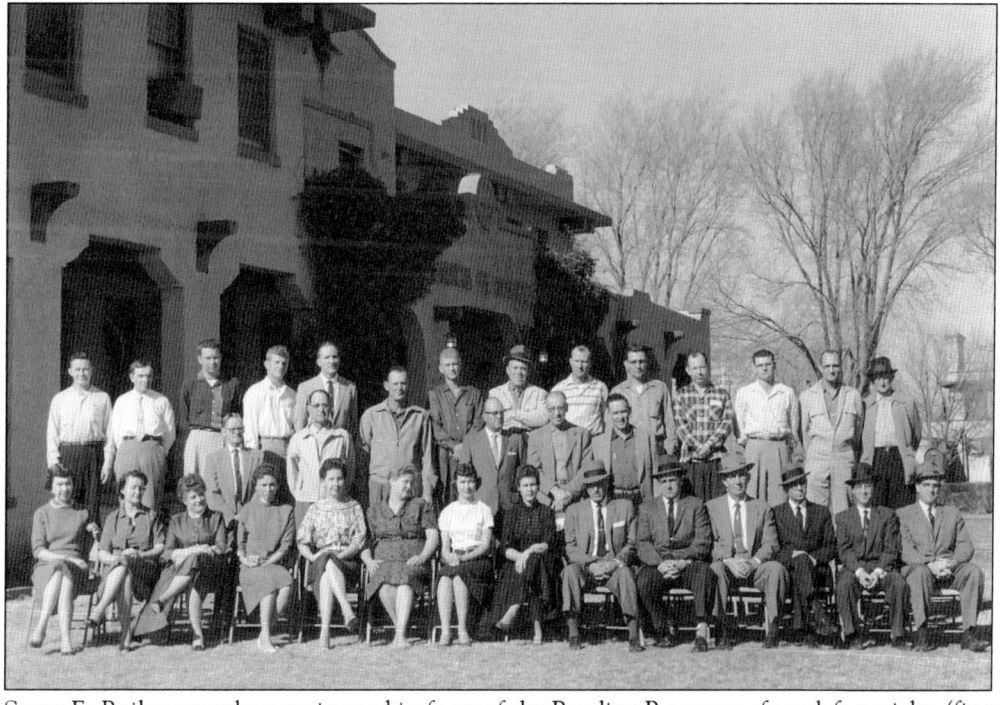

Santa Fe Railway employees pictured in front of the Reading Room are, from left to right, (first row) June Spikes, Doretha Harden, Vivian Williams, Ann Gay, Lori Ann Lamb, Bonnie Jones, Kay Ella Buxkenper, Mary Lee Schuette, W.A.J. Carter, E.O. Chaddock, Elmer Nelson, J.W. Bagby, Joe Miles, and E.D. Cummings; (second row) Jack Shepard, C.H. Green, T.M (Shorty) Wright, R.D. Bisbee, H.W. (Bob) Roberts, O.D. Diad, Back Row, Bill Brown, Gus Seel, Dwayne Tefertiller, Bobby Taylor, L.D. Langham, W.T. (Tinker) Taylor, Bob Fondy, Joe Wicker, Walter Moser, Allard Wendell, Norman Spears, Ray Bowman, and W.H. (Hammer) Dawson.

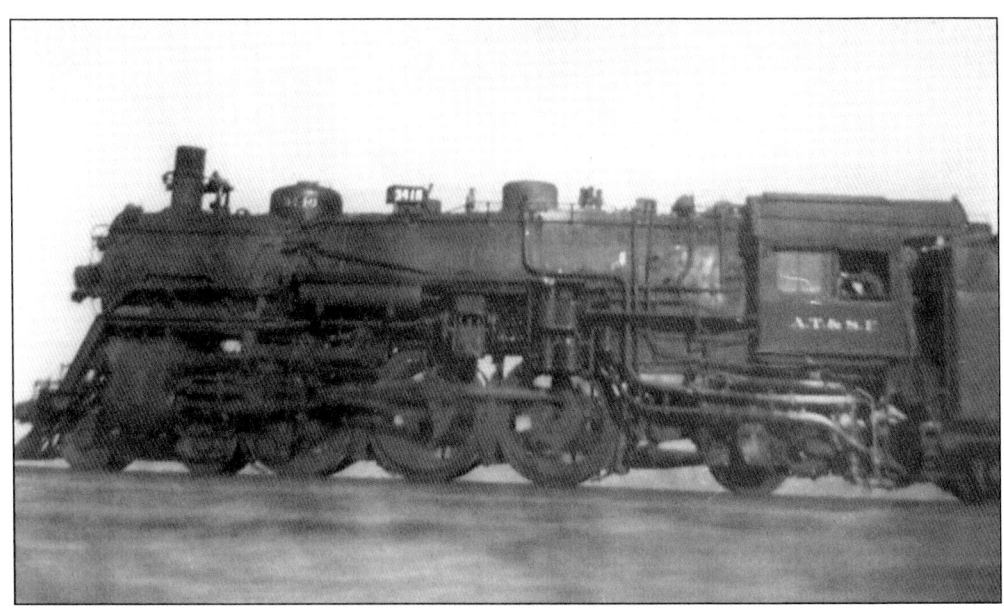

The history of the town of Slaton is intertwined with that of the Santa Fe Railway. The Pecos & Northern Texas branch of the railroad reached Slaton in May 1911, and one month later, lots were sold. Slaton grew rapidly as the Santa Fe established a division point in Slaton that included a Harvey House, a roundhouse, a two-story freight and passenger depot, and machine shops. Slaton incorporated in 1912, and R.J. Murray was elected mayor of the town. Joe H. Teague Sr. served as the first city marshal. Pictured below are Santa Fe employees doing repairs.

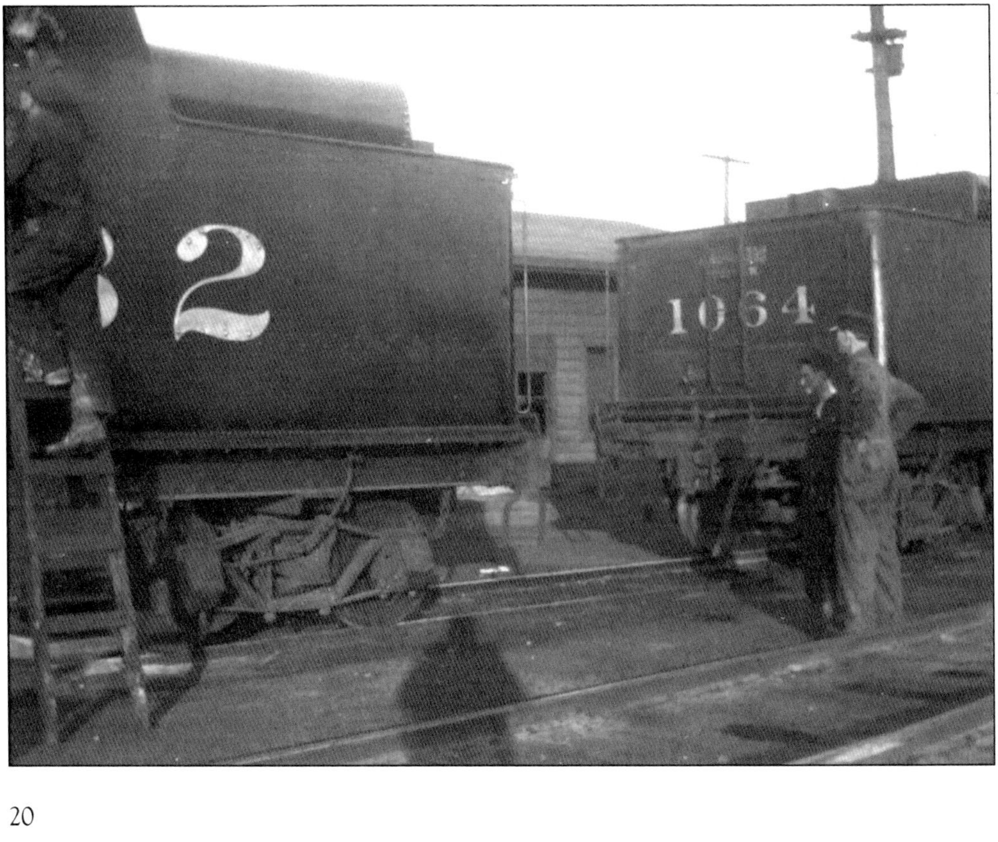

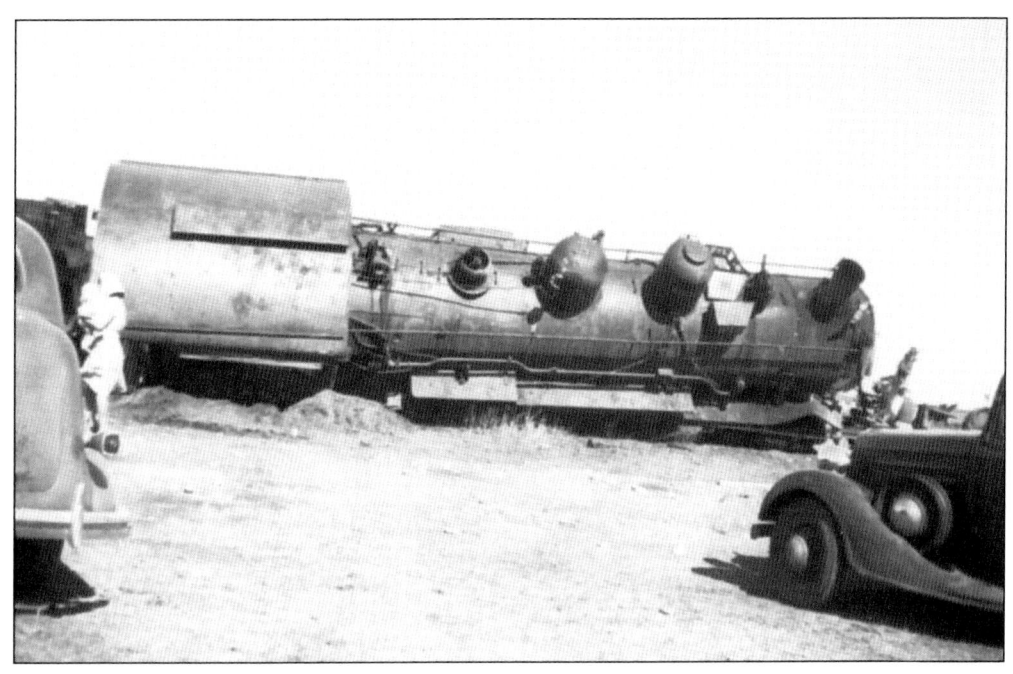

In 1938, the Santa Fe Railway had a tragic accident—with a fatality—near Posey, which is just outside of Slaton. The engineer, named Shelby, was killed in the accident. These photographs are from the 1938 train wreck.

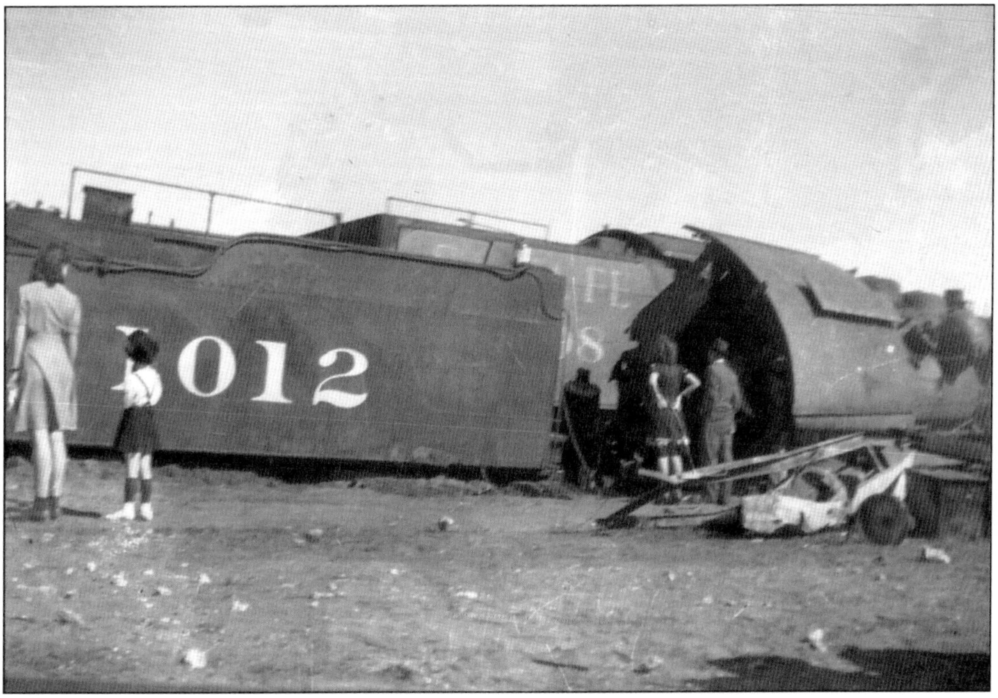

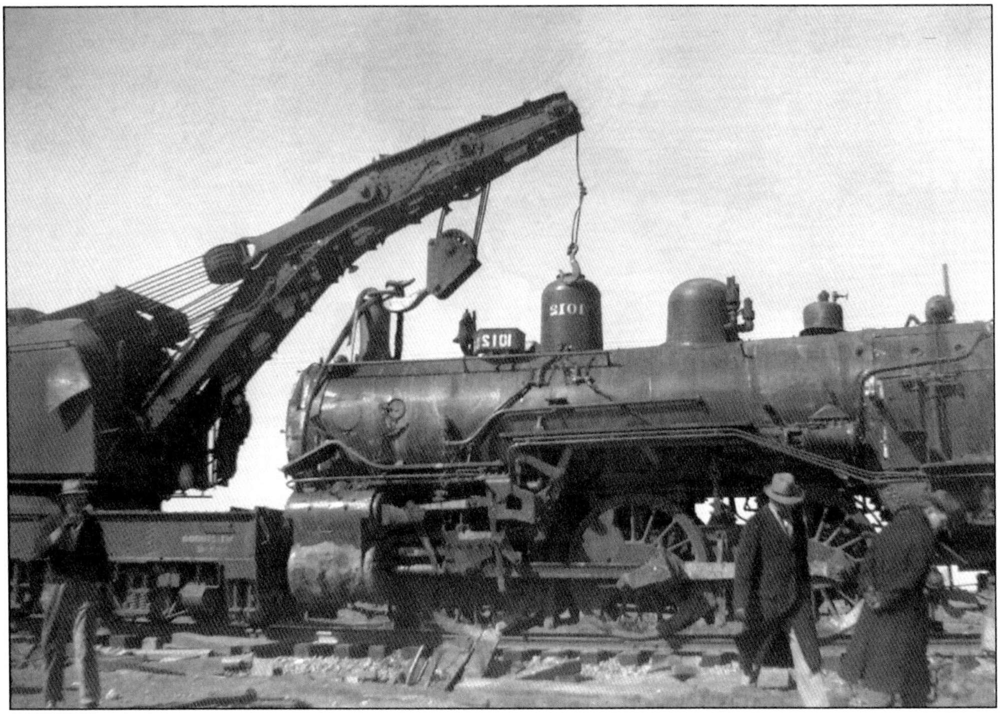

Here are two more pictures of the train wreck that took place in 1938 in Posey, just outside of Slaton.

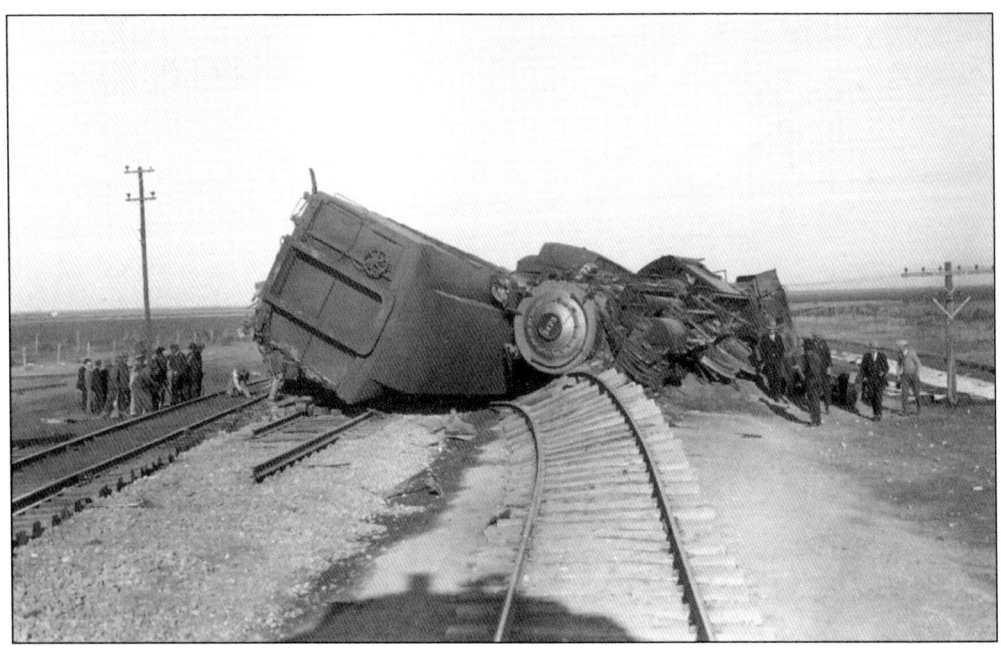

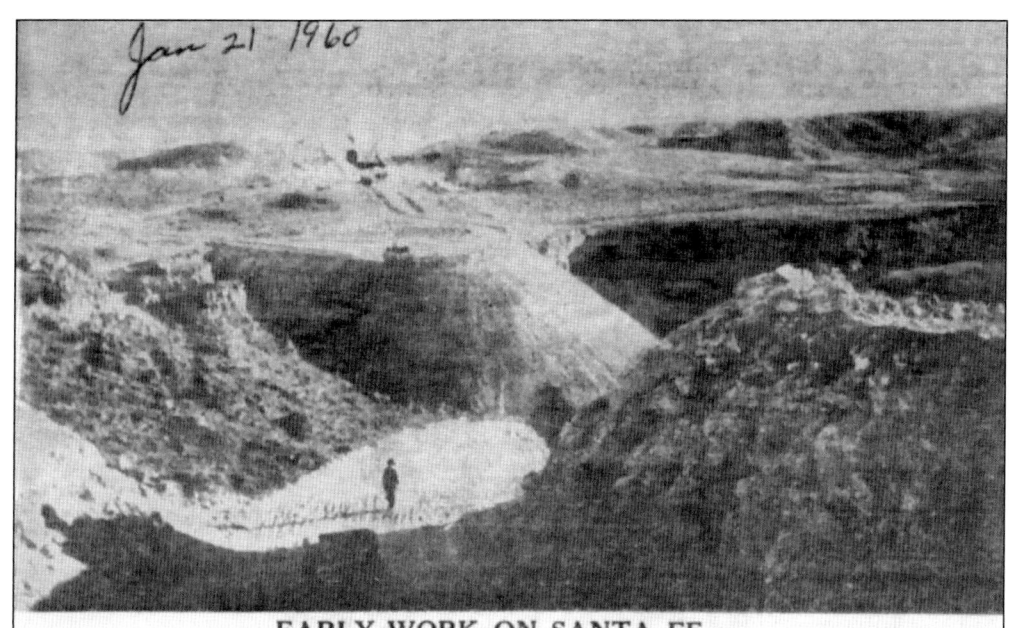

EARLY WORK ON SANTA FE

Here is a picture of early-day work on the Santa Fe Railroad in the Slaton area. If our information is correct, the picture was taken about 49 or 50 years ago near Southland. Can you recognize the place and remember the time? If so, let us know and we'll save the picture for next year's big 50th anniversary edition.

This image is from an advertisement printed in *The Slatonite* on January 21, 1960. This picture was taken about 50 years prior and shows early work on the Santa Fe Railway near Southland, which is a short distance from Slaton.

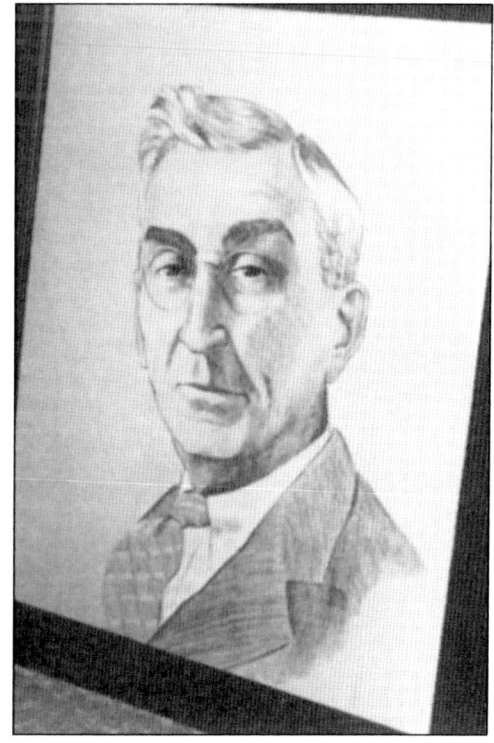

Businessmen like Monroe Abernathy, H.B. Reid, B.O. McWhorter, J.J. Dillard, Don Biggers, and Oscar Lowe (O.L.) Slaton had the foresight to develop the railroads that enhanced the prosperity of the entire plains area. This is a drawing of Slaton—rancher, banker, and the namesake of the town of Slaton. He was born on November 21, 1867, and passed away in 1946. In 1902, after living in other areas of Texas for most of his life, he moved to Lubbock and opened a real estate office. In 1905, he married Sally Wilkinson, whose parents were early Slaton settlers. In 1907, O.L. became active in administration of First National Bank, and was elected president in 1908. In March 1909, Santa Fe Railway had reached a decision to build a railroad and secure the right-of-way from Lubbock to Sweetwater. Slaton was so impressive to railroad executives that they decided to name this newly founded town after him. The information in this caption comes from the book *Slaton's Story*, compiled by the Slaton Museum Association in 1979. (Courtesy of the Slaton Museum.)

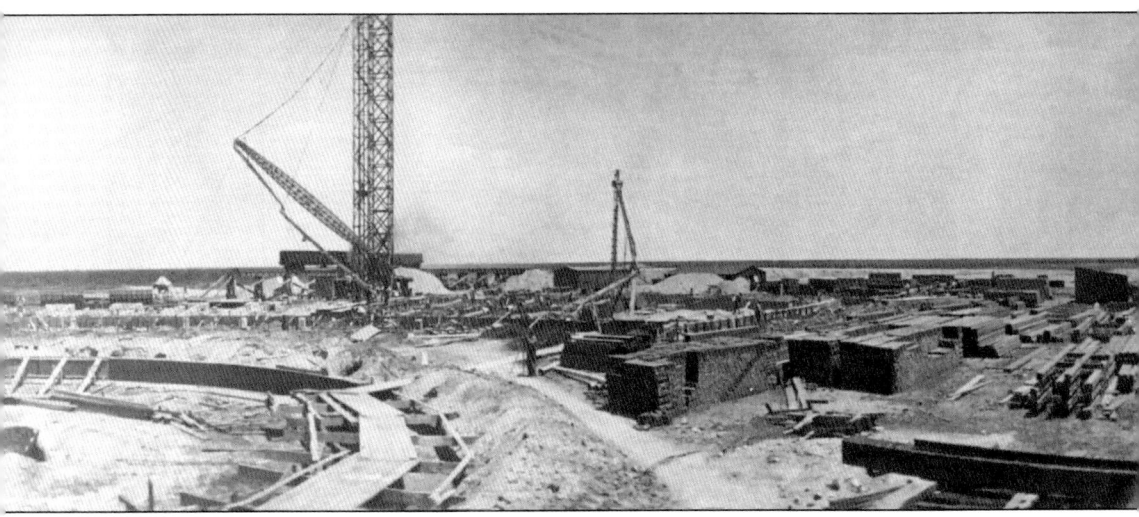

This is a c. 1911 photograph of the construction of the Santa Fe Railway turntable. When Santa Fe executives decided to locate a division point 15 miles southeast of Lubbock, some promoters of the rail line in Lubbock were afraid that it was too close to Lubbock and might detract from their development. The vice president of the railway, W.B. Story Jr., was in charge of construction and continued to assure Lubbock that the railroad did not wish to establish a new station that would hurt their progress. By June 1910, the Santa Fe was operating freight and passenger service south of Lubbock to Lamesa, and by June 1911, it was operating passenger service from Amarillo to Sweetwater. This new line could connect with the Texas & Pacific Railway to give service to Fort Worth.

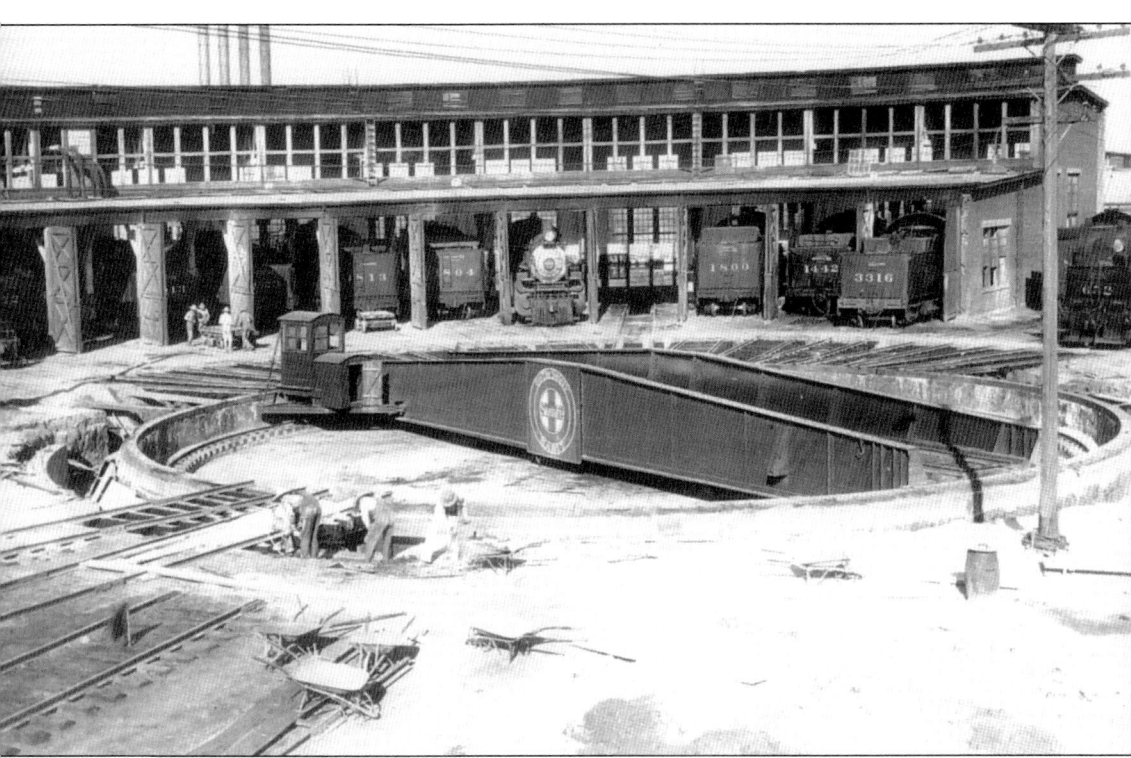

The Santa Fe Railway brought with it hopes and dreams of a fresh life filled with new opportunity. Ultimately, the Santa Fe is the reason Slaton exists. (Courtesy of Slaton Harvey House and Slaton Railroad Heritage Association.)

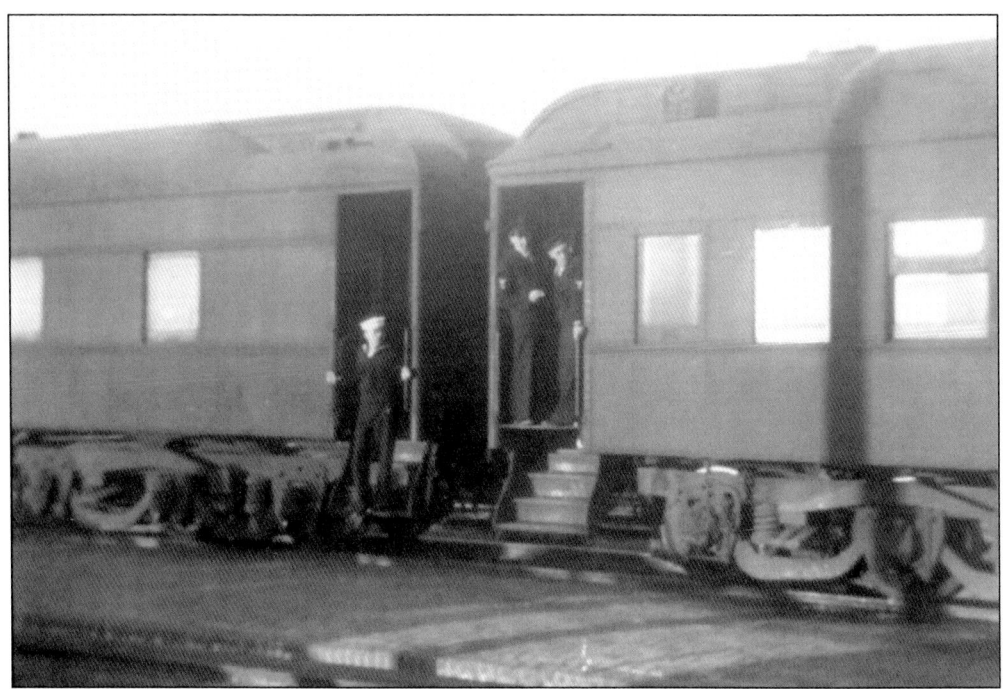

During World War II, Slaton was a rest stop for troop trains going cross-country toward the West Coast. The traveling soldiers would march from the Santa Fe Railway station to town and back for exercise. There were many hundreds of soldiers, and many of them enjoyed the Slaton Bakery.

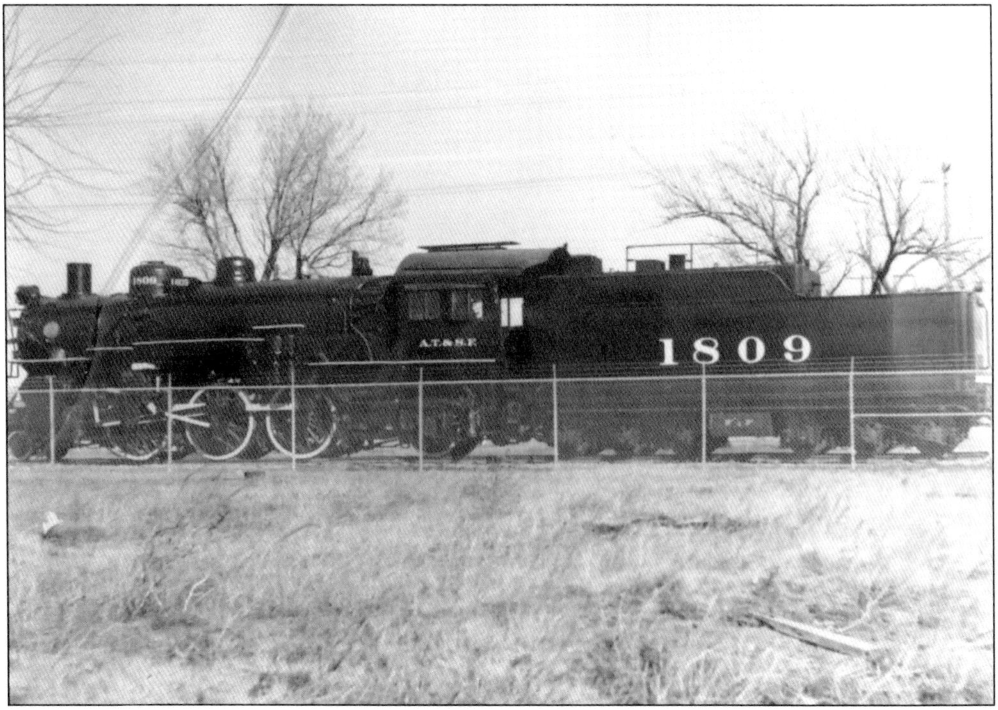

Santa Fe Railway engine No. 1809 played a key role in Slaton's agricultural economy, making runs that delivered bales of cotton from the Slaton area to the ports on the Gulf.

ATCHISON TOPEKA AND SANTA FE RAILWAY COMPANY

F. N. STUPPI,
General Manager,
Amarillo, Texas.

J. H. BLAKE,
Asst. General Manager,
Amarillo, Texas.

K. C. MAY,
Superintendent,
Amarillo, Texas.

TRAINMASTERS
C. T. HERZOG . . . . Wellington, Kan.
D. R. WARREN . . . . Amarillo, Tex.
W. C. SPANN . . . . Amarillo, Tex.
P. R. BUCHANAN . . . . Slaton, Tex.

TRAINMASTER-ROAD FOREMAN OF ENGINES
W. K. FRY . . . . San Angelo, Tex.

ASST. TRAINMASTER
H. E. DeREMER . . . . Amarillo, Tex.

ROAD FOREMEN OF ENGINES
W. W. GENTRY . . . . Amarillo, Tex.
R. O. SMITH . . . . Wellington, Kans.
B. R. TUCKER . . . . Slaton, Tex.

CHIEF DISPATCHER
D. H. HOLDAWAY . . . . Amarillo, Tex.

ASST. CHIEF DISPATCHERS—AMARILLO
B. L. BRANT   H. E. COWLES   A. DEATON, JR.

DISPATCHERS—AMARILLO
V. H. FARSCHON	C. L. ANDERSON	L. A. STEWART
W. LAWSON	W. R. DAUNER	J. M. STANDIFER
E. R. BOYER	J. E. SMITH	A. B. CAUDLE
V. L. ROCHE	W. H. MORGAN	K. G. LITTON
D. F. CARDER	F. E. YOCK	H. L. LOVELADY
A. C. BURK	J. E. McMEEKAN	K. D. GRUBB
M. J. TRAFFAS	G. C. BRUNSON	W. A. FARRELL
R. B. SIDMAN	W. D. PARKER	J. N. ISCH
M. COLE	D. L. HODGES	H. C. WHITE
W. HELLMAN	J. W. OLSON	V. L. COLBERT
R. WOOD	A. C. WESTBROOK	J. D. WILDE

YARDMASTERS' SENIORITY ROSTER
Whitney, P.	Day	Lubbock	1-17-50
Faulkner, D. J.	Evening	Lubbock	8-10-50
Odom, J.C.	Night	Lubbock	3-14-56
som, R.L.	Reg. Relief	Lubbock	11-25-56
Morrison, L.T.	Extra	Lubbock	1-05-58
Allison, J.R.	Extra	Lubbock	6-16-63

Pinkie's — Serving West Texas

Lubbock

Canyon Road Store

½ mile south of Acuff Road on Texas FM 1729

(Lubbock) PO 2-2091

Tahoka Highway Store

1.3 miles south of Lubbock city limits on U.S. Highw[ay]

(Lubbock) SH 4-4386

Lake Store

Buffalo Lakes Road

(Lubbock) SH 4-7177

Post

503 East Main on U.S. Highway 380

(Post) 495-2769

This is a 1978 Atchison, Topeka & Santa Fe Railway company roster featuring employees from Amarillo, Slaton, Lubbock, and Wellington, Kansas.

FORREST LUMBER COMPANY

HOMES REPAIR REMODEL HOME LOANS

... STREET — MAIN STREET
...763-4335 — PHONE: 828-6106
..., TEXAS — SLATON, TEXAS

BRAKEMEN'S SENIORITY ROSTER
JANUARY 1, 1971

	BRAKEMEN Santa Fe Seniority	BRAKEMEN Seniority	YARDMEN Seniority
...ory ...ster Service Foreman			
...ter, C.E.	9-17-25 (2)	8-01-29	5-01-60
...tis, W.C.	4-18-26	"	"
...kel, P.S.	8-01-29		
...ggett, D.D.		10-08-36	"
...ompson, R.H.		11-07-36	"
...rry, M.D.		11-08-36	"
...e, W.O.		12-14-36	"
...wman, A.E.		5-01-37	"
...omas, W.J.		5-15-37	"
...liburton, J.P.		5-30-37	"
...ghes, L.O.		5-31-37	"
...bbard, W.O.		6-01-37	"
...tterlee, H.K.		6-02-37	"
...elby, J.H.		6-04-37	"
...elch, E.F.		6-17-37	"
...ndrus, H.G.		7-09-37	"
...ountree, J.D.		10-01-37	"
...avis, D.H.		10-02-37	"
...ickson, C.E.		6-25-39	"
...oyd, F.C.		5-16-41	"
...ay, O.W.		6-08-41	"
...oster, L.N.		7-19-41	"
...ooter, F.D.		10-18-41	"
...ark, O.L.		10-19-41	"
...ill, F.E.		12-17-41	"
...ones, E.W.		1-10-42	"

(BRAKEMEN'S SENIORITY ROSTER CONTINUED)

		BRAKEMEN Seniority	YARDMEN Seniority
27.	Wampler, V.L.	2-02-42	5-01-60
28.	Kitten, C.V.	6-09-42	"
29.	Reed, J.L.	6-14-42	"
30.	Chapple, F.E.	6-16-42	"
31.	Martin, C.J.	6-26-42	"
32.	Felty, C.J.	6-27-42	"
33.	Henry, R.L.	6-29-42	"
34.	Wike, J.N.	7-12-42	"
35.	Privett, G.W.	7-15-42	"
36.	Banks, H.B.	7-27-42	"
37.	Stansell, R.F.	10-08-42	"
38.	Shafer, A.A.	10-16-42	"
39.	Hogue, C.E.	11-02-42	"
40.	Glasscock, W.H.	12-07-42	"
41.	Enloe, L.A.	1-03-44	"
42.	Dunn, J.W.	11-28-44	"
43.	Childers, W.V.	12-04-44	"
44.	Watkins, J.M.	12-15-44	"
45.	Sharp, T.A.	5-19-45	"
46.	Hatch, C.L.	6-07-45	"
47.	Traweek, A.A.	6-18-45	"
48.	Fisher, F.	7-25-45	"
49.	Bryant, H.A.	1-28-46	"
50.	Lamb, E.C.	7-17-46	"
51.	Perdue, L.	9-06-46	"
52.	Bradford, G.E.	9-24-46	"
53.	Smith, I.V.	9-28-46	"
54.	Hodges, R.G.	9-30-46	"
55.	Wells, C.A.	10-02-46	"
56.	Hogue, H.S.	10-08-46	"
57.	Brake, C.V.	10-11-46	"
58.	Davidson, E.C.	6-06-47	"
59.	Busby, B.G.	6-24-47	"
60.	Isbell, H.E.	8-09-47	"
61.	Kroll, E.W.	10-08-47	"
62.	Modawell, E.A.	10-11-47	"
63.	Neill, S.M.	10-25-47	"
64.	Breland, J.M.	11-04-47	"
65.	Bradford, C.F.	11-25-47	"
66.	Davis, C.J.	12-09-47	"
67.	Tumlinson, E.B.	6-01-48	"
68.	Green, W.L.	6-25-48	"
69.	Hartley, G.L.	6-19-49	"
70.	Moore, T.H.	11-12-49	"
71.	Merriman, H.R.	7-29-50	"
72.	House, J.L.	8-04-50	"
73.	Scurlock, H.T.	8-05-50	"
74.	Simmons, C.M., Jr.	9-22-50	"
75.	Longtin, F.T.	10-10-50	"
76.	Paschall, A.L.	11-15-50	"

This is a brakemen's seniority roster for the Santa Fe Railway in Slaton from January 1, 1971.

Two

The Harvey House

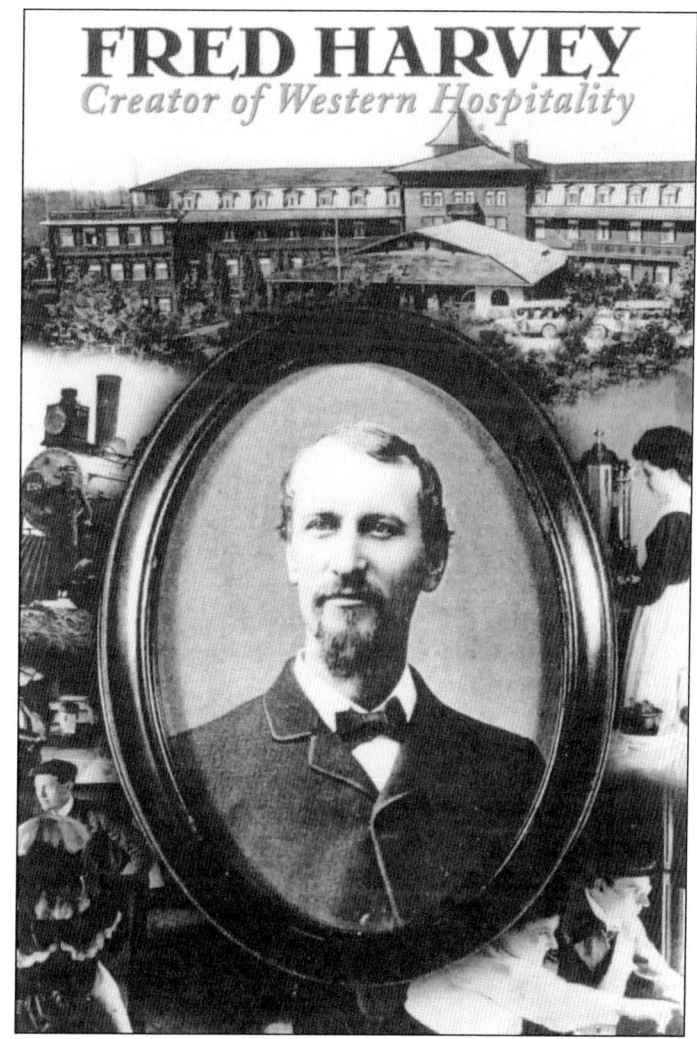

Fred Harvey was born June 27, 1835, in London, England. He came to the United States when he was a teenager and became a dishwasher. As he observed the poor quality of the food served on trains, he found a partner and, in 1876, opened up a railway restaurant in Topeka, Kansas, that proved successful. He later partnered with Atchison, Topeka & Santa Fe Railway to begin his Harvey House empire. When the Slaton Harvey House opened in 1912, it served elegant meals to 42 passengers at a time around a horseshoe-shaped counter. Waitresses known as Harvey Girls provided cheerful service and delicious meals and were required to exemplify high standards in service, attire, and appearance. (Courtesy of Slaton Harvey House and Slaton Railroad Heritage Association.)

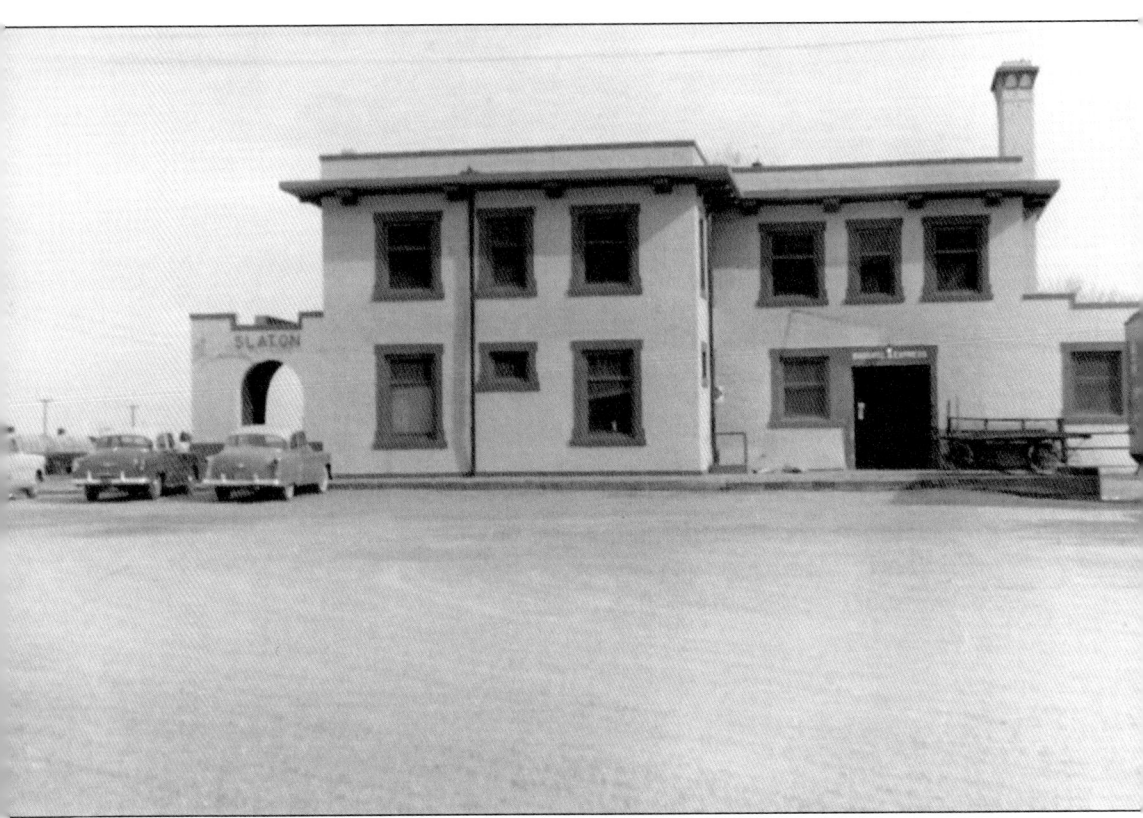

The Slaton Harvey House, built for $75,000 in 1912, contained a kitchen, a bakery, a gift shop, and a manager's office. This photograph of the Slaton Harvey House was taken in 1920. The two-story structure provided railroad passengers and others with delicious meals and a pleasurable dining experience. The manager, his family, and the Harvey Girls roomed on the second floor. The Slaton Harvey House operated for 30 years—from 1912 until 1942. It briefly reopened to serve troops during World War II. The building remained a passenger depot until 1969 and was later converted into a freight depot and operations center that functioned until the mid-1980s.

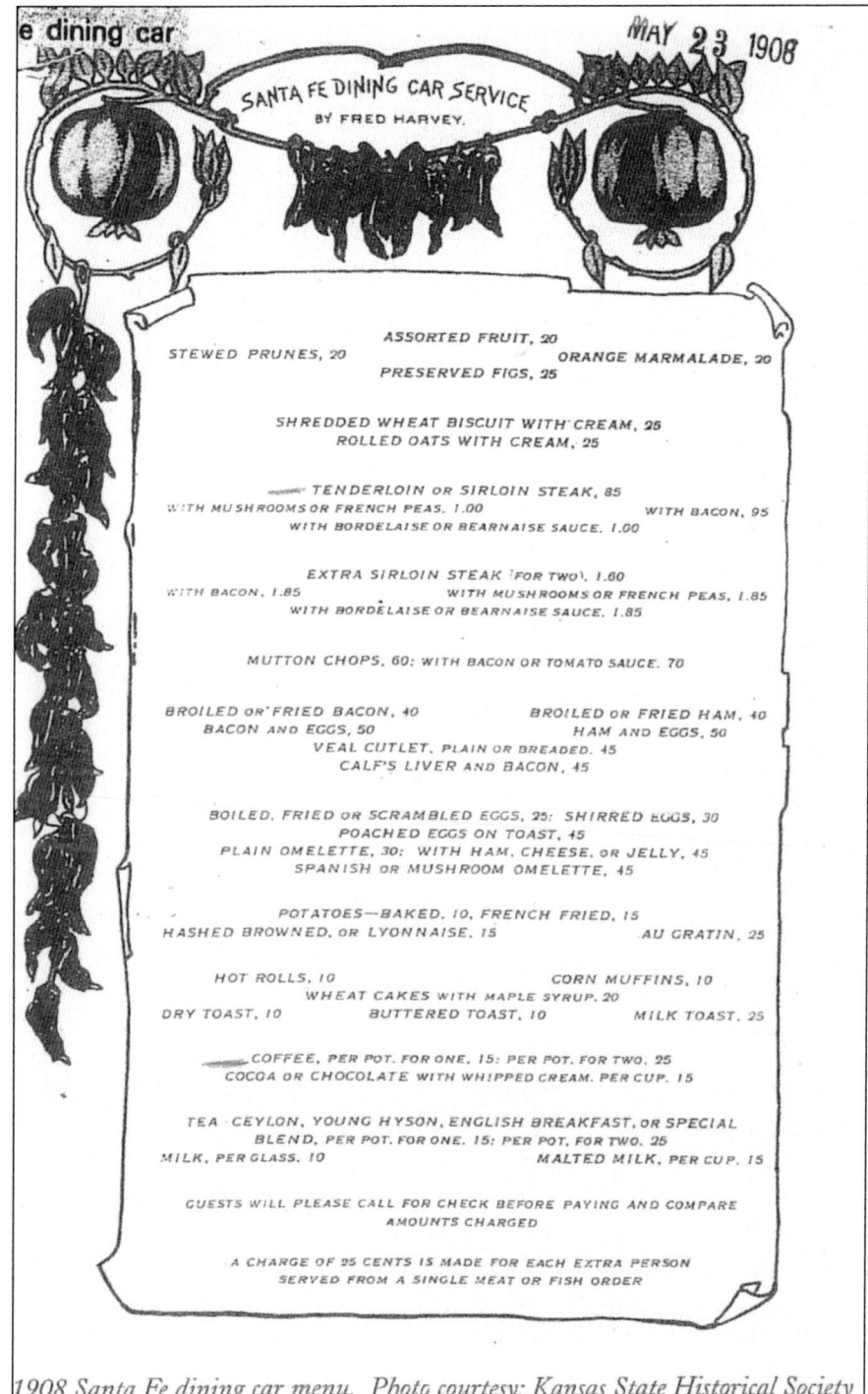

1908 Santa Fe dining car menu. Photo courtesy: Kansas State Historical Society

This 1908 menu from a Santa Fe Railway dining car was created by Fred Harvey. The food was elegant and set new standards for railroad dining. Harvey eventually had 80 Harvey Houses built along railroads across the country. He successfully married the Santa Fe with his Harvey Houses. (Courtesy of the Kansas State Historical Society.)

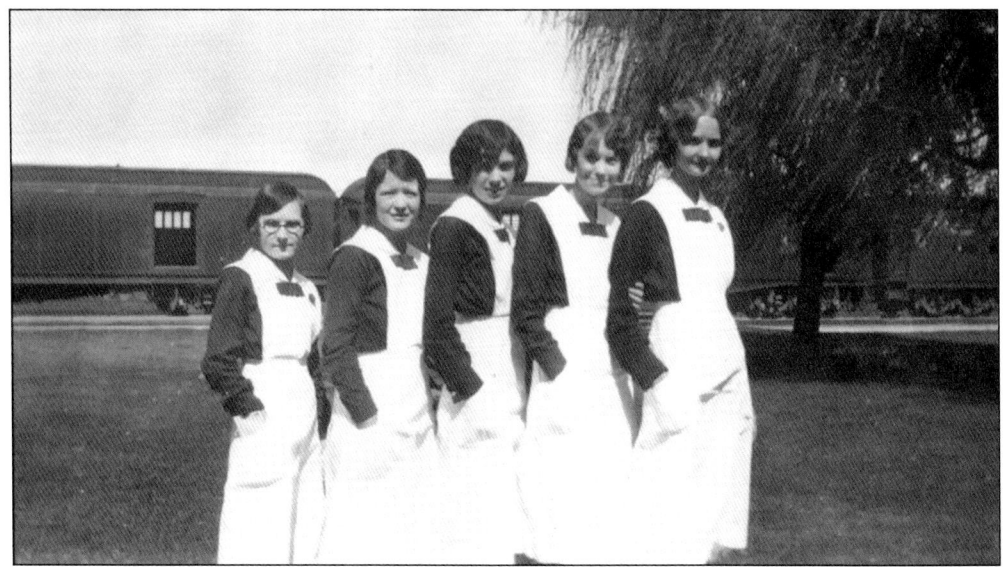

The Harvey Girls of Slaton Harvey House pictured here are, from left to right, Bertha Garragus, Patsy Hoffman, Grace Squares, Cleo Ruth, and Alma Russell.

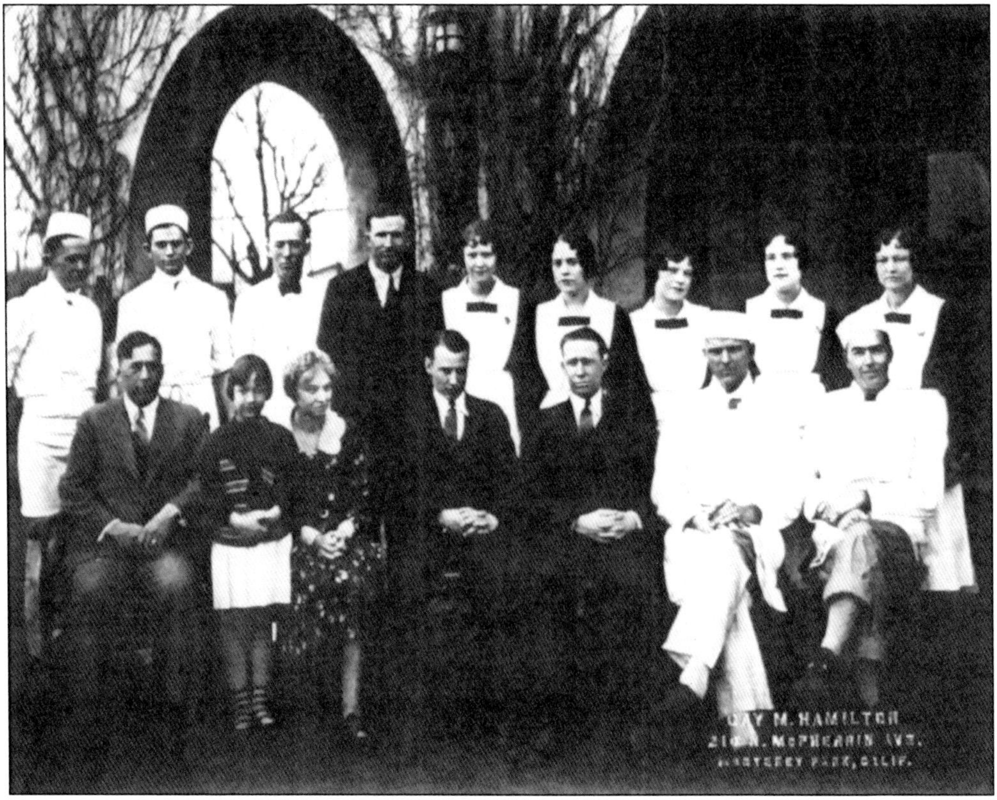

The first crew of the Slaton Harvey House gathers for a picture. From left to right are (first row) Mr. W.H. Bowman (manager), Virginia, Mrs. Bowman, Norman Miller, Red Shelton, Floyd Wells, and H.T. Carr; (second row) Ira McCarver, Jimmy McCall, John Shelton, Royce Hill, Cleo Wolf, Jo Short, Verna Tabor, Mable Reno, and Blanche Tabor.

Pictured at right is Joseph Warren "J.W." Tate in April 1919. At age 16, he started working as a busboy for the Harvey House. He later became a brakeman, then a conductor who ran an entire train for the Santa Fe Railway. While working at the Harvey House, he met (and later married) a Harvey Girl named Ethel Louise Reeves, from Sweetwater. She is pictured below. Their daughter, Jolene Fondy of Slaton, recalls that when she was a teenager, her dad was a butcher at the Slaton Harvey House and her mother was a Harvey Girl at the Sweetwater Harvey House. Fondy said, "Everything was so elegant. The desserts were always beautiful. There was fine china, and the linens came from Ireland, the silver from England." Fondy remembered her mother telling her that when she signed the contract to work for Harvey House, she could not marry for a year. Harvey House employees also had to honor a strict curfew and other rules. J.W. Tate passed away at age 44. (Both, courtesy of Jolene Fondy.)

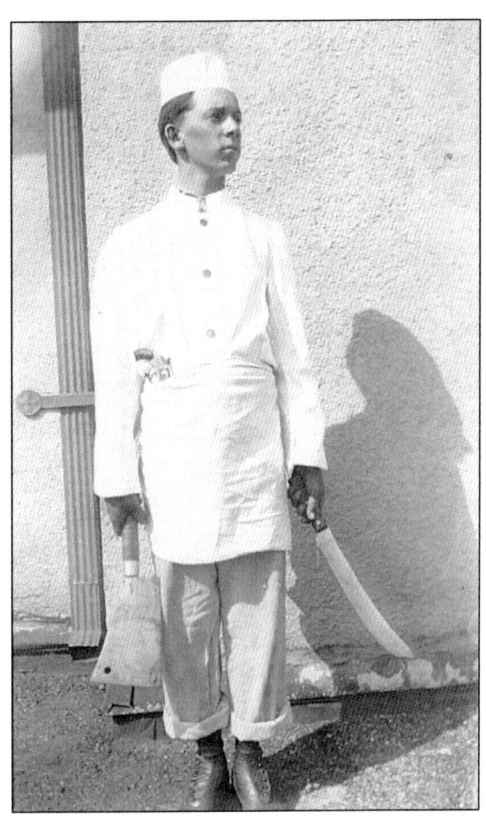

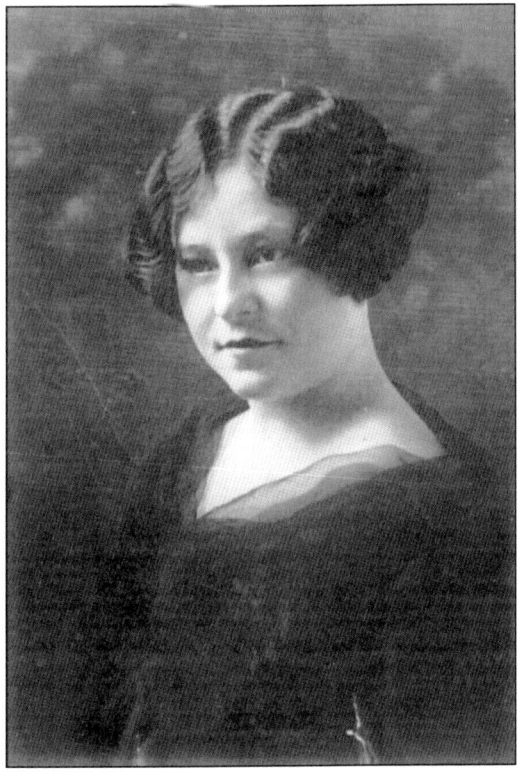

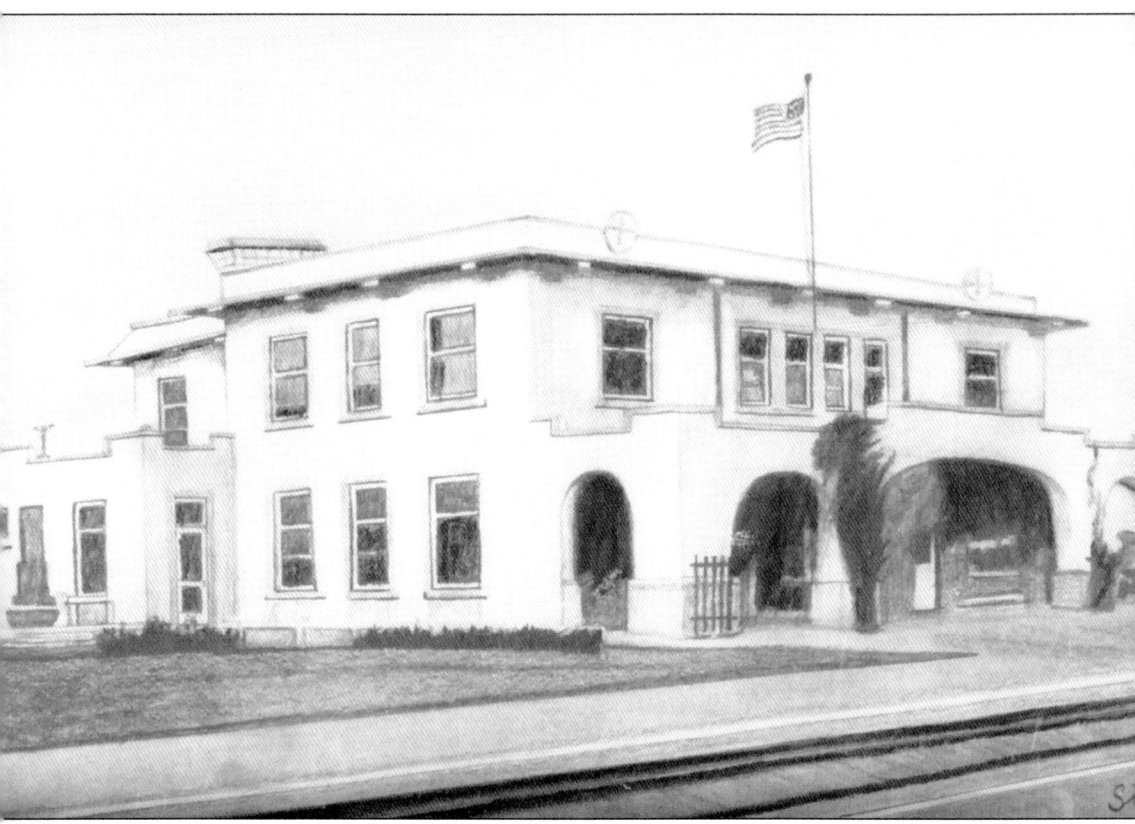

This image of the Santa Fe Eating House, in Slaton, is from 1934. This picture was given to the Slaton Museum by Scharlene Yandell Morris in memory of her father, Archie Yandell (a Santa Fe Railway engineer for 30 years), and her husband, O.D. Morris (a Santa Fe Railway clerk for 41 years). (Courtesy of the Slaton Museum.)

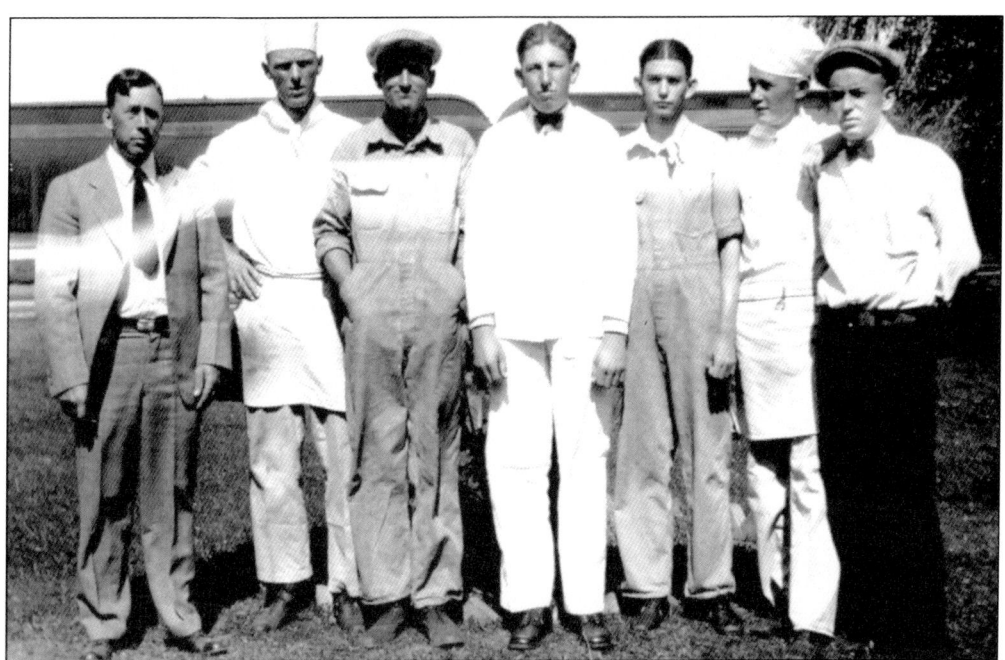

This 1930s Harvey House crew includes Bowman Wells, Cader Kennedy, Jimmy and Ira McCarver, and ? Hill.

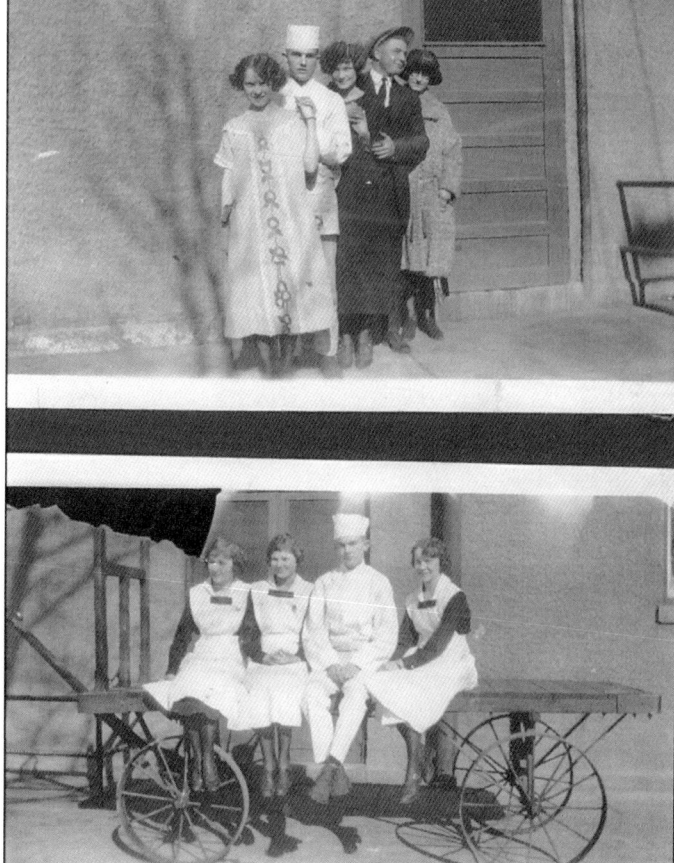

These pictures from the Slaton Harvey House collection show several people who worked there. The only person identified is the man in the suit and tie—he worked for Harvey House, and his name is Lafayette Bruce Burnett. (Courtesy of Slaton Harvey House and Slaton Railroad Heritage Association.)

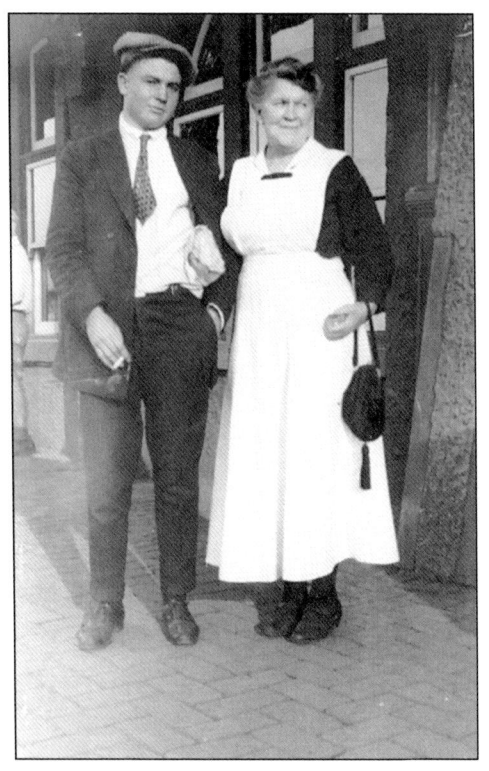

This is another picture of Lafayette Bruce Burnett (left) at the Harvey House. The Slaton Harvey House served passengers from three trains beginning at 7:00 a.m. They also served railroad employees and anyone who wanted a meal until 6:00 p.m. Each Harvey Girl received a two-hour break each afternoon and one day off per week. (Courtesy of Slaton Harvey House and Slaton Railroad Heritage Association.)

Harvey Girls were required to wear a specific outfit—starched black shirt and white smock—and be well groomed. They had to wear opaque black hose and black shoes. The hems of their uniforms had to be eight inches from the floor. Harvey Girls had to display good morals, be reasonably attractive, modest, and well-mannered. They kept themselves neat but did not overdo the makeup. They could not wear jewelry. Some have said that Harvey Girls "tamed" the West. Over 20,000 Harvey Girls went on to marry cowboys, miners, ranchers, merchants, and railroad men. It was hard for women to find jobs in those days, so becoming a Harvey Girl was an aspirational goal. The Harvey Girls were paid $1 per day plus tips. They also received room and board. The hours were long, but being a Harvey Girl was considered a privilege.

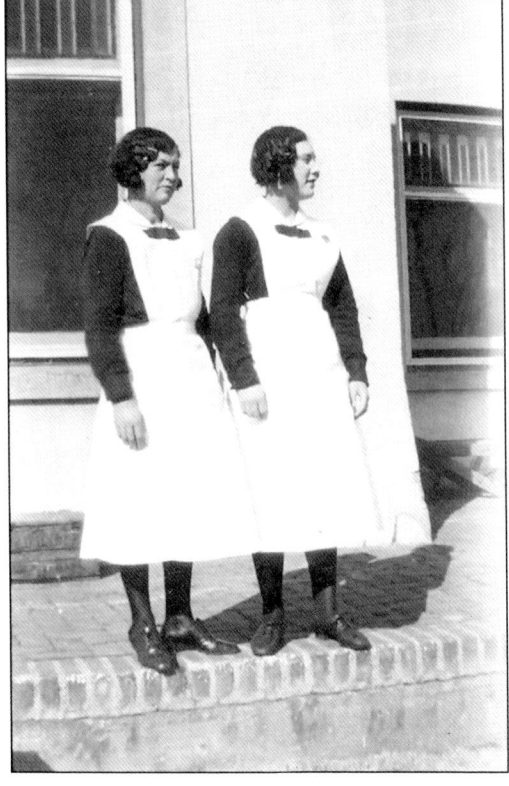

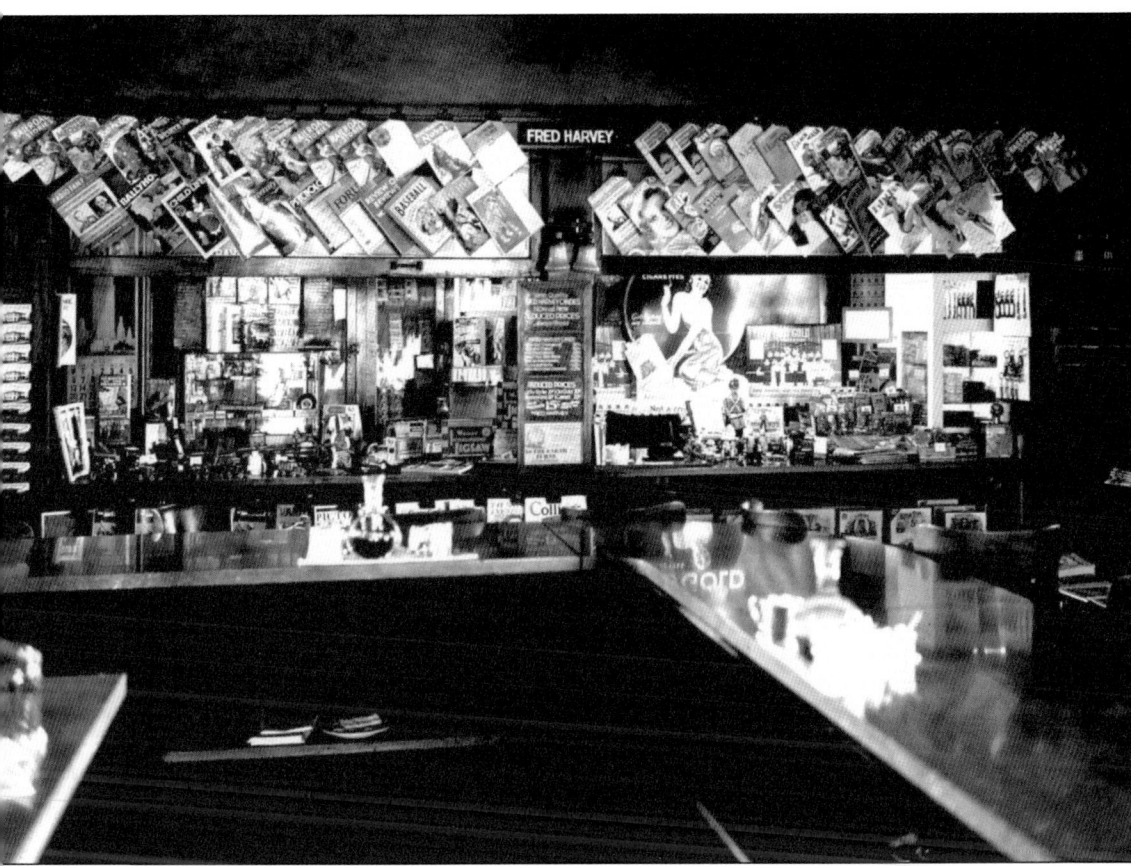

This is the horseshoe-shaped counter at the Slaton Harvey House. The counter and large dining room with a rose-colored top at the Slaton Harvey House hosted thousands of meals served by the impeccably groomed Harvey Girls. Trains could even telegraph passengers' orders ahead so that they would have a meal waiting for them upon arrival. The food was fresh and was brought in daily by train. Beef came from Kansas City, and seafood and produce came from California. The Santa Fe and Harvey Houses also tried to buy locally as often as possible to help local economies and serve the freshest food possible. Though the Harvey House in Slaton was meant for the railroad, it was open to everybody. Some wealthy Lubbock residents would drive to Slaton just to dine there for the food and dining experience, and Slatonites would dine there on special occasions.

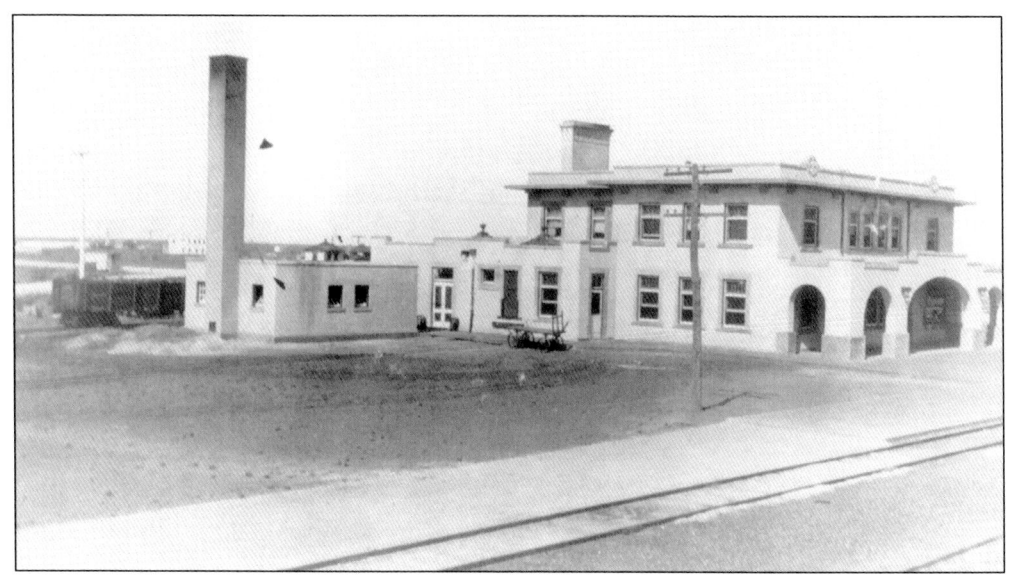

Fred Harvey, who created the Harvey Houses, became a national legend. He partnered with the Santa Fe Railway when he saw a need for better food and service. He provided the trains with food and supplies, plus equipment, management, and hospitality staff. The Harvey House in Slaton housed a dining room featuring a horse-shoe shaped counter that could feed 42 diners at a time, a kitchen, bakery, gift shop, and manager's office. It became a commercial and social center and operated for 30 years from 1912 to 1942. The Harvey House in Slaton is pictured here.

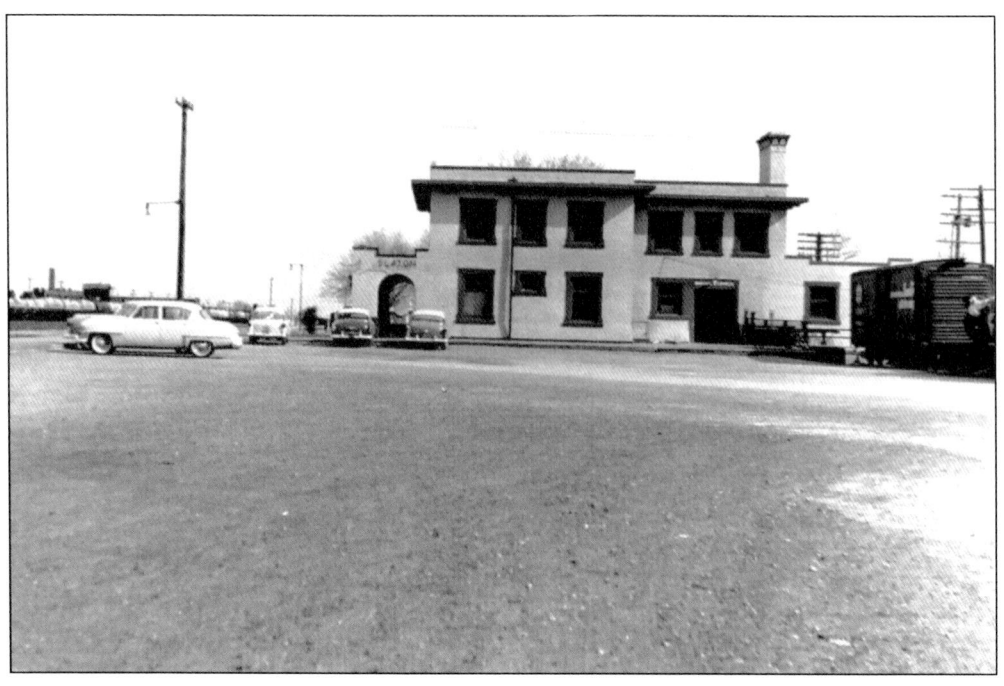

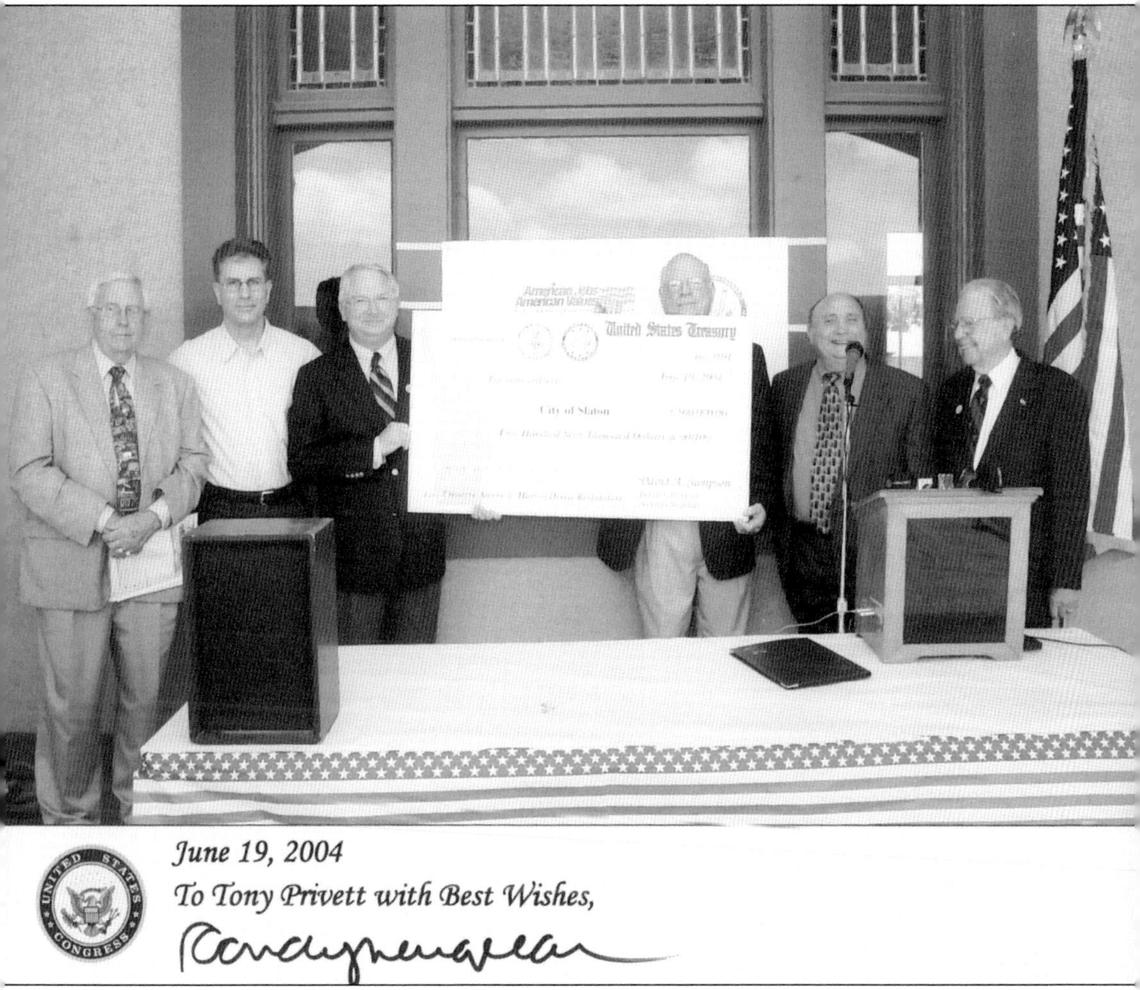

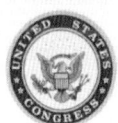

June 19, 2004

To Tony Privett with Best Wishes,

Randy Neugebauer

After the Santa Fe Railway stopped using the Slaton Harvey House building in the late 1980s, it was scheduled to be torn down in 1990. It still stands today because a local plumber, Bill Burks, was asked to salvage fixtures after a Santa Fe demolition crew arrived unannounced to tear down the building; Burks immediately contacted city officials to let them know. This incident led to the formation of the Slaton Railroad Heritage Association by local citizens. The association didn't pay anything for the building; they initially borrowed funds from Citizens Bank of Slaton to begin renovations. The association did what they could to restore the Harvey House as they filed for grants to do a complete restoration. On June 19, 2004, the City of Slaton was awarded $500,000 toward the $1.2 million restoration of the Harvey House. The Slaton Harvey House reopened in September 2007 as a bed and breakfast, as well as a museum and community center. (Courtesy of Slaton Harvey House and Slaton Railroad Heritage Association.)

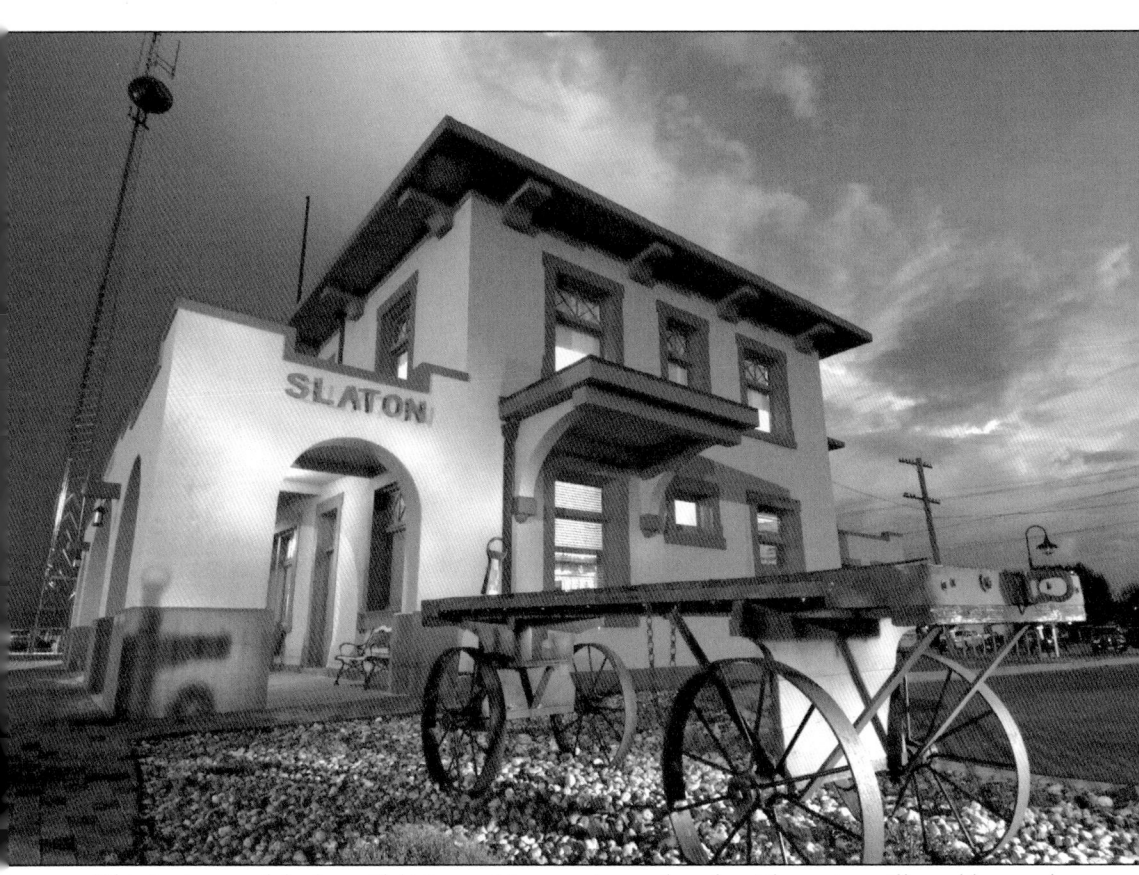

This is picture of the beautiful Harvey House as it stands today. The trains still rumble past, but now it is a bed and breakfast and museum and community center. This building is a life-size piece of history that offers a glimpse into the golden age of American railroads. It has also been designated a Texas Historical Marker. It has been featured on Bob Phillips' *Texas Country Reporter* television program and is still open every Wednesday for lunch. (Courtesy of Kevin Stillman, TxDOT.)

Three
BOOMTOWN IS BORN

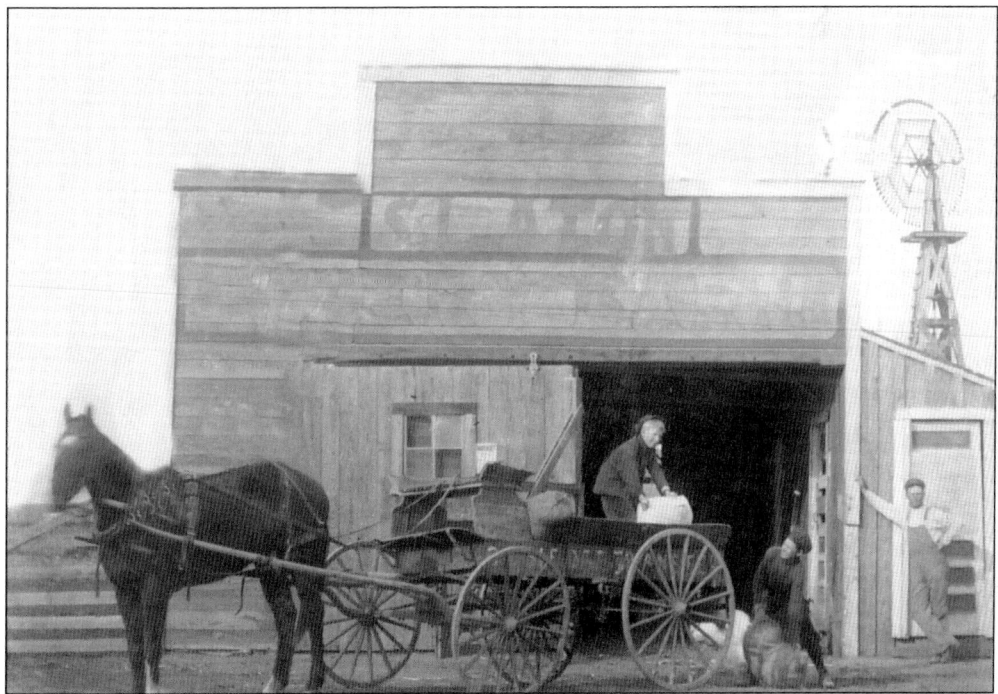

This 1912 photograph shows the Slaton livery barn. The G.L. Sledge transfer wagon is parked outside the doors. Livery stables were popular before automobiles and trains took over as the most popular forms of transportation. The Santa Fe Railway started with a dream. Though some thought he was crazy, a man by the name of Cyrus K. Holliday had an improbable dream to build a railroad paralleling the famous Santa Fe Trail. His idea was to replace mules and wagons with something faster and more efficient—the railroad. In 1859, Holliday single-handedly wrote the charter for the Atchison, Topeka & Santa Fe Railroad. He had setbacks—including the Civil War, financial trouble, and drought—but never gave up. Holliday stated that the railroad would reach the Pacific Coast and Gulf of Mexico and was laughed at for his big ideas, but his dream evolved into an industrial giant. The Santa Fe continued to expand, and reached the town that would become known as Slaton in 1911. There, a boomtown was born.

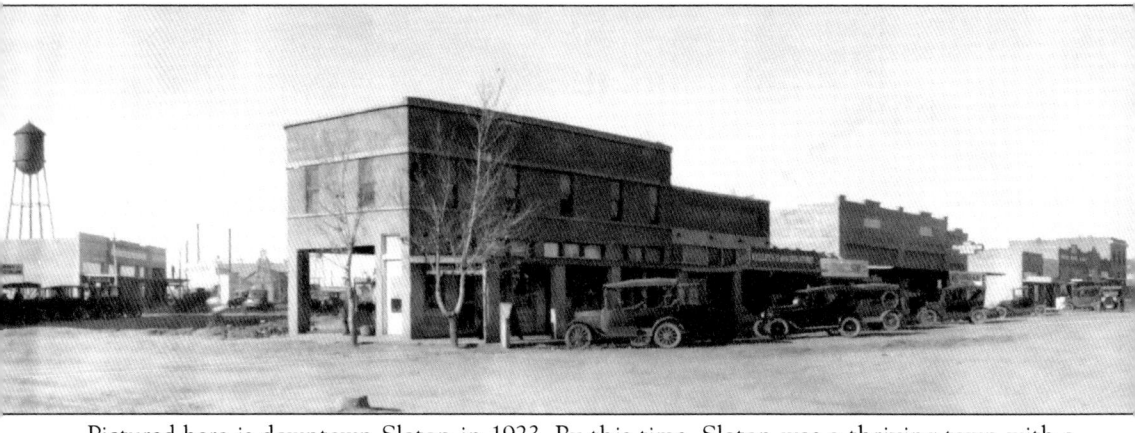
Pictured here is downtown Slaton in 1923. By this time, Slaton was a thriving town with a population of over 6,000. Area businesses included a drugstore, a candy shop, service stations, a grocery store, a hardware store, clothing companies, and more. It was the "Roaring Twenties," and many were enjoying the successes of the time.

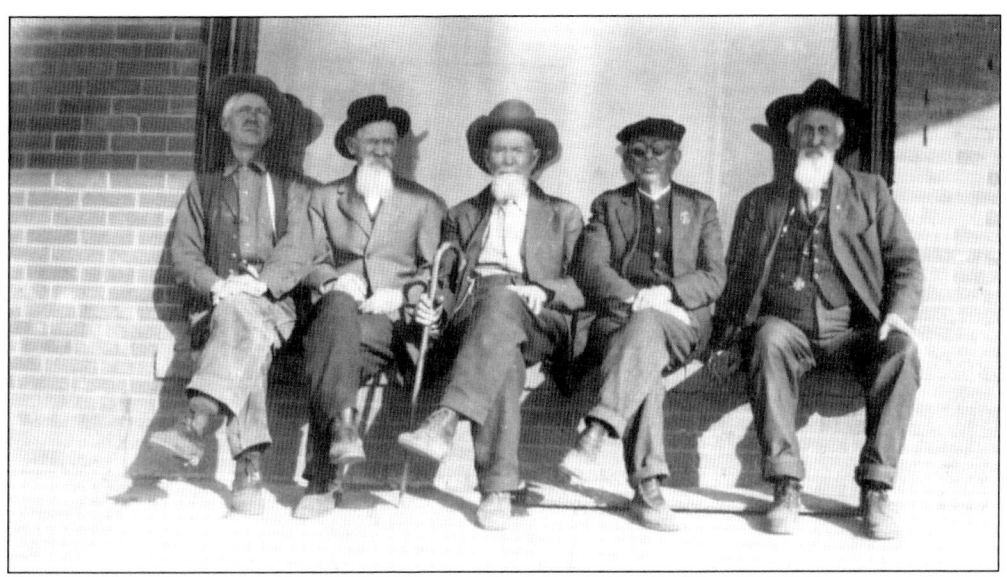

The pioneers of Slaton pictured here are, from left to right, Captain Murray, Dr. S.H. Adams's father, Mr. Kuykendall, Colonel Smith, and T.A. Worley's father.

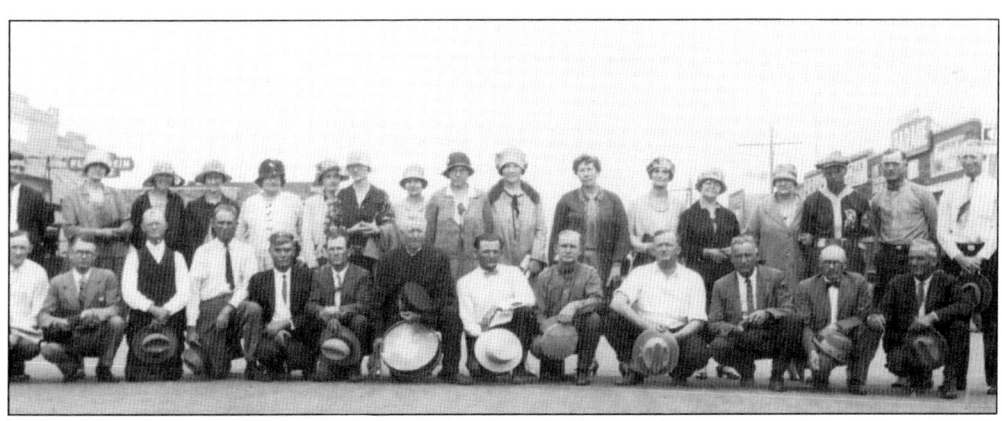

This picture—from a June 16, 1927, parade of Slaton "old timers"—was taken during Slaton's 16th birthday celebration. Pictured are, from left to right, (first row) Wiley Martin, Mrs. E.P. Nix, Mrs. Chas Yeats, Mrs. Terry Austin, Mrs. P.H. Whalen, Mrs. C.V. Young, Mrs. John Simmons, Mrs. Ed Tonn, Mrs. J.W. Wallace, Anna Higbee, Mrs. Lee Green, Mrs. A.E. Roberts, Mrs. J.E. Eckert, Mr. J.E. Eckert, Mr. Clyde Shaw, Bill Sledge, and W.E. Martin; (second row) R.H. Tudor, R.A. Baldwin, George Sledge, E.P. Nix, W.P. Florence, Brown Bishop, Paul P. Murray, R.T. Williams, Fred B. Tudor, Alex DeLong, C.A. Coleman, C.V. Young, and John Simmons. (Courtesy of the Slaton Museum.)

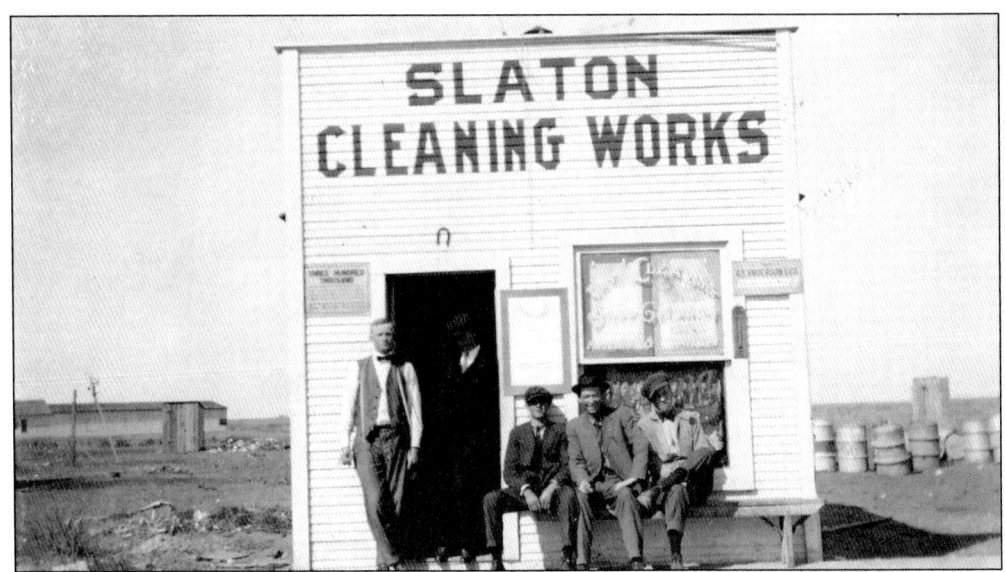

This 1914 image shows a few gentlemen sitting in front of the Slaton Cleaning Works on Texas Avenue. From left to right are Alex DeLong and an unidentified man standing in the door; seated from left to right are DeLong's brother, Joe Kirkendall, and Vern Johnson.

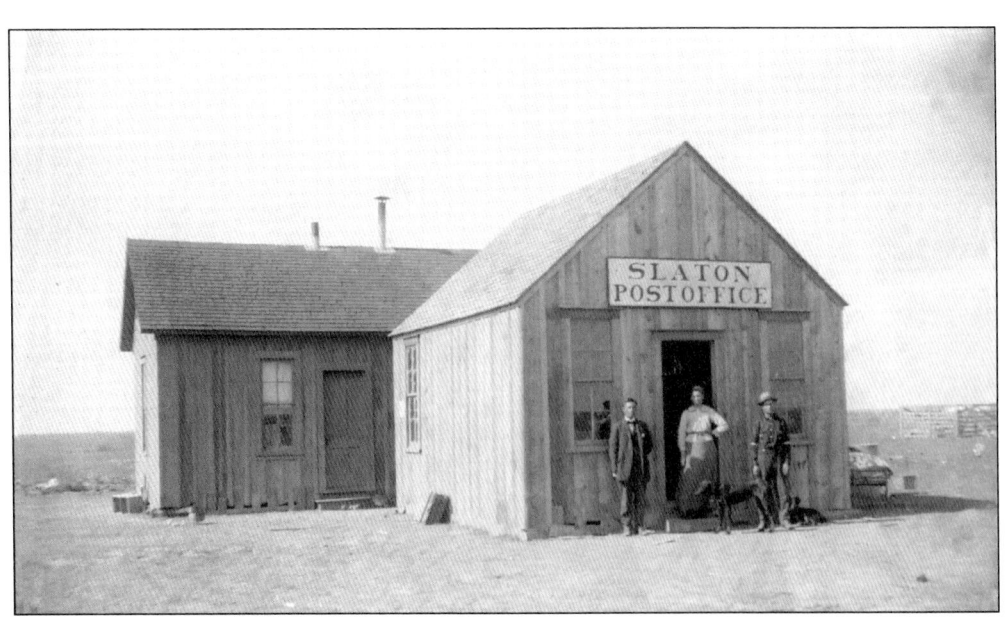

This 1911 picture of the Slaton post office includes, from left to right, Fred Higbee, Annie Higbee (Fred's wife), and their son Freddie. Fred Higbee served as postmaster of Slaton from 1910 until 1912, and Annie served as postmistress from 1912 until 1918. Annie Higbee was the first woman in Slaton, and when her husband passed away, she because the first postmistress.

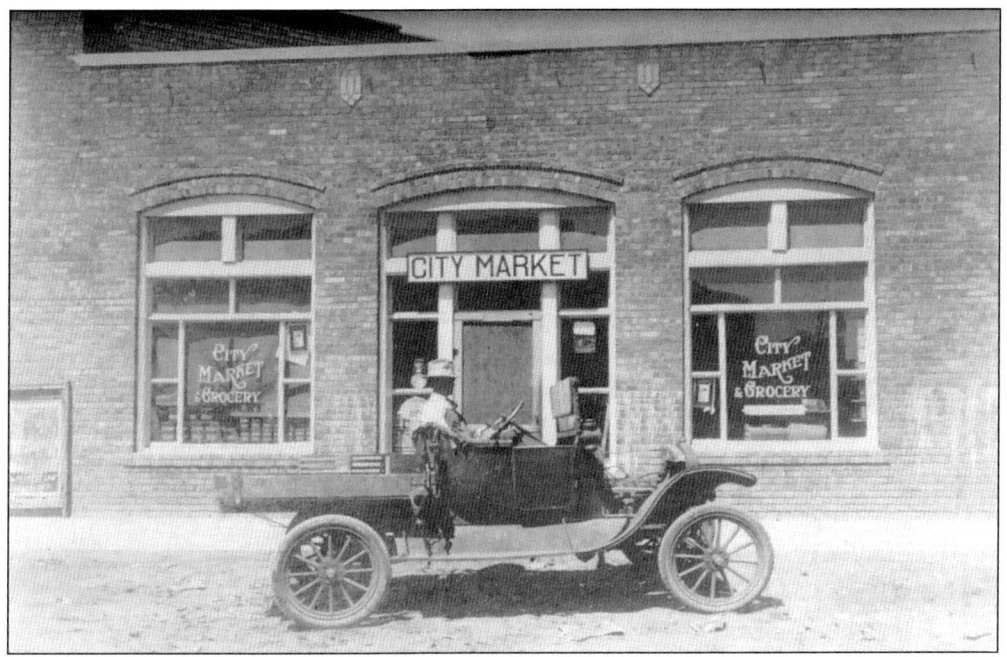

Robert Terry (Tee) Williams (1892–1950) is pictured here in a Model T delivery truck at the city market, one of four businesses owned and operated by three Williams brothers in buildings they constructed in Slaton in 1920. (Courtesy of the Slaton Museum.)

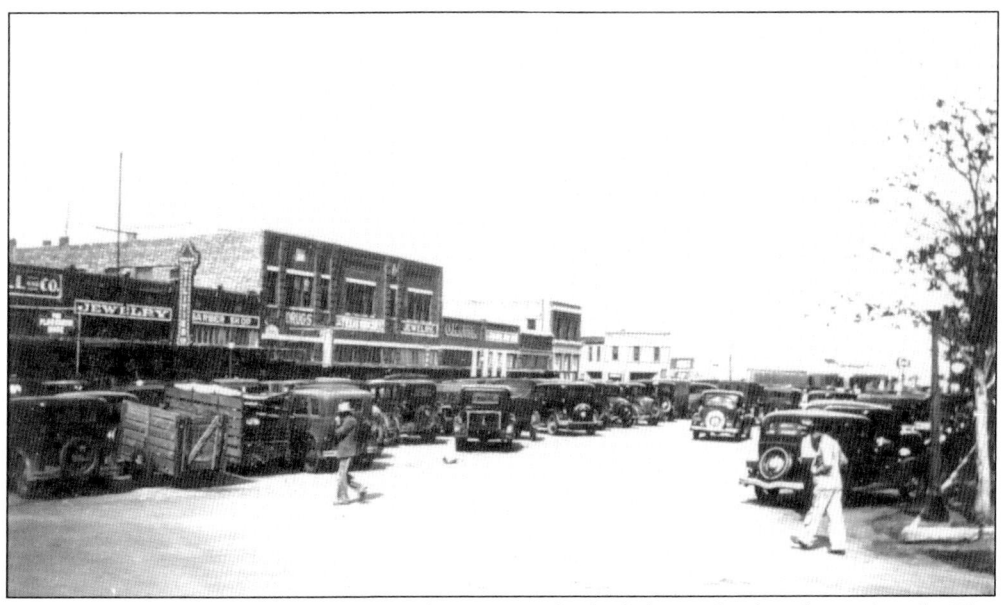

This is a picture of downtown Slaton in the 1920s. A lot had changed in less than a decade. This photograph depicts a thriving town full of people and businesses.

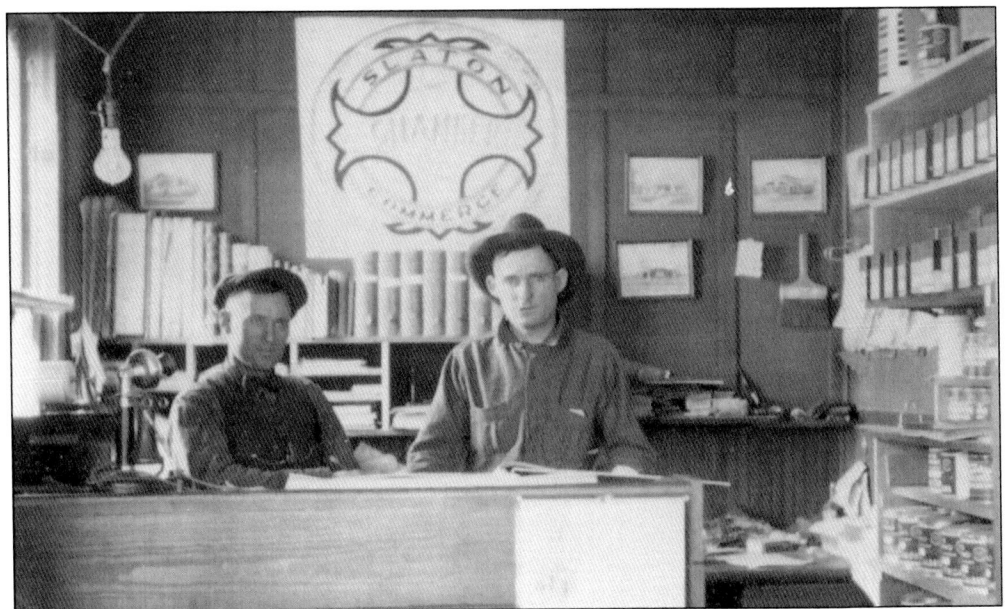

This 1915 photograph shows Rockwell Lumber Company, located at the corner of Lynn and North Seventh Streets. The building contractors at this time could barely keep pace with the demand in Slaton. Building supplies were purchased here. Pictured are Henry McGee (left) and Jerry Simmons. Other local lumber companies at the time included Alfalfa Lumber Company and Slaton Lumber Company.

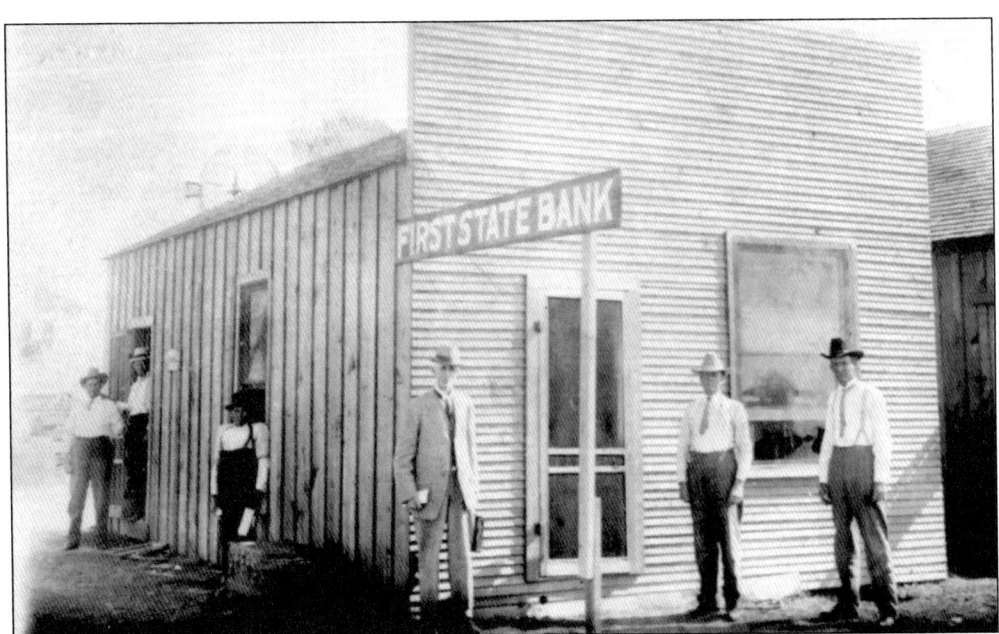

This is the First State Bank in 1911. Pictured are, from left to right, H.D. Talley, J.S. Edwards Sr., Shorty Helm, ? Drummer, A.B. Ellis, and P.E. Jordan. On July 20, 1911, the bank advertised that it held a capital of $15,000. O.L. Slaton was the first president of the bank.

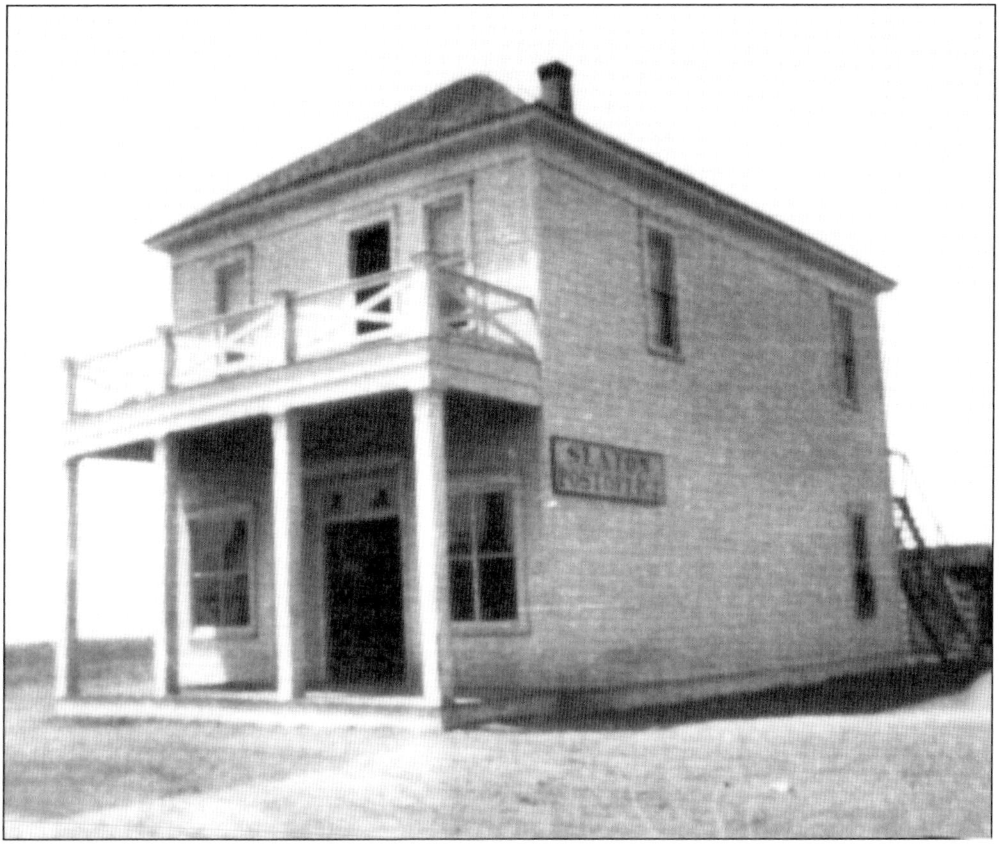

The inside and outside of the Slaton post office, located at 235 West Lubbock Street, are pictured here in 1912.

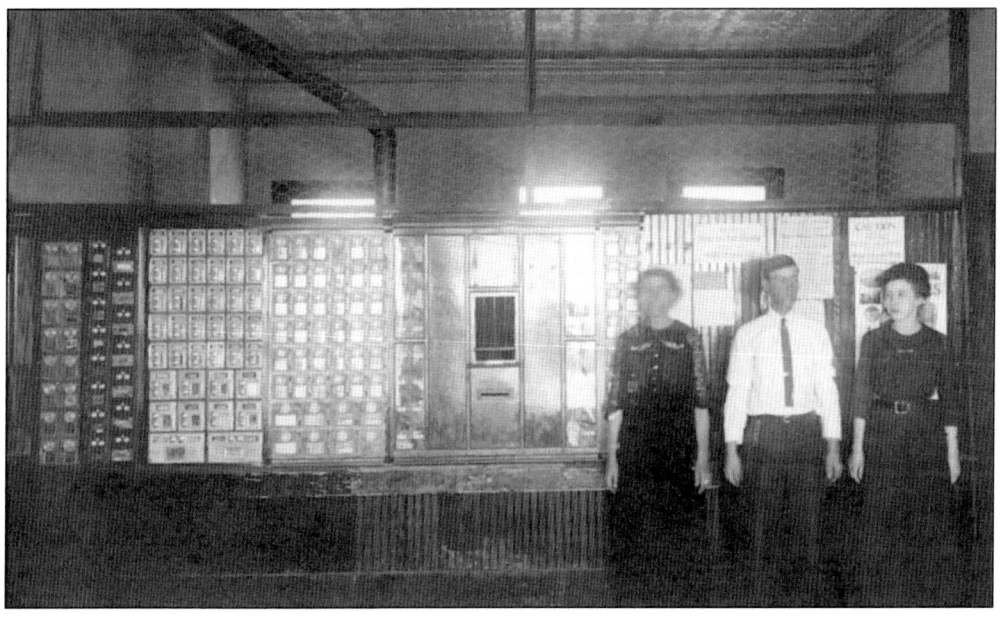

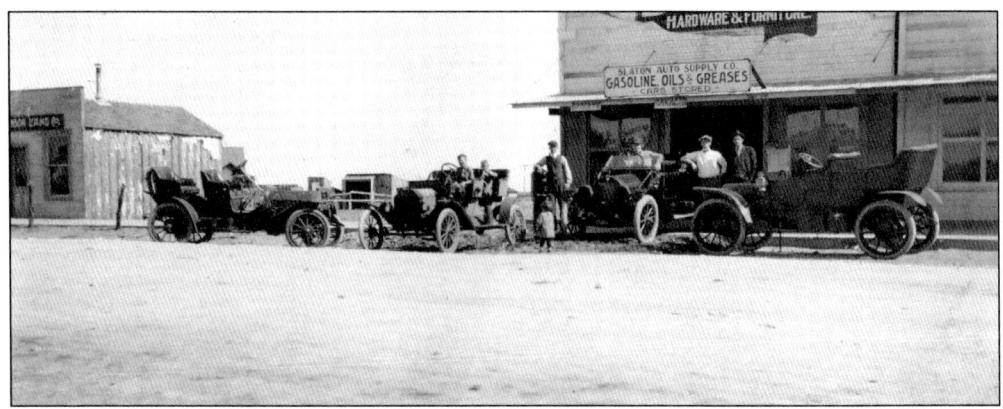

Here is a picture taken in 1915 in front of the Slaton Auto Supply Company. The four cars are, from left to right, a four-cylinder, four-passenger Buick; a four-cylinder, four-passenger Ford; a four-cylinder Hudson; and a four-cylinder Franklin. DeLong is standing by the gas pump, and Vern Johnson is in the car. The other two men are Alex DeLong and Herschel Magee. Standing in front of the first DeLong is Cordelia Grantham.

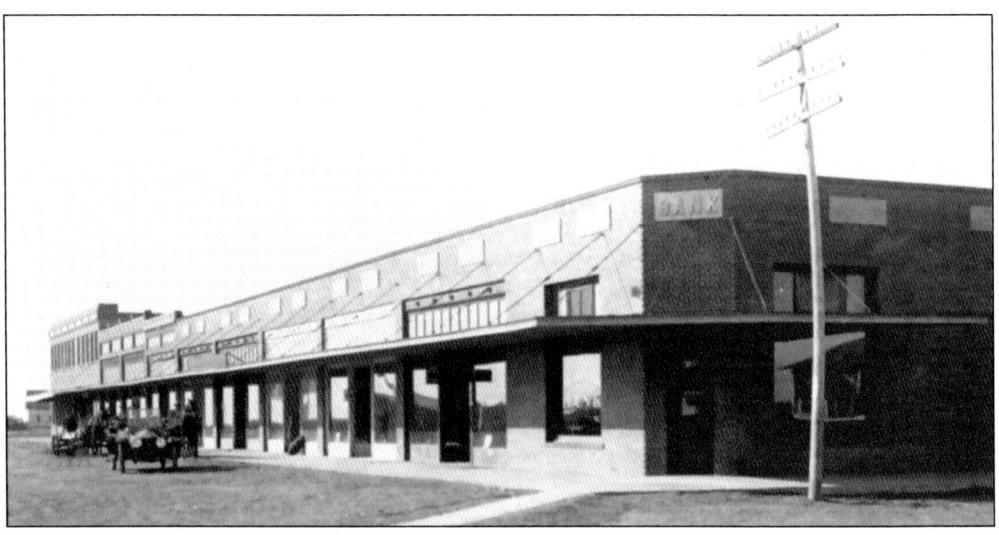

Pictured here are nearly empty downtown Slaton streets in 1919.

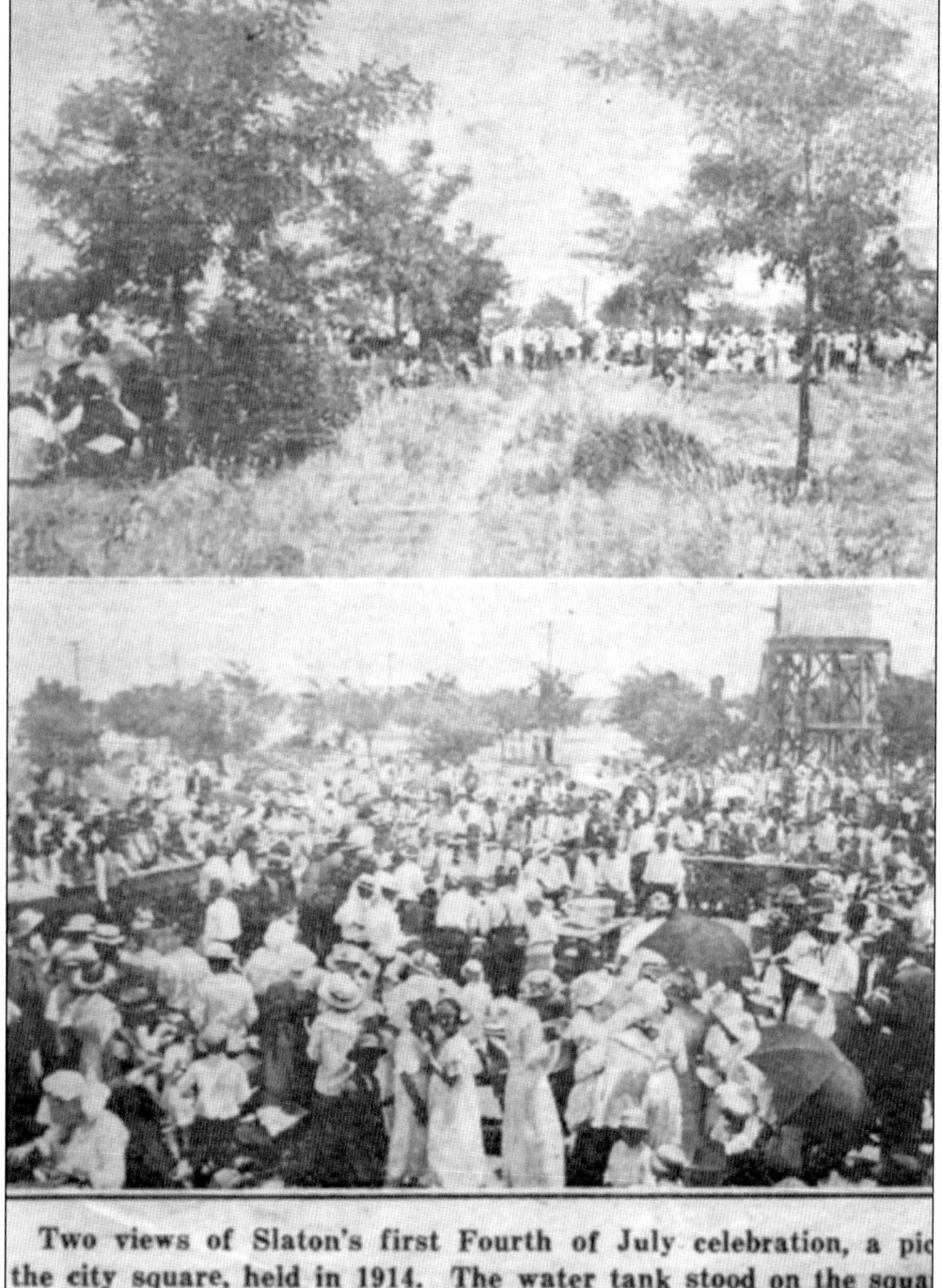

Two views of Slaton's first Fourth of July celebration, a pic the city square, held in 1914. The water tank stood on the squa the city hall had not been built. Old timers with a good memor 'e able to pick out themselves and friends.

These images from *The Slatonite* captured Slaton's very first Fourth of July celebration, which was held in 1914. City Hall had not yet been built.

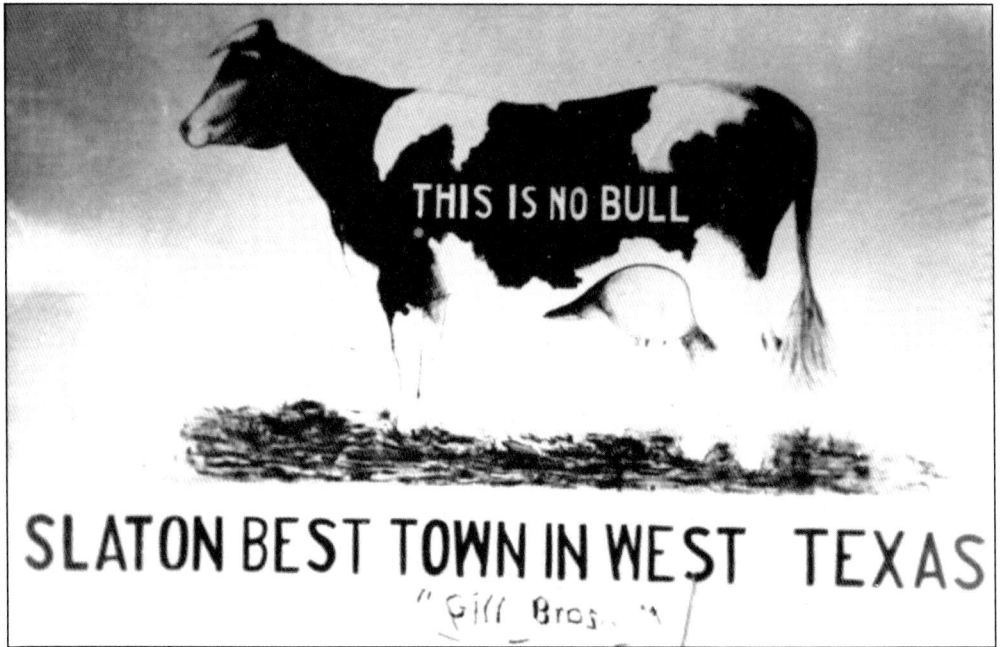

This 1910 postcard promoting Slaton is no bull. This was part of the preparations for the official opening day, June 15, 1911, which included an ambitious advertising program, printed circulars, and this postcard. The advertisements, which described the area and promised ample water, were distributed from Lubbock to Kansas via the Santa Fe Railway.

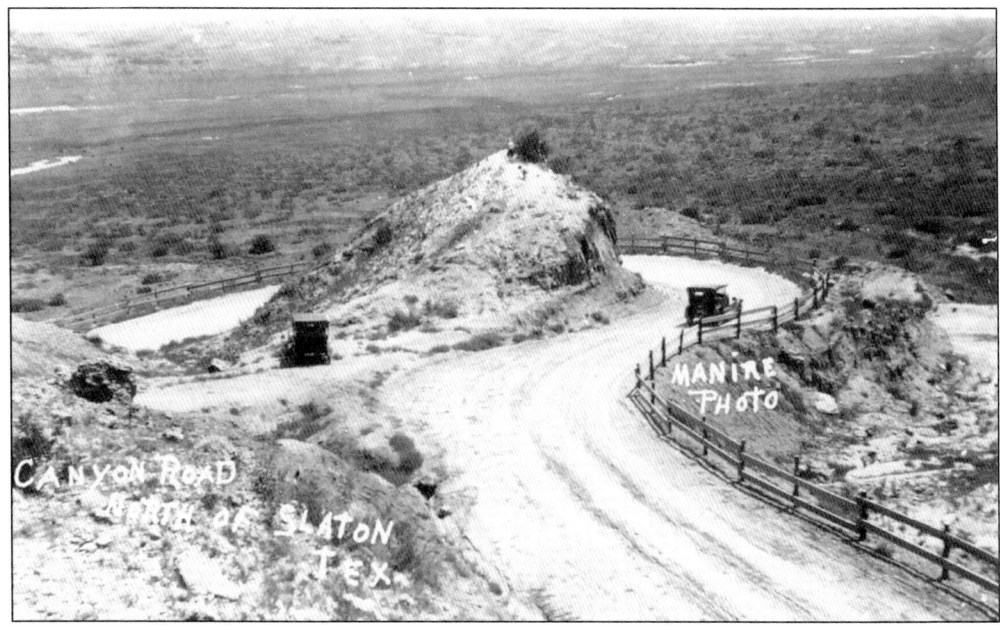

This picture of Horseshoe Bend in Yellow House Canyon was taken in the 1910s. Yellow House Canyon is about 20 miles long at the junction of Blackwater Draw and Yellow House Draw and is about 6.2 miles east of Slaton. Yellow House Canyon is one of three major canyons along the east side of the Llano Estacado and carries the waters of the North Fork Double Mountain Fork Brazos River.

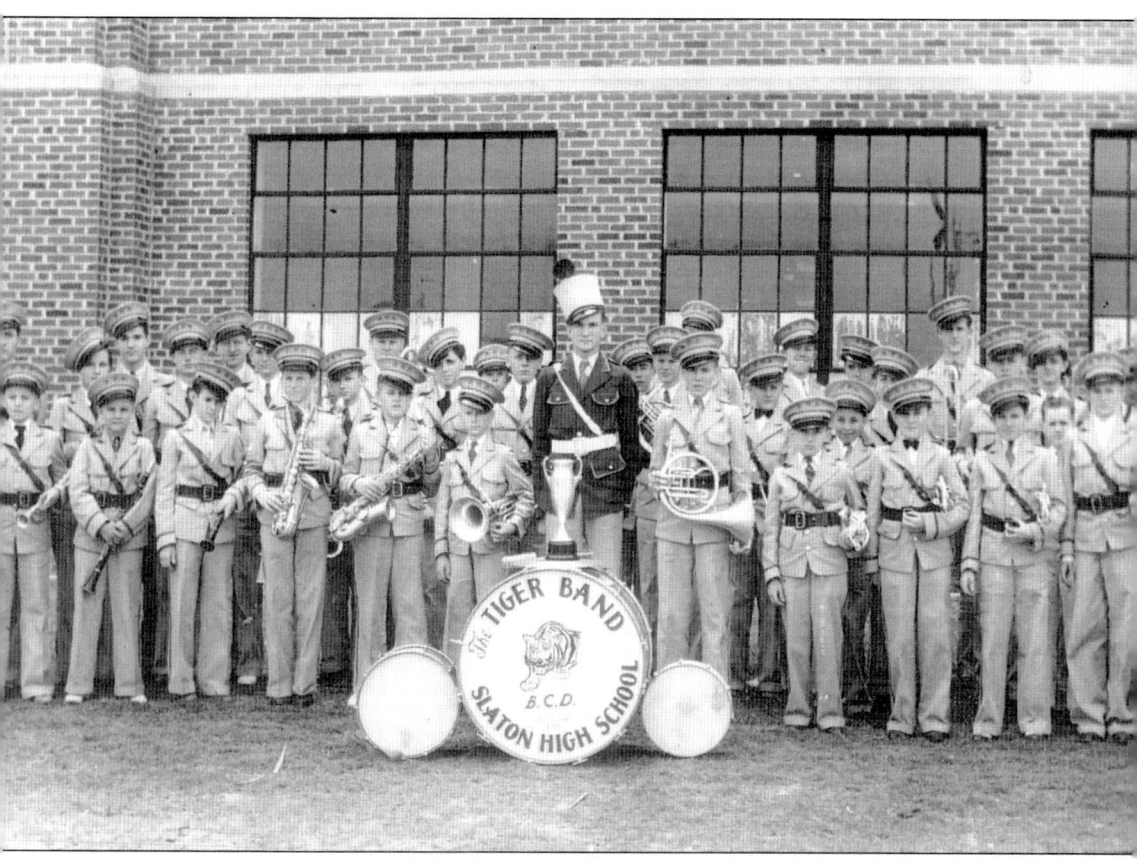

The first school class was held in Slaton in 1911 at the Methodist church. School also took place that year at area Baptist churches. W.P. Florence was instrumental in beginning the public school system in Slaton. This 1937 photograph shows the Slaton High School band, the members of which went to the tri-state competition in Oklahoma City. They traveled by train, picking up band members along the way. This band placed first in the competition. Some of the members pictured here include, in no specific order, Wesley Jones, Bill Ball, Paul Melton, Don Hatchett, Harold Tucker, Toy Dial, Joe Walker, Curtis Brown, Rodney McReynolds, Kenneth Tanner, Perry Moss, Billie Rust, Margie Brown, Levi Self, and Joe Ward. (Courtesy of the Slaton Museum.)

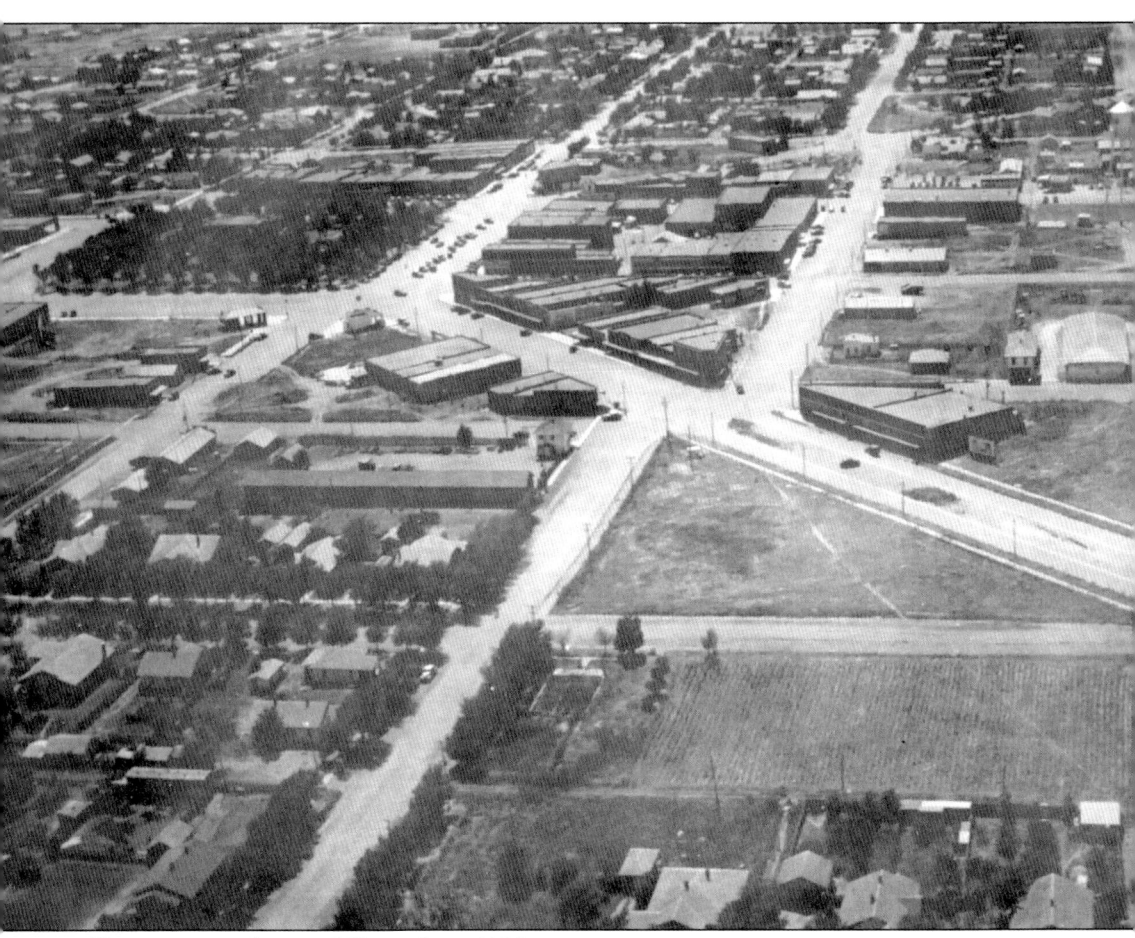
Here is an aerial view of Slaton from 1936.

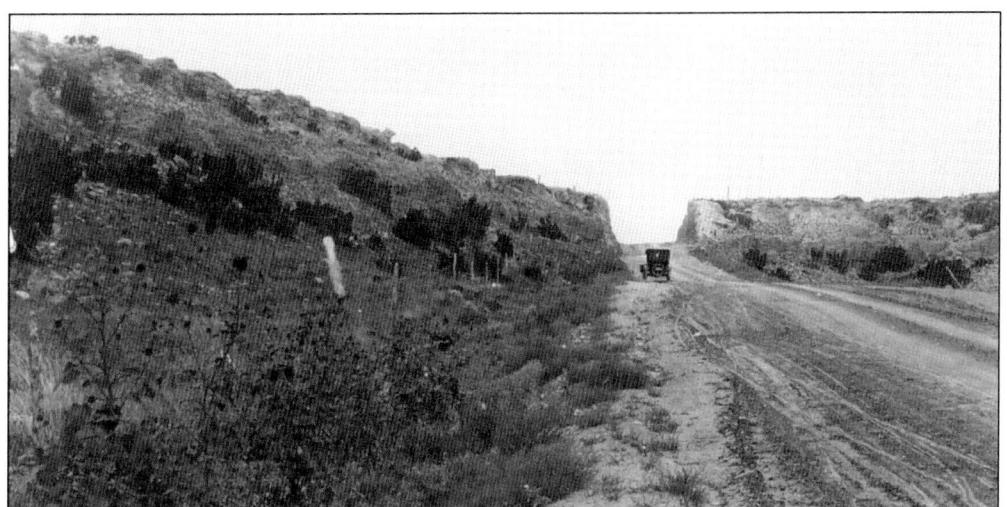
This picture captures a memory from 1920—a lonely old Model T heads down a dirt road on the Caprock Escarpment, the edge of the plains.

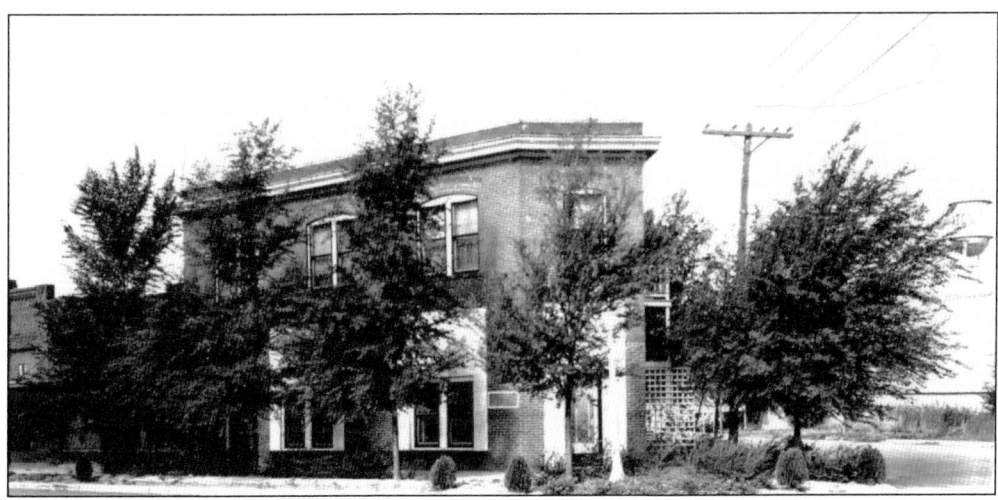
This 1911 photograph shows the historic McCrea Building. It housed the E.N. Twaddle Grocery from 1912 to 1921, then the Blue Front Grocery from 1922 until 1924. It then became a boardinghouse, and later, an apartment building.

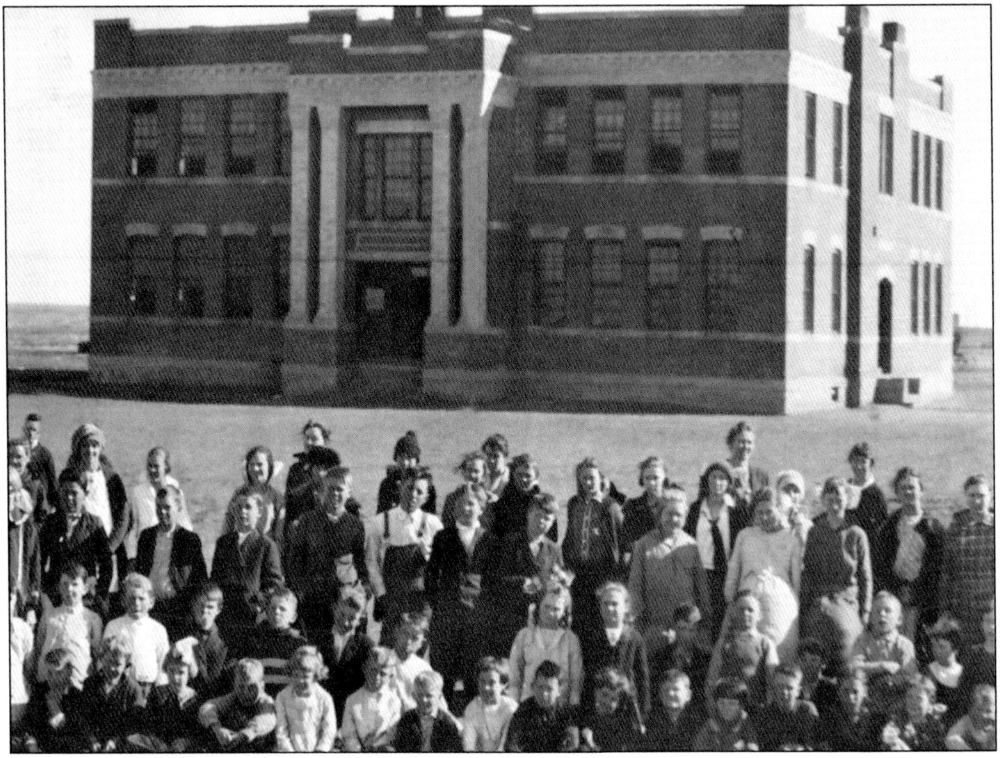

Although school in Slaton began in churches, it did not take long before the city built a new two-story brick structure to house a school. This 1915 photograph shows the two-story Slaton Independent School District building with many children out front. At the time, non-school activities for children included A Russian Thistle literary society, Campfire Girls, and Boy Scouts.

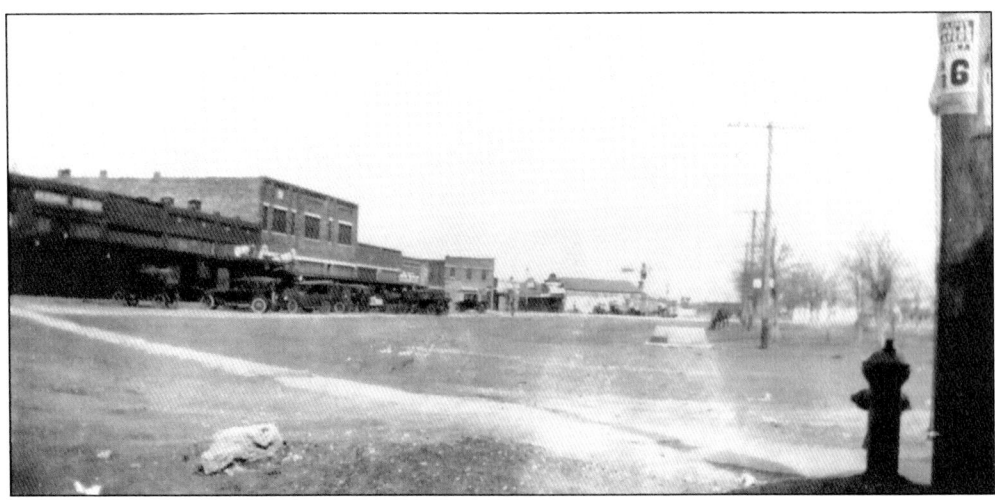

This is what downtown Slaton looked like in 1920—several businesses, a horse grazing at the edge of the street, a fire hydrant, and a promising future for this Santa Fe Railway town. The first homes in Slaton were small frame houses. Early settlers remember many frame buildings, board sidewalks, streets that were unpaved, and plenty of mudholes, but they also look back on this time of their life with fond memories.

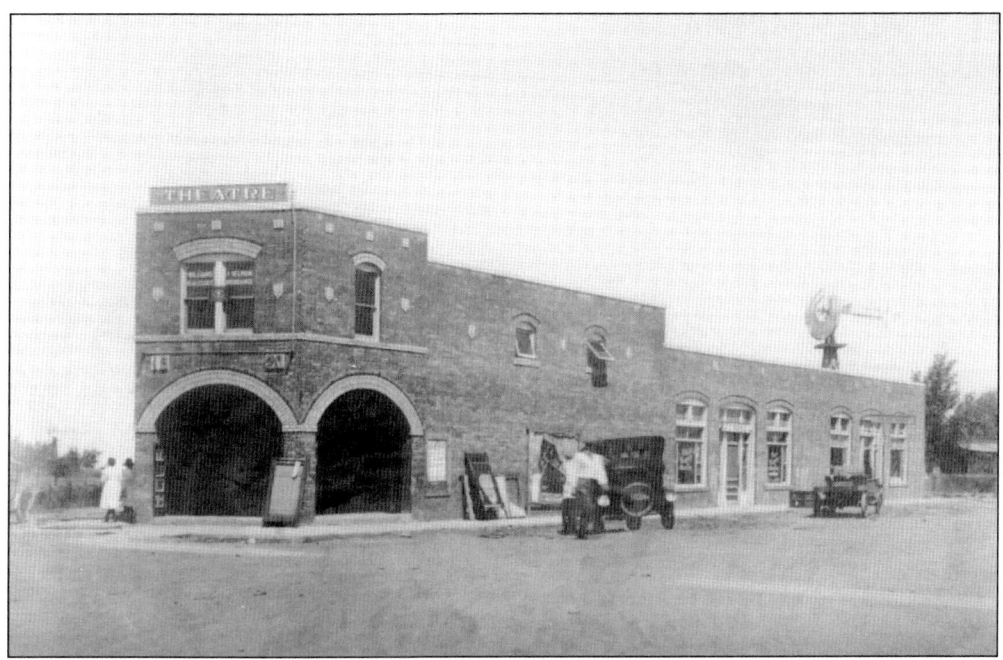

This 1919 picture shows the Wilselma Theatre on the corner of Ninth Street. The theater, opened by Floyd Williams and Sam Selman, was in business from 1919 until 1923; the business's name was a combination of both of the men's last names. The building, constructed by brothers R.T. and Floyd Williams, also housed a city market and a tailor shop. A two-story addition was later built at the end of the complex by a third Williams brother, Lafayette (Fate). The Wilselma Theatre was oriented toward City Hall Square, while the other businesses faced Ninth Street.

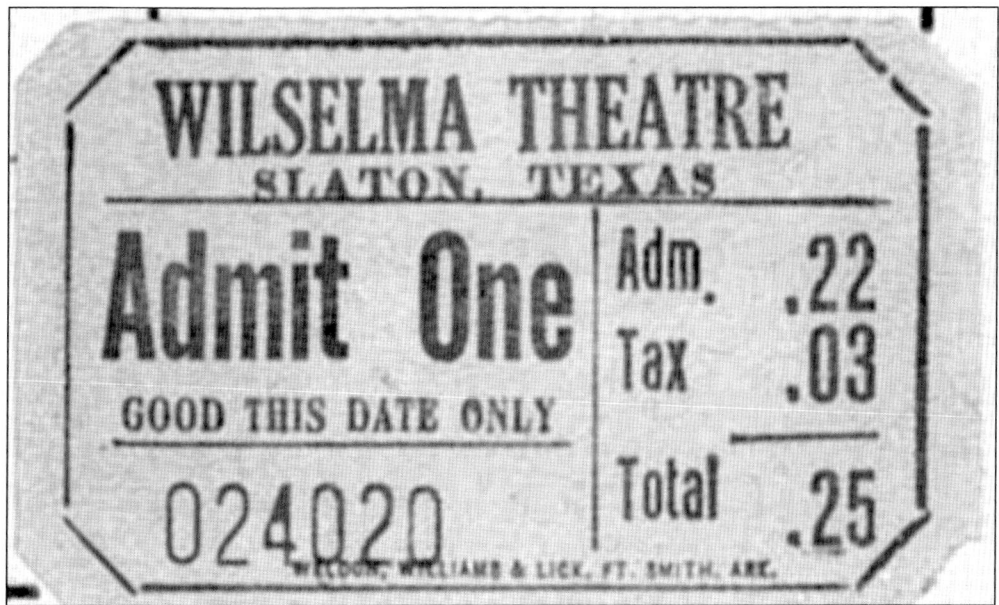

This is a ticket used to get into a movie at the Wilselma Theatre. Note that it only cost 25¢ to see a movie in those days. (Courtesy of the Slaton Museum.)

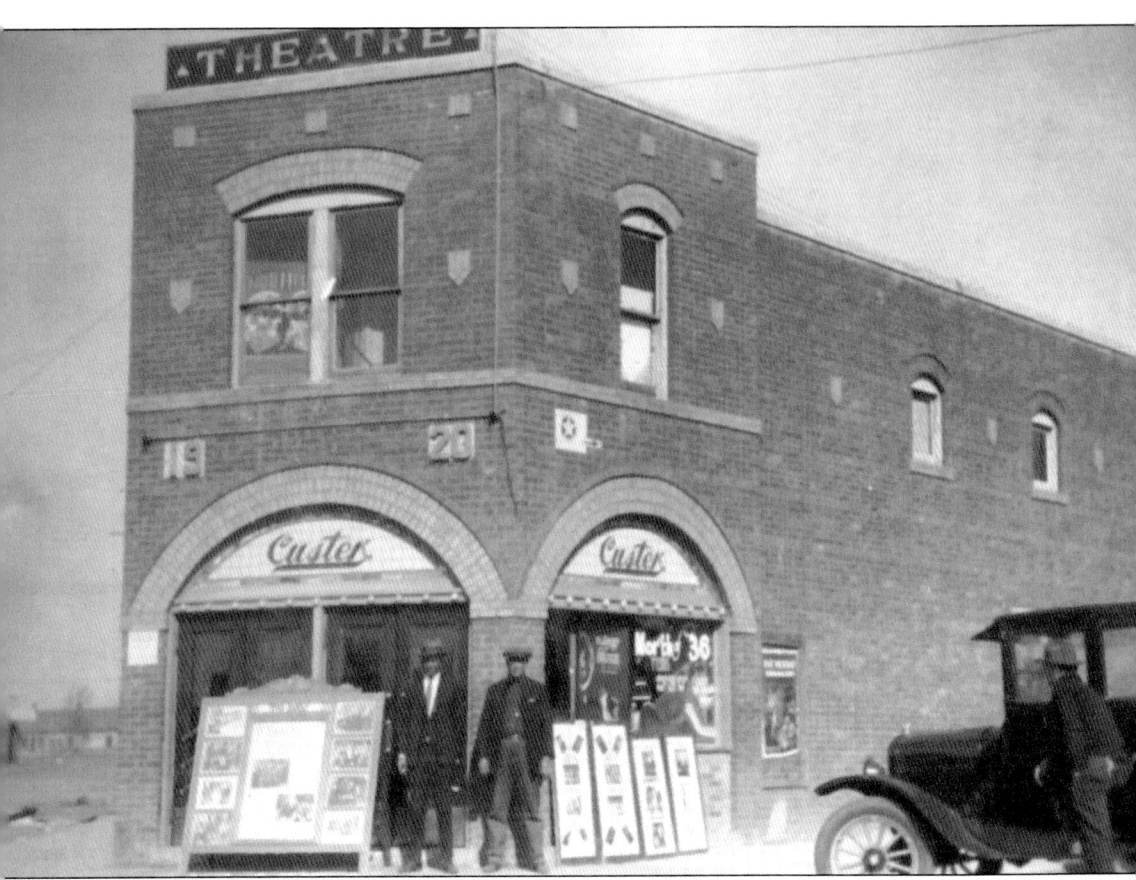

In 1920, the Wilselma Theatre was sold to Ford Taylor, who briefly owned it until he sold to Jeff Custer. Custer operated the theater under the name Custer Theatre until 1925. It seated 740 people.

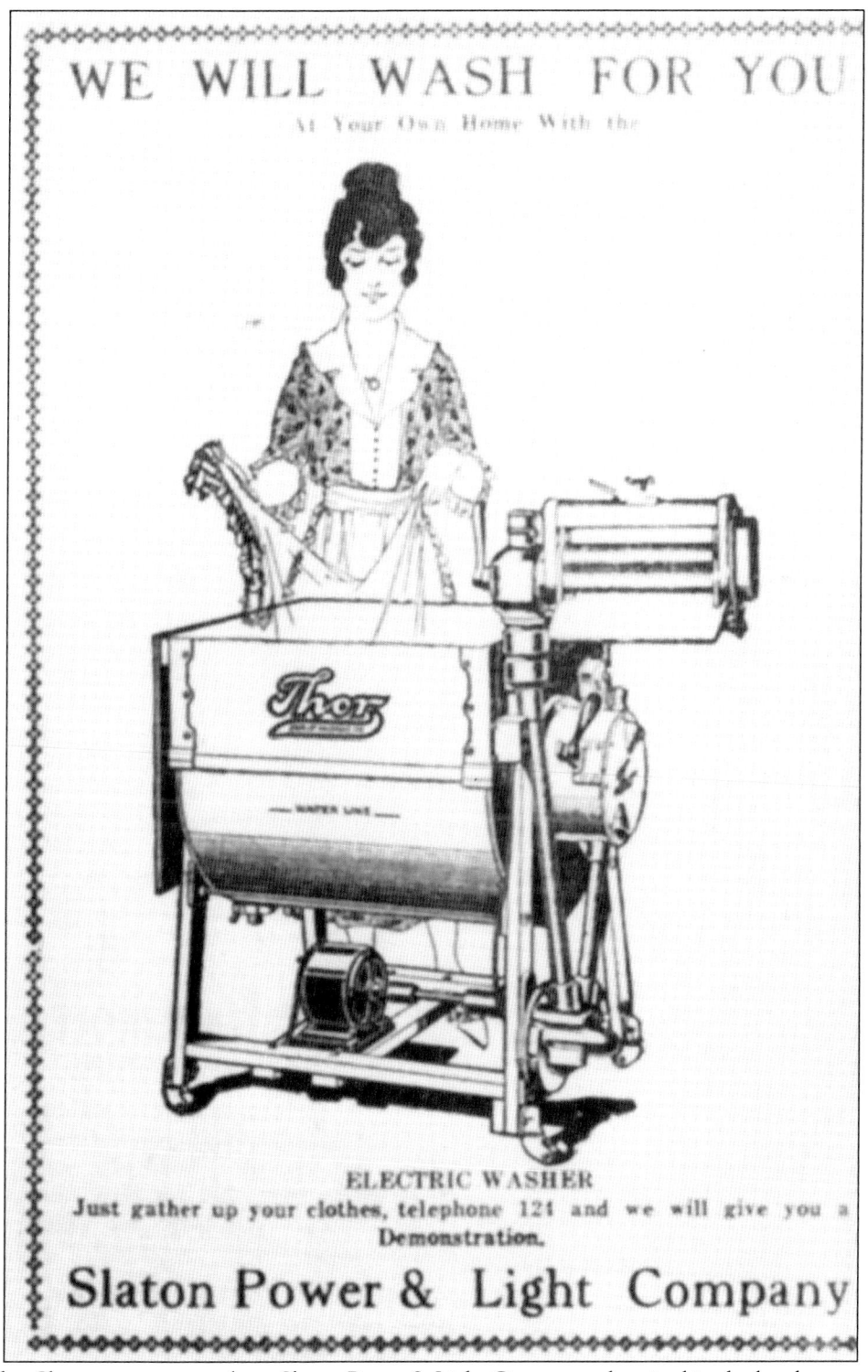

After Slaton got a power plant, Slaton Power & Light Company advertised in the local paper to promote its in-home electric washer demonstrations.

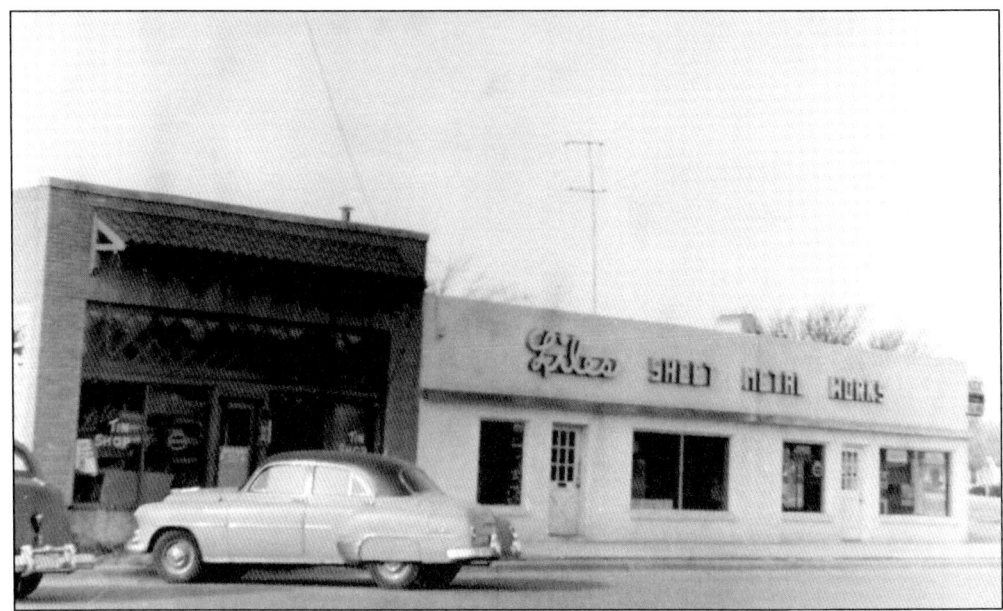

Dan Liles and his wife, Sue, arrived in Slaton by train from Vernon, Texas, in April 1923. They wanted to start a new home and business. Their son, Wayne, was three years old at the time. Dan had been discharged from the US Navy after serving overseas in England and France in World War I. He was a tinner by trade and established Liles Sheet Metal Works. He did metalwork for structures such as grain elevators, oil mills, and cotton gins. He also made clothes boxes for the Santa Fe Railway in Slaton. This picture shows Liles Tin Shop and Liles Sheet Metal Works in 1955. Dan and Wayne operated the businesses.

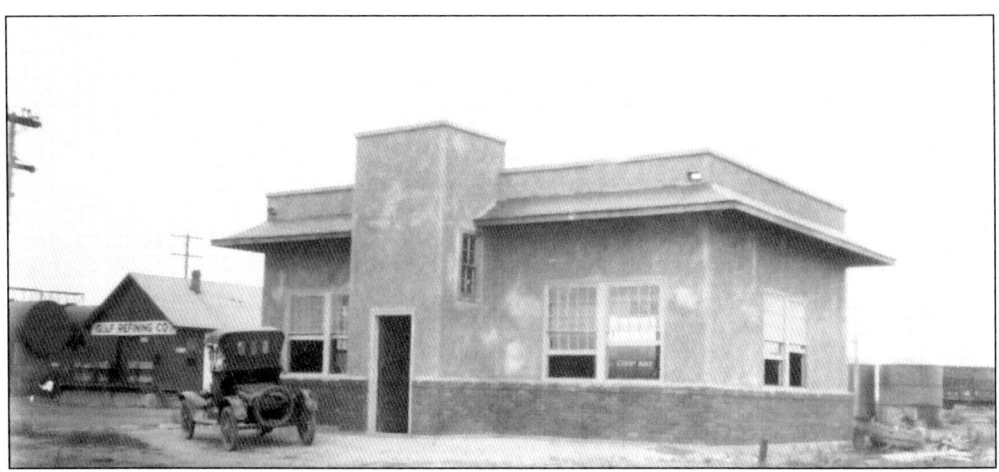

In July 1920, Slaton's first power plant opened, with J.A. Elliott as the manager. It all began with a 25-horsepower Fairbanks Morse engine. This 1920 image shows the outside of the plant. When it opened, it only offered electric service from dusk to midnight, but this changed the lives of Slatonites from that moment on. Instead of oil lamps, residents could now use electric bulbs. Prior to the establishment of the power plant, businesses such as movie theaters had to operate using low-voltage generators.

O.D. Kenney and Bessie Kenney are pictured here on their wedding day—February 11, 1925. O.D. came to Slaton with his family in 1920; they lived south of town. He was the oldest of eight children born to James Wiley and Leta Kenney. They moved to Slaton thinking the climate of the plains would help their ill daughter who had tuberculosis. O.D. and Bessie were married by pastor Jasper Bogue in the pastor's home on Tenth Street. They had four children: Pauline Faye, Oliver Wayne, Alton Daniel, and Peggy Sue.

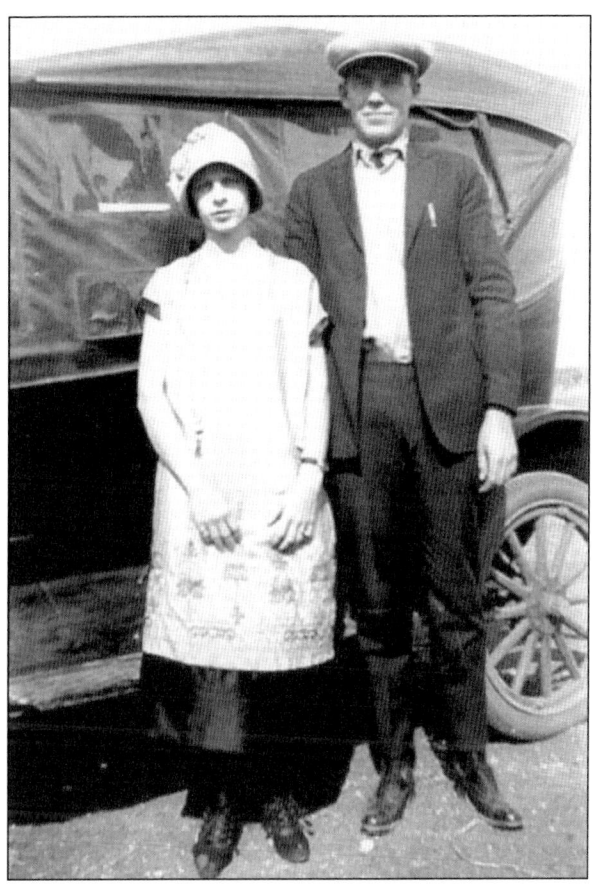

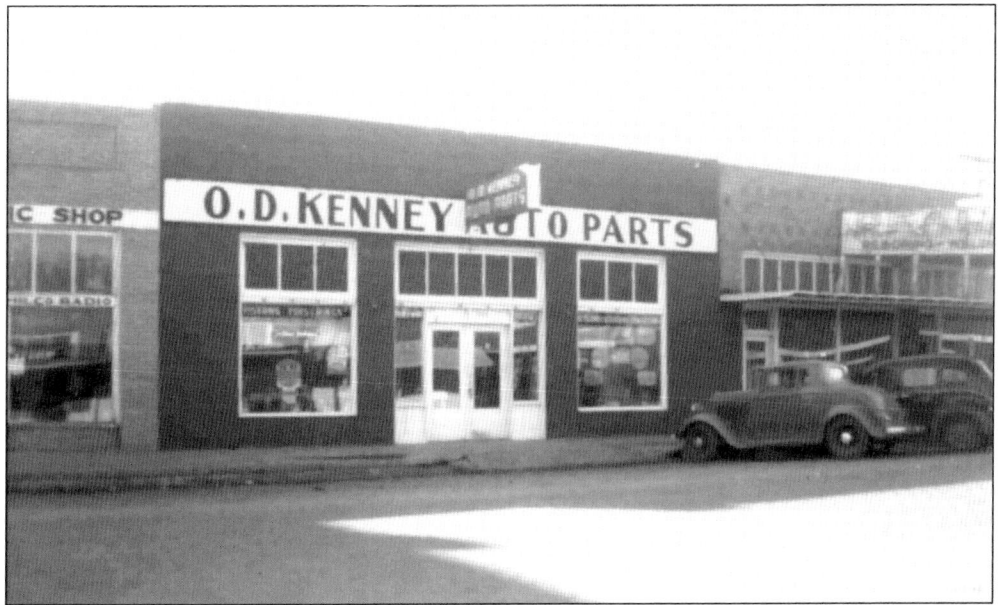

This picture was taken in 1938. O.D. Kenney Auto Parts, started in 1929 by O.D. Kenney, is still in business today in downtown Slaton.

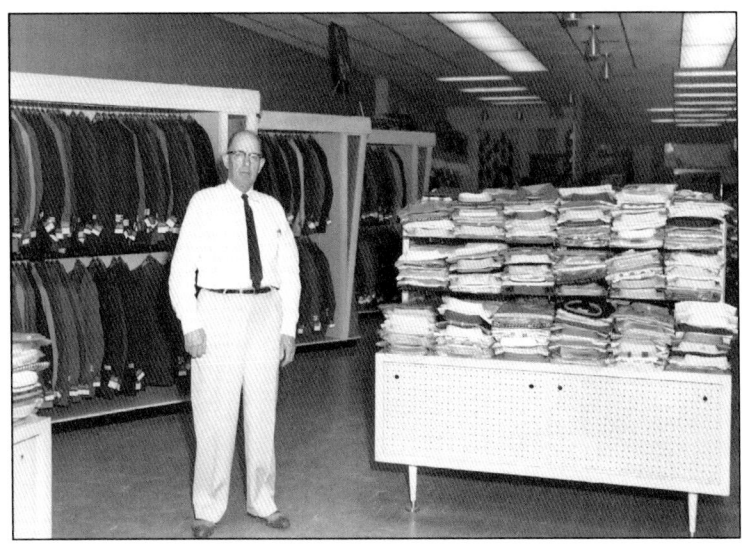

O.Z. Ball is pictured here in 1936 in his clothing store, O.Z. Ball Men's Store. He came to Slaton in 1918 during one of the biggest snowstorms the town has ever had and worked for the Santa Fe Railway for three years before going into the clothing business. Most of his business came from the railroad. He sold his business to his son, Bill, in 1967.

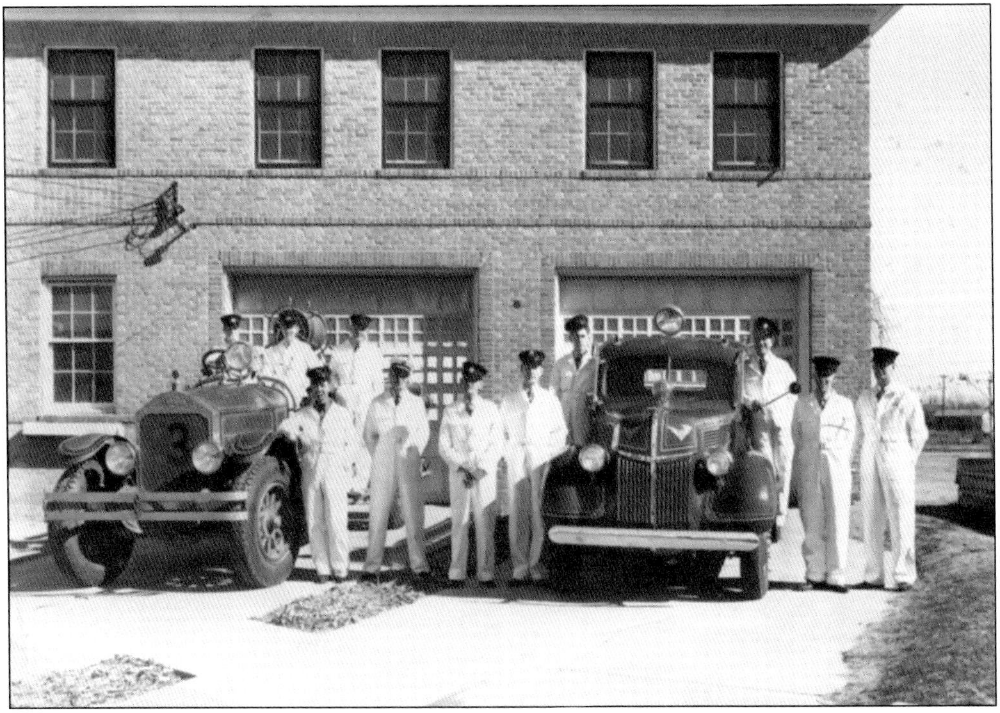

The Slaton Fire Department is pictured here in the 1930s. The first fire department in Slaton was a bucket brigade. When asked how they gave the alarm, the reply was that they did not. They said the first man who saw the fire grabbed a bucket and made for the nearest water tank, then yelled to the nearest passing man to pass it on to the fire. Everybody grabbed buckets—some shot pistols—and soon, they had a string of buckets going from the tank to the fire. From that modest beginning, the Slaton Fire Department grew to owning a hose cart with chemicals, then a small truck. From left to right are Jack Cooper, Bart Jones, Jess Burton, C.C. Kenney, Elbert Wilson, Tom Thompson, Kirk Dowell, Wallace Cooper, Ottis Browning, L.B. Hagerman, and Carl Sartain.

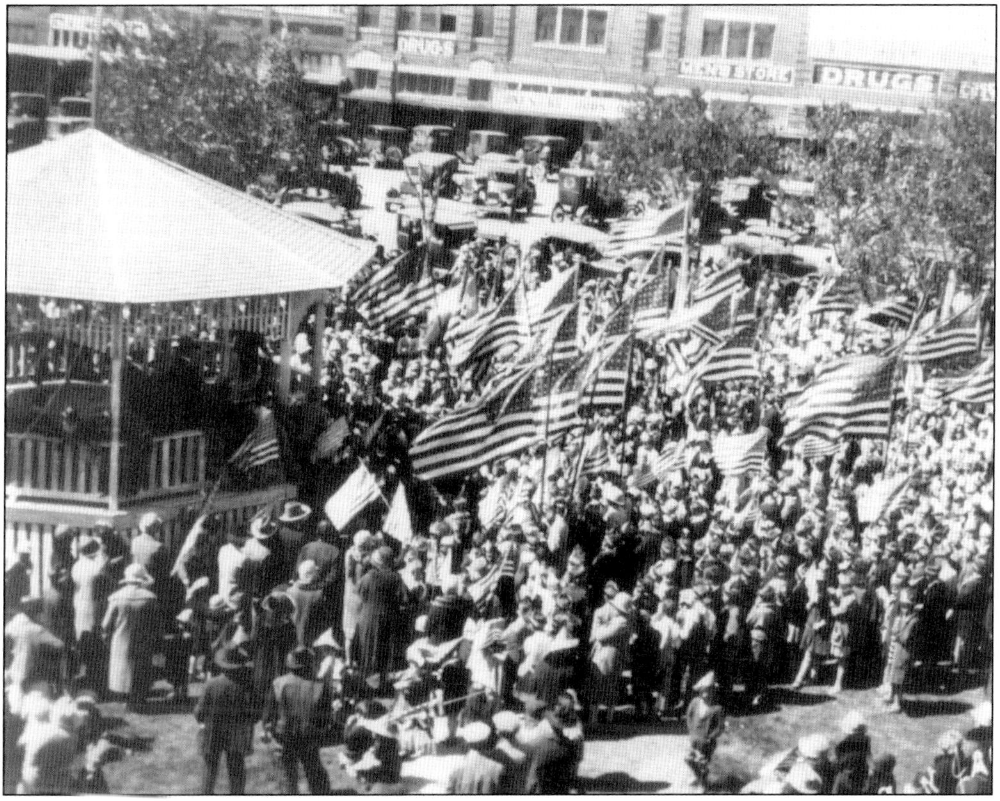

Locals gather around the gazebo in downtown Slaton in 1925 for San Jacinto Day. San Jacinto Day is the celebration of the Battle of San Jacinto, which was fought on April 21, 1836. It was the final battle of the Texas Revolution, in which Texas won its independence from Mexico.

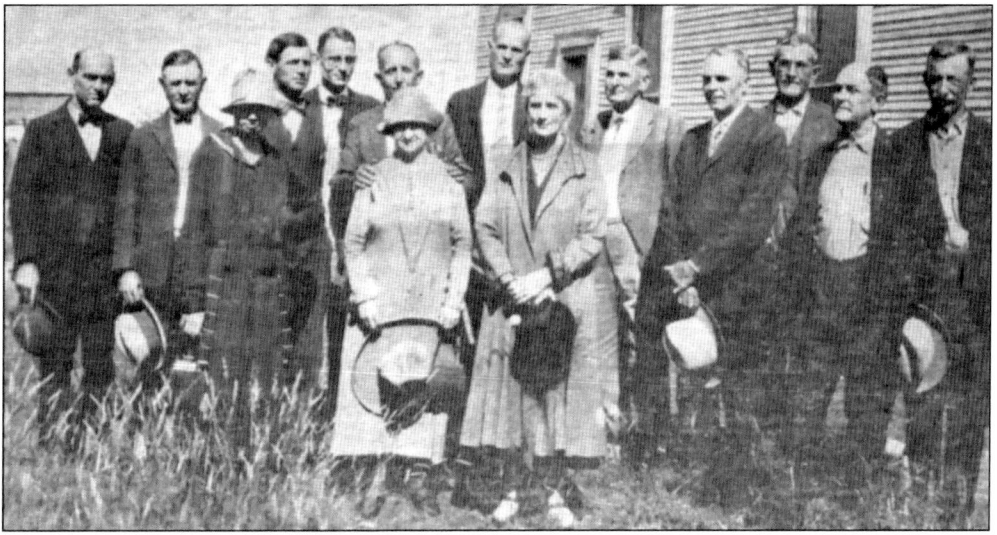

This picture shows a committee appointed in 1926 to hold a fair in Slaton. From left to right are (first row) S.H. Adams, Mrs. J.J. Ross, and Mrs. Lee Green; (second row) Dr. ? Roberts, George W. Bourland, Floyd Williams, J.H. Brewer, J.J. Ross, C.L. Stone, H.D. Talley, J.W. Nesbitt, Nick Gentry, ? Binion, and L.J. Strube.

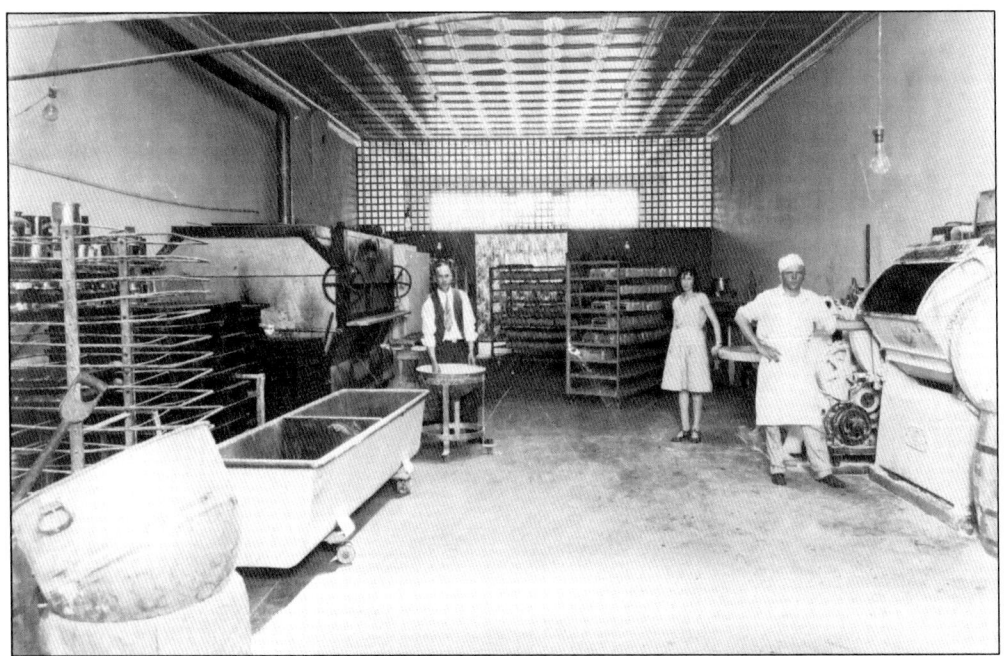

Ray Hickman purchased the City Bakery from C.C. Carr in 1930. It was then named Slaton Bakery Company and located at 155 N. Garza Street. In 1943, Barney and Ollie Mae Wilson purchased the bakery from R.D. Hickman. Pictured here in 1929 are Ray Hickman (left) and Barney Wilson (right).

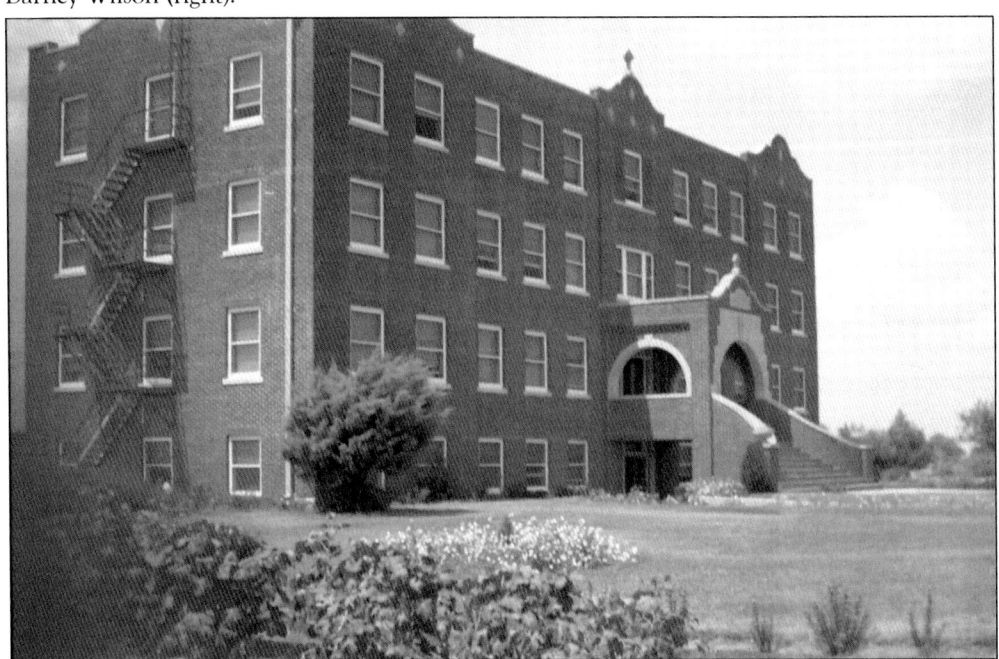

Mercy Hospital operated from 1928 until 1983. T.D. O'Brien invited the Sisters of Mercy to erect the hospital in Slaton to offer care, nursing, and relief to everyone regardless of national origin, age, or race. The Sisters of Mercy reluctantly turned over operation of this hospital to the Slaton Hospital Memorial Foundation in 1971.

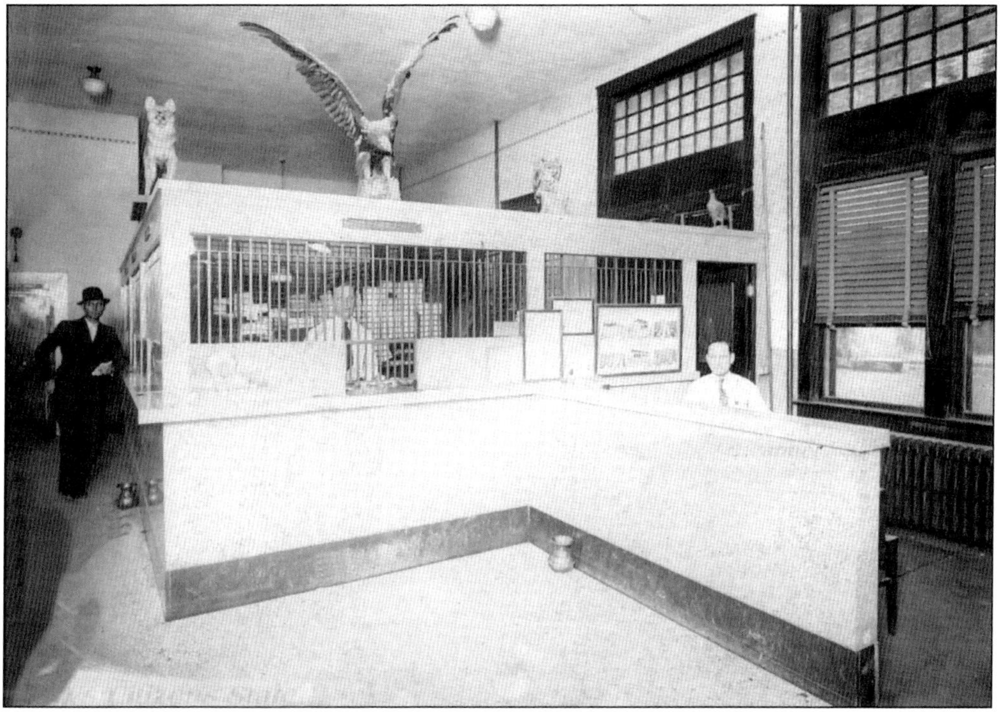

J.S. Edwards was the senior president of First State Bank, which opened in 1911 in Slaton but collapsed during the Depression in the 1930s. Edwards rebuilt his banking career and opened Citizens State Bank, which is pictured here in 1932. It opened its doors for business at 100 West Garza Street in October 1932. The bank's original board members included Edwards, A. Kessel, Bob Merrell, C.F. Anderson, G.H. Orr, and H.G. Sanders. The bank started with $25,000, which was very difficult in those hard times when few people had any money. The bank's name changed to Citizens Bank of Lubbock County in the late 1970s, and it continued to be an important part of the community.

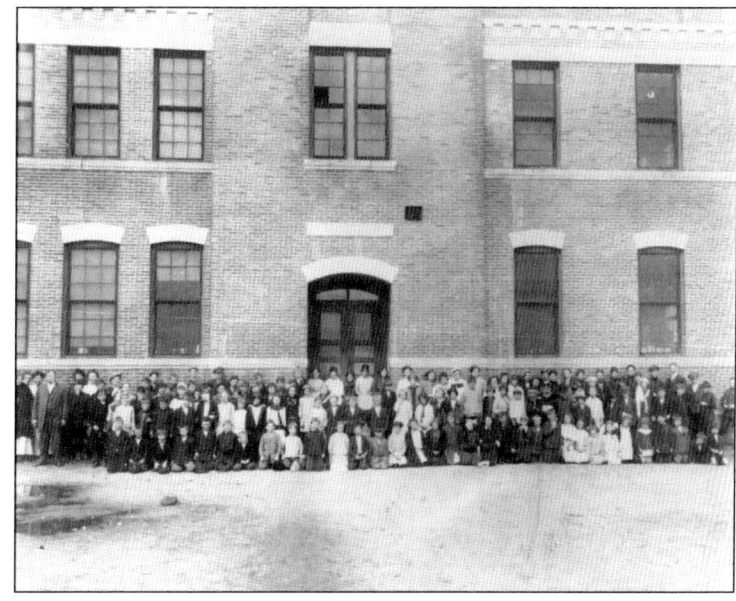

As Slaton continued to thrive, so did the Slaton school system. Here is a picture of the Slaton Independent School District school and children in the 1920s.

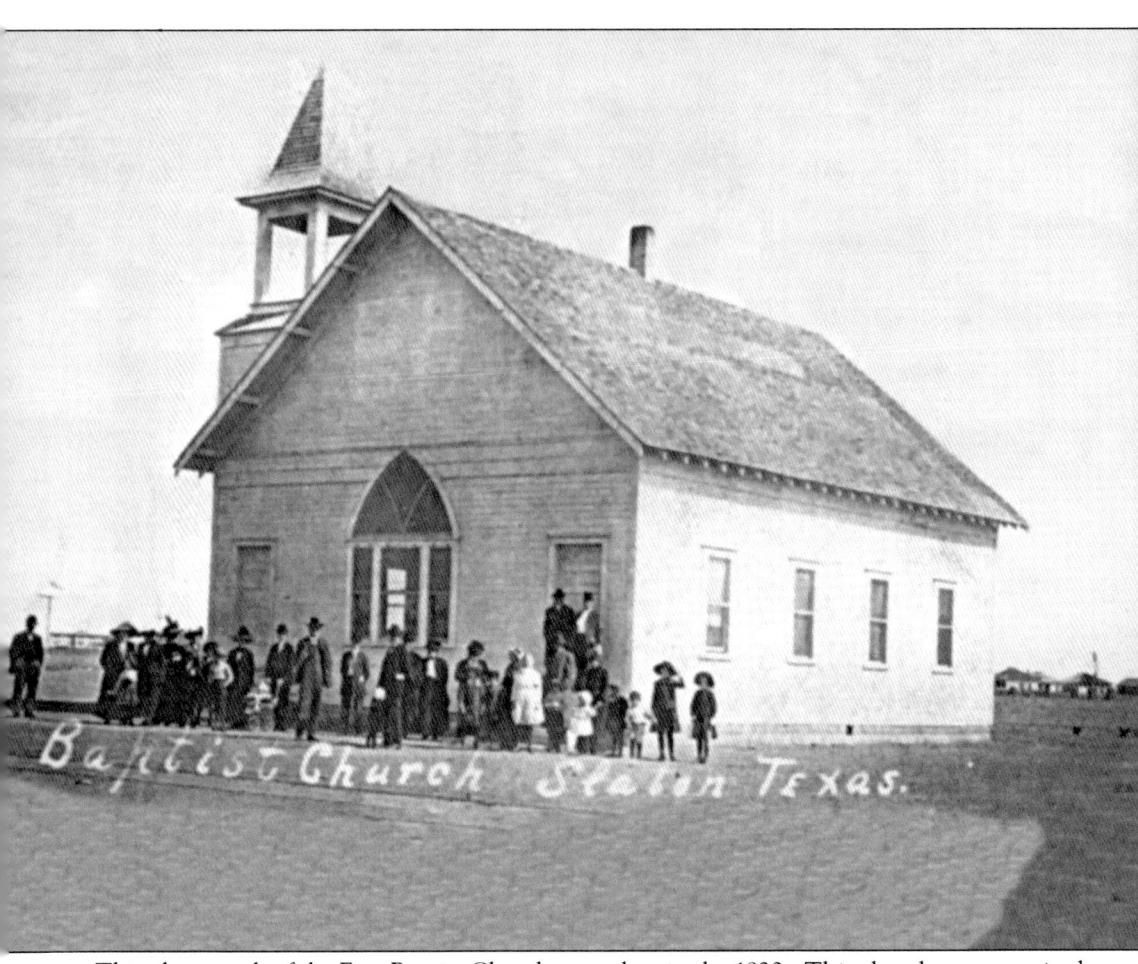

This photograph of the First Baptist Church was taken in the 1920s. This church was organized on July 2, 1911, with five members. The first pastor was J.R. Balch of Tahoka, and by the end of the year, the congregation had grown to 40 members. Church was a staple in the Slaton community from the beginning. In fact, the month after Slaton became an official town, the town's first church, Slaton Methodist Church, was organized under Rev. G.B. Overton. Church was originally held at what is now the corner of West Garza and Ninth Streets. A fundraising effort began in 1919 to build a church, and the building was completed in 1922 at a cost of $34,000.

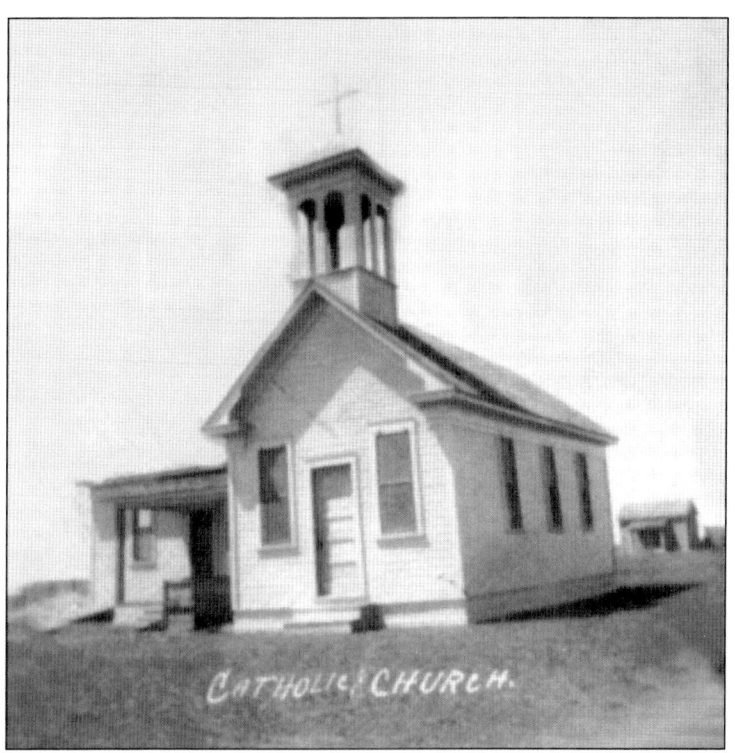

This picture of St. Joseph's Parish Catholic church is from the 1920s. The Santa Fe Railway donated the land for the church on December 30, 1911, and it was erected by Western Investment Land Company and cost around $1,500, which was paid for by the company. By 1917, the church had grown so much that they appointed a new pastor and built a new church. The new church opened in June of that year. In 1919, a third and even larger church was built for $10,000.

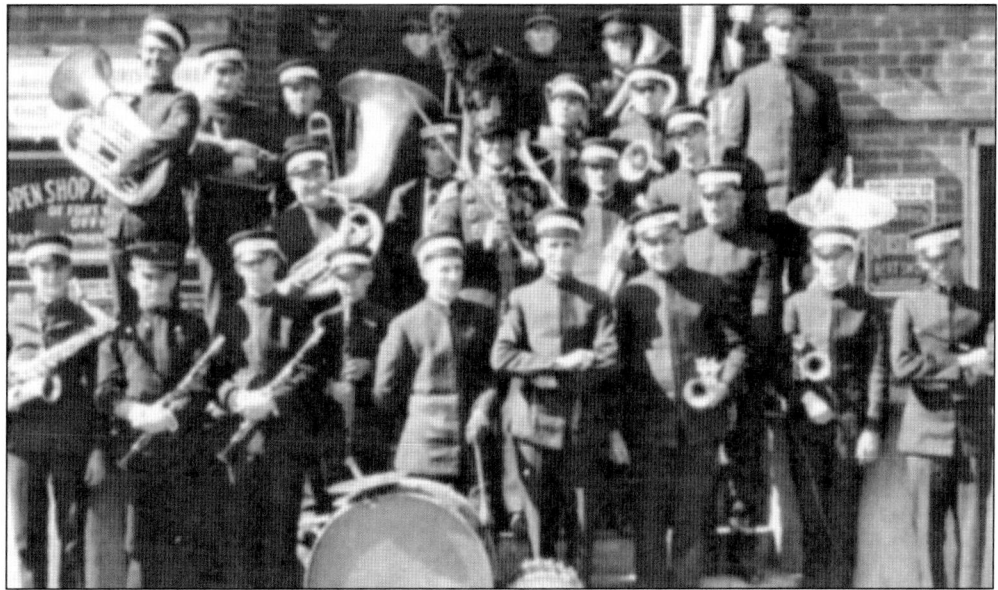

This is the 1922 Slaton Chamber of Commerce band. Scully Pogue was the director, and Jack Wadley was the drum major. Among those pictured are Wyle Burnes, Charles Splawn, Hugo Sanders, Harvey Tunnell, Charles Yeats, Jack Wadley, Guy, Vannota, Joe Heinrich, Forrect Payne, C.C. Hoffman, T.A. Worley, J.W. McKirahan, Tex Easterledge, Woody Rogers, and Cy Pettus.

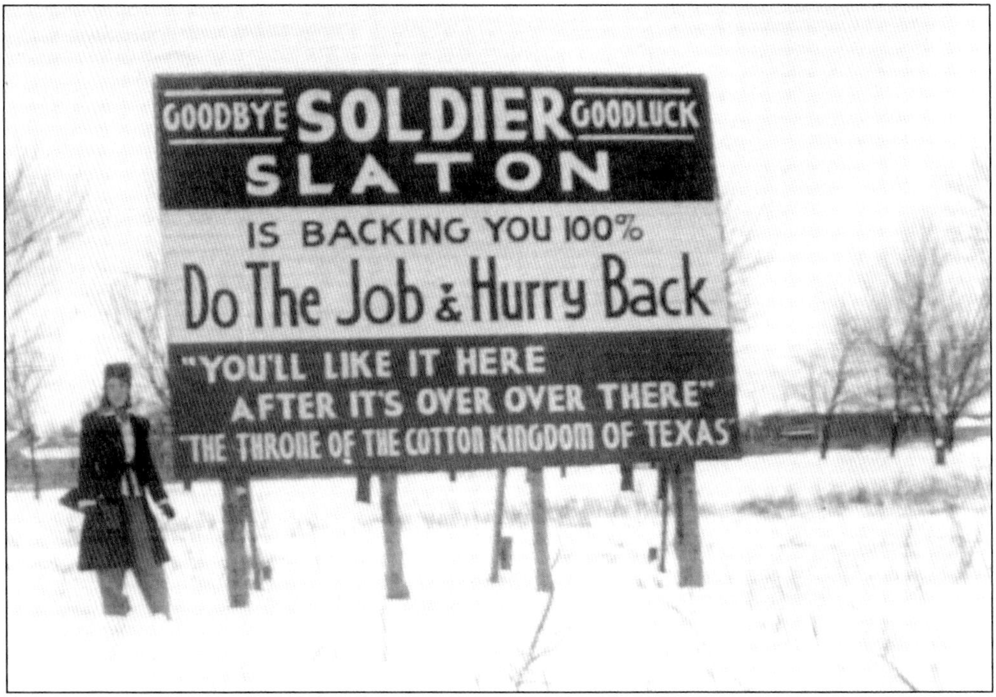

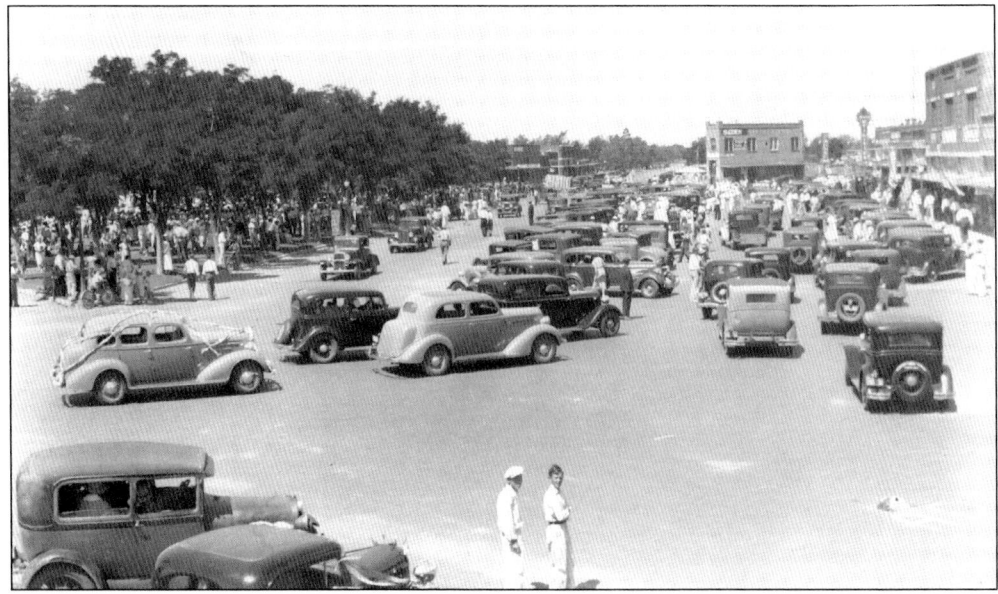

During World War II, this sign near the Harvey House encouraged troops to make a home in Slaton after the war was over. By the time World War II had begun, the Slaton Harvey House had closed. The Slaton Harvey House was both a commercial and social center and had operated for 30 years. It briefly reopened to serve troops during World War II. The building remained a passenger depot until 1969, and the Santa Fe Railway later converted it to a freight depot and operations center before vacating the property in the 1980s.

As shown here, downtown Slaton on the square was the place to be in the mid-1930s. It was thriving and full of life and activities.

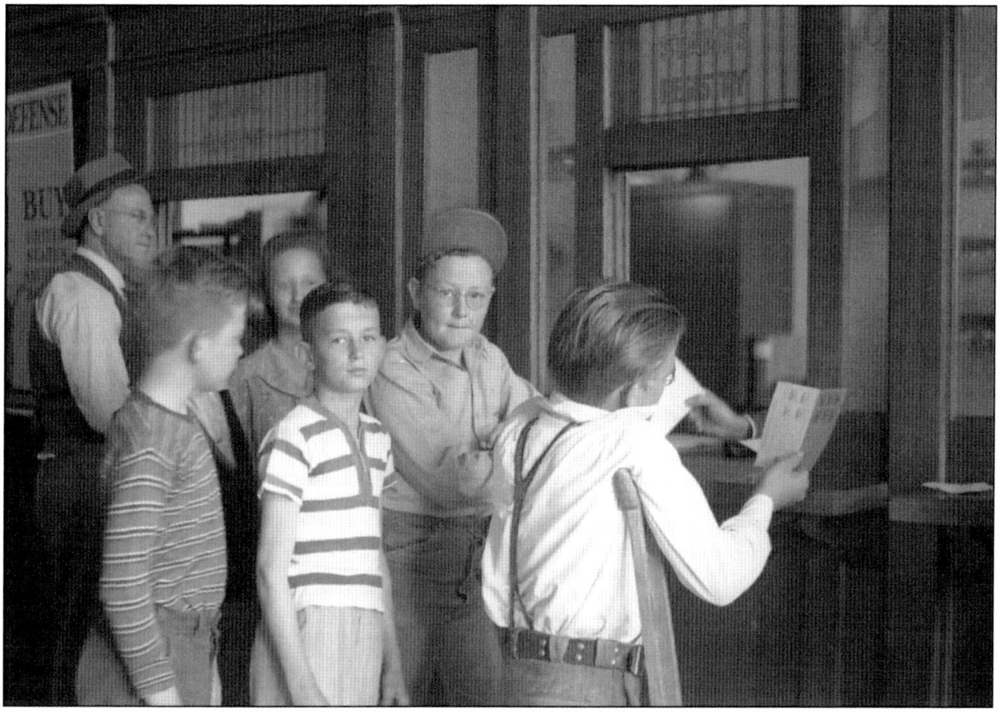

Among those pictured buying war bonds in 1943 are Bill Layne, Grady Burnett, and possibly Brian Sartan. The federal government spent over $300 billion on World War II—twice as much as it had spent in its entire existence before the war. The US Treasury Department needed to come up with a lot of money fast to meet expanding financial demands. Pres. Franklin D. Roosevelt decided on increased taxes and borrowing through the sale of massive amounts of war bonds. The decision aimed to help with the massive costs of war and also to eliminate excess wages and other spendable money in this time of shortages, helping to minimize inflation.

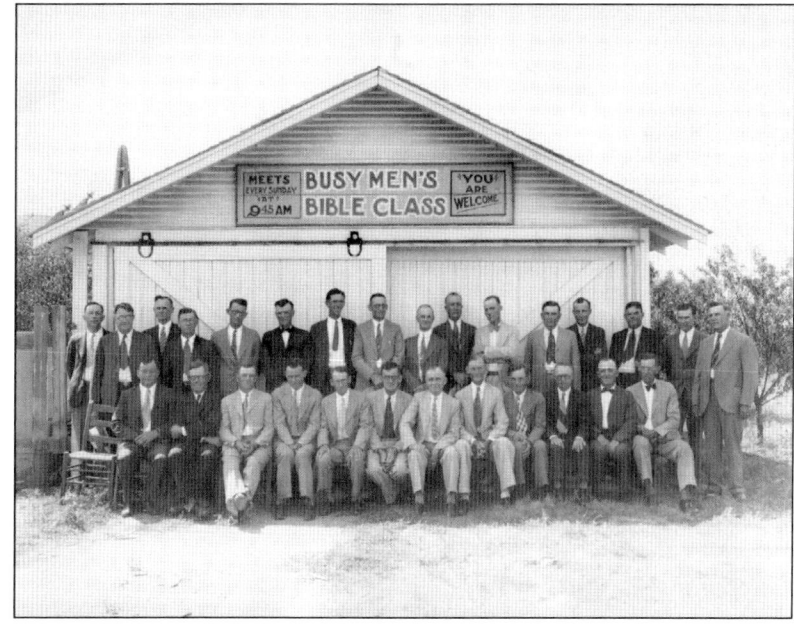

The Busy Men's Bible Class is seen at the garage behind the First Methodist Church.

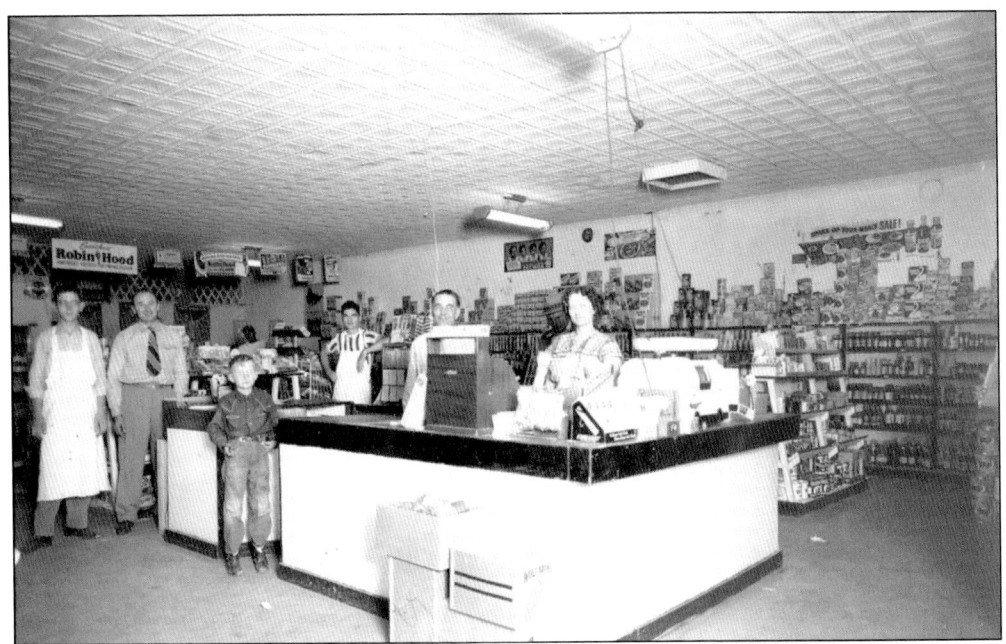

The Drive In Food Market is seen in the 1940s. From left to right are Jimmy Lovelady, Ben Sokoll, Gerald Heinrich, H.R. (Shorty) Donaldson, Herbert Heinrich, and Marie Heinrich.

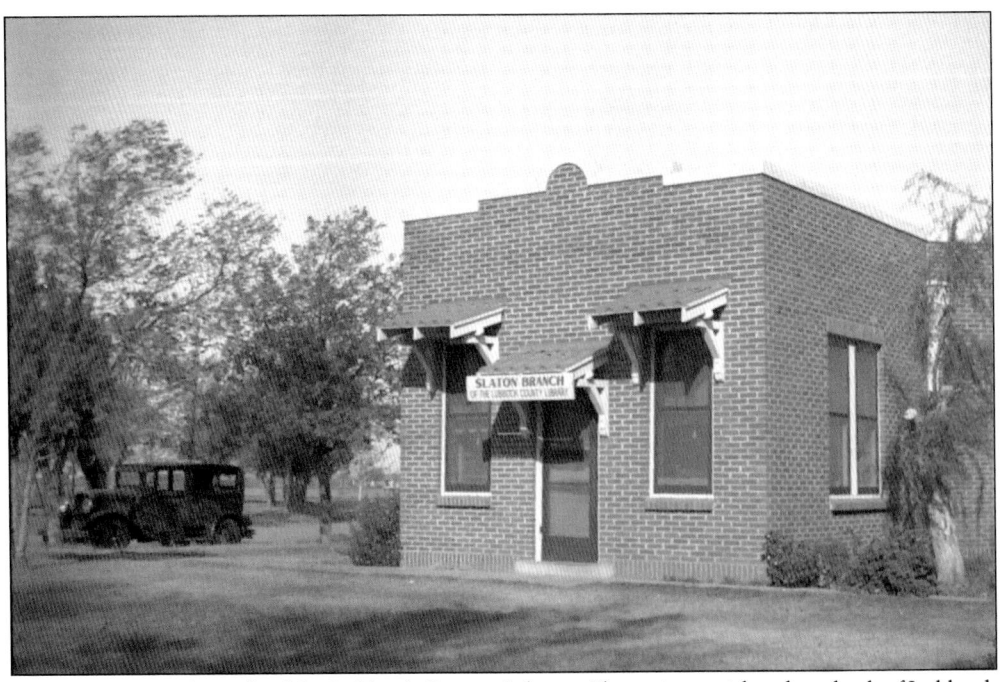

This is the Slaton branch of the Lubbock County Library. Slaton is considered a suburb of Lubbock and is part of the Lubbock Metropolitan Statistical Area. Slaton is located in the southeast corner of Lubbock County and is only 15 miles from Lubbock.

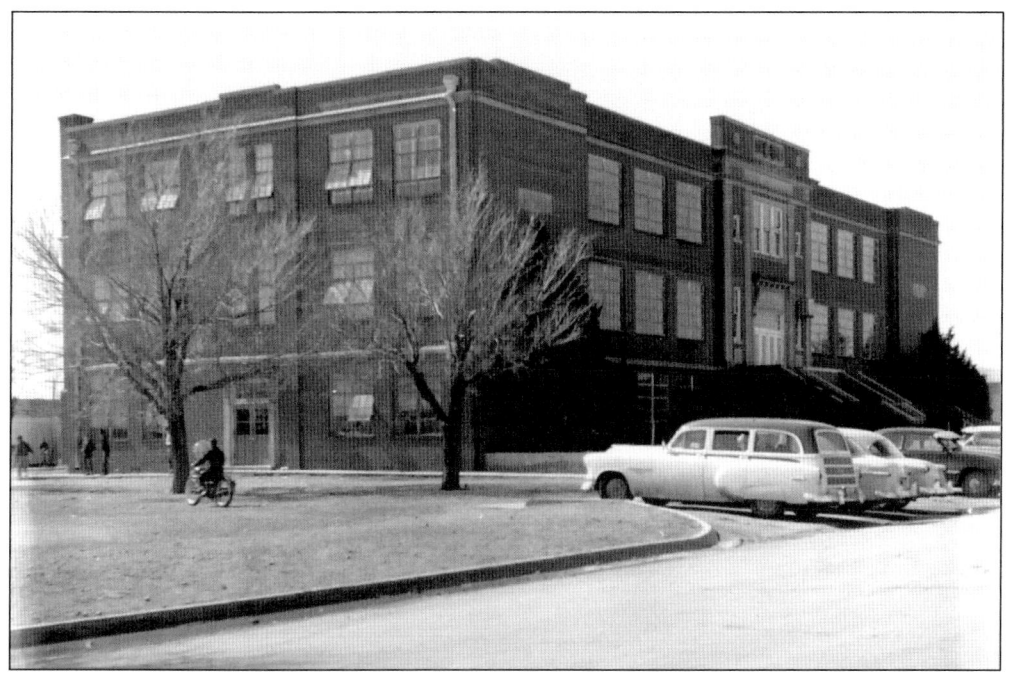

This picture shows Slaton High School in 1955. At the time, the high school superintendent was P.L. Vardy Jr., the principal was John M. Gilbert, and the board of directors consisted of Robert Hall Davis (president), Joe Walker Jr. (secretary), Clark Self Sr., Travis Reynolds, M.M. Brieger, and J.C. Smith Jr. This was the year that Sonny Curtis, well-known country music songwriter and singer, graduated from Slaton High.

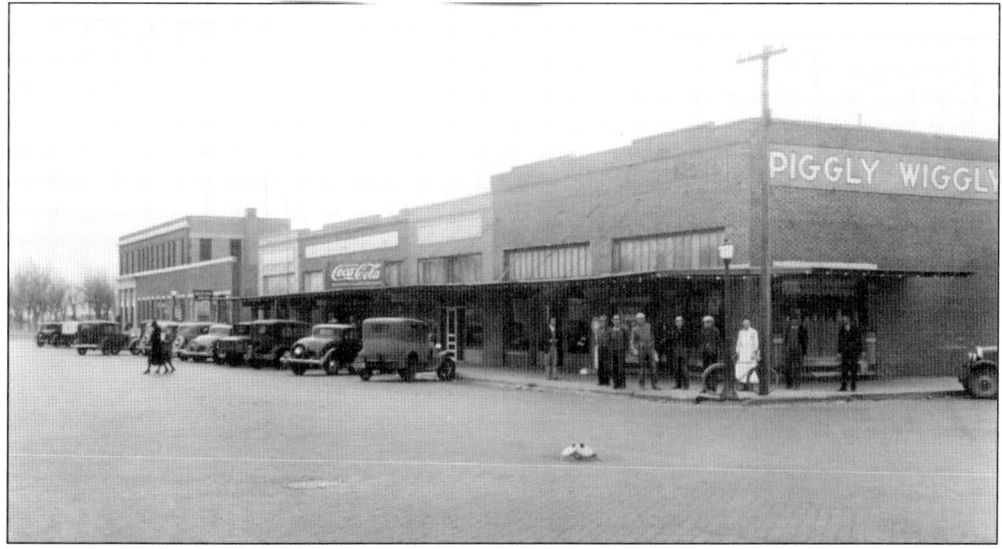

Slaton City Square is seen here in 1923. By this time, the Slaton Chamber of Commerce and the Women's Chamber of Commerce had been formed to assist in the advancement of Slaton. There was also a Retail Merchants Association to help with the growth of this young West Texas railroad town. This picture was taken from the 100 block of North Eighth Street on the west side of the street. The Piggly Wiggly grocery store was operated by Hack Lasater. In the 1950s, it offered double S&H Green Stamps every Tuesday with a purchase of more than $2.50.

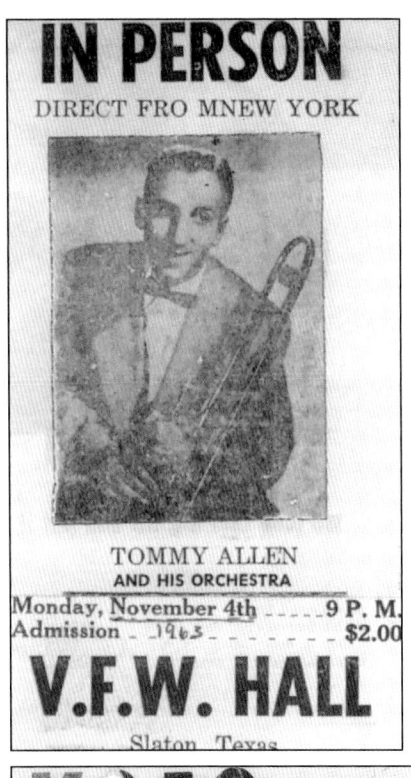

This is a 1963 advertisement for an upcoming show at the VFW hall. Tommy Allen and his orchestra from New York played there, and it was only $2 to get into the show. The Slaton chapter of the Veterans of Foreign Wars was organized and chartered on April 2, 1946. It was named for Aaron Luman, a war veteran. (Courtesy of Slaton Museum.)

Slaton had a radio station with call letters KCAS from 1962 until 1987; this "coffee-gram" was published in 1965. It is difficult to find much record of the station, but KCAS's coffee-grams kept listeners and the community up to date on events and news. (Courtesy of Slaton Museum.)

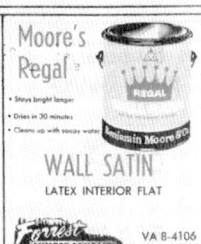
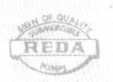
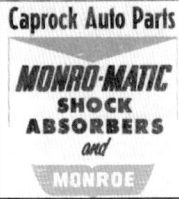

Four
MEMORY LANE

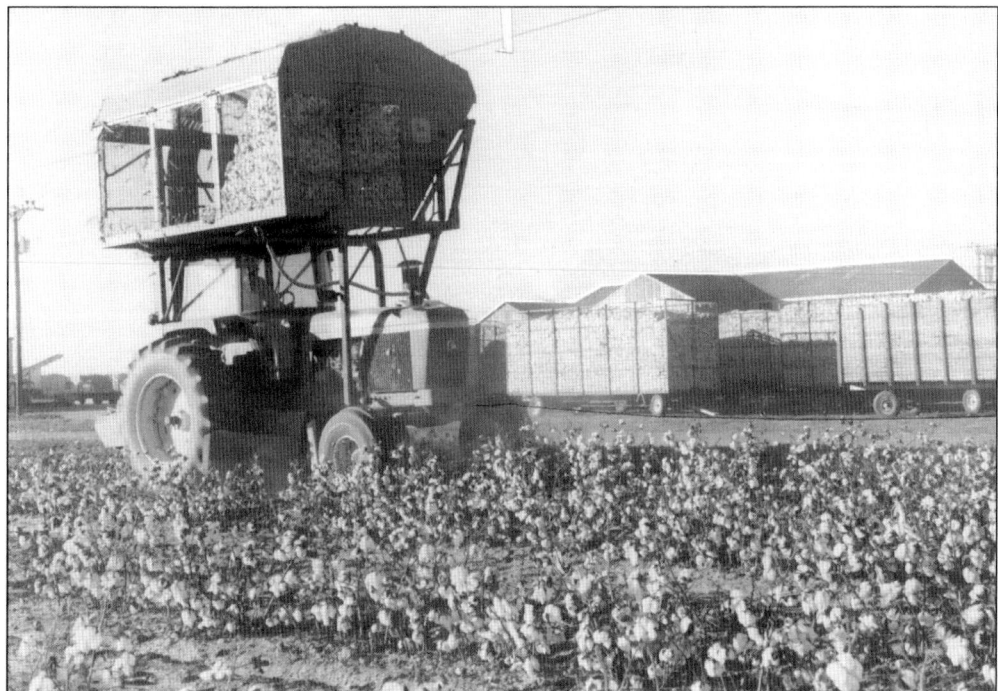

Slaton definitely owes its existence to the Santa Fe Railway, but farming existed in the area even before Slaton officially became a town. Farming continues to be a mainstay of the economy of Slaton and the entire West Texas area. There is no doubt that the Santa Fe brought builders and dreamers to town, along with many profitable enterprises like lumberyards, drugstores, restaurants, hardware stores, car dealerships, cotton gins, hotels, and many other businesses. There is no way to mention every business that has been successful in Slaton and contributed to the town's success, but this stroll down memory lane will allow readers to peek into the past at some of the businesses that left a mark on this West Texas town that continues to thrive because of the railroad, farming, local businesses, ranching, and the people who live in it.

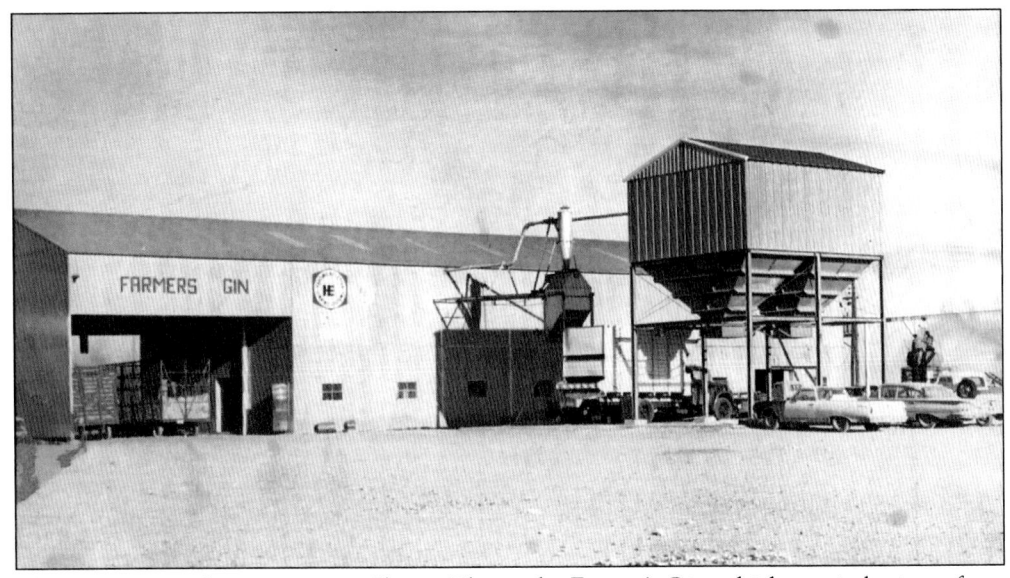

There were several cotton gins in Slaton. This is the Farmer's Gin, which was in business from 1965 until 2003.

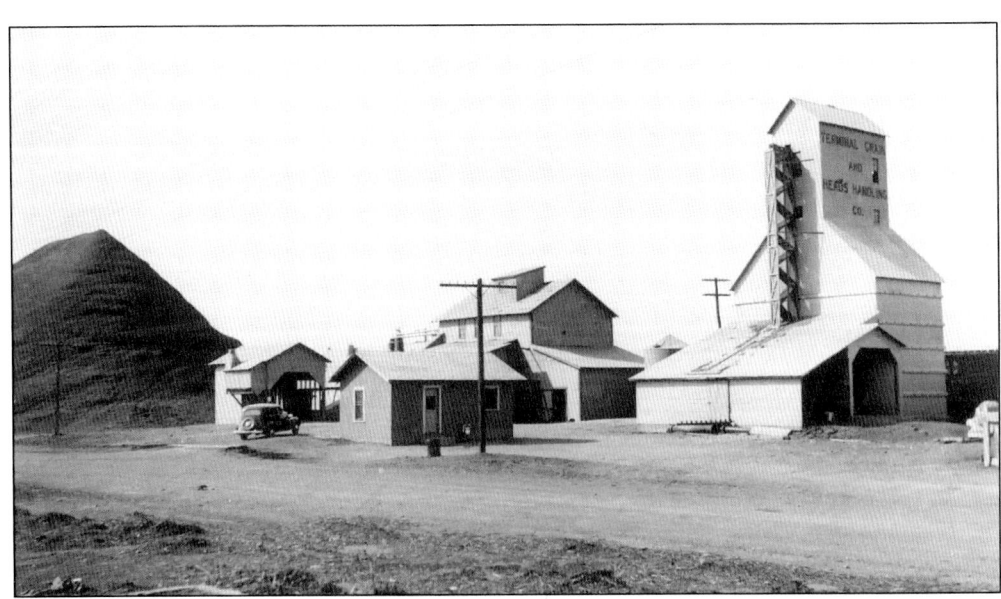

Plains Grain is pictured here in 1928. Ray C. Ayers came to Slaton in 1928 to open his grain company. While it was being built, he lived at the Forrest Hotel. Ayers developed a patent to thresh the grain from milo heads that had been harvested by hand. This method left a byproduct of cracked grain and stalk residue. Ayers opened a 6,000-head cattle feedlot, which was located on the east edge of Slaton and was one of the largest feedlots in Texas during the mid-1930s.

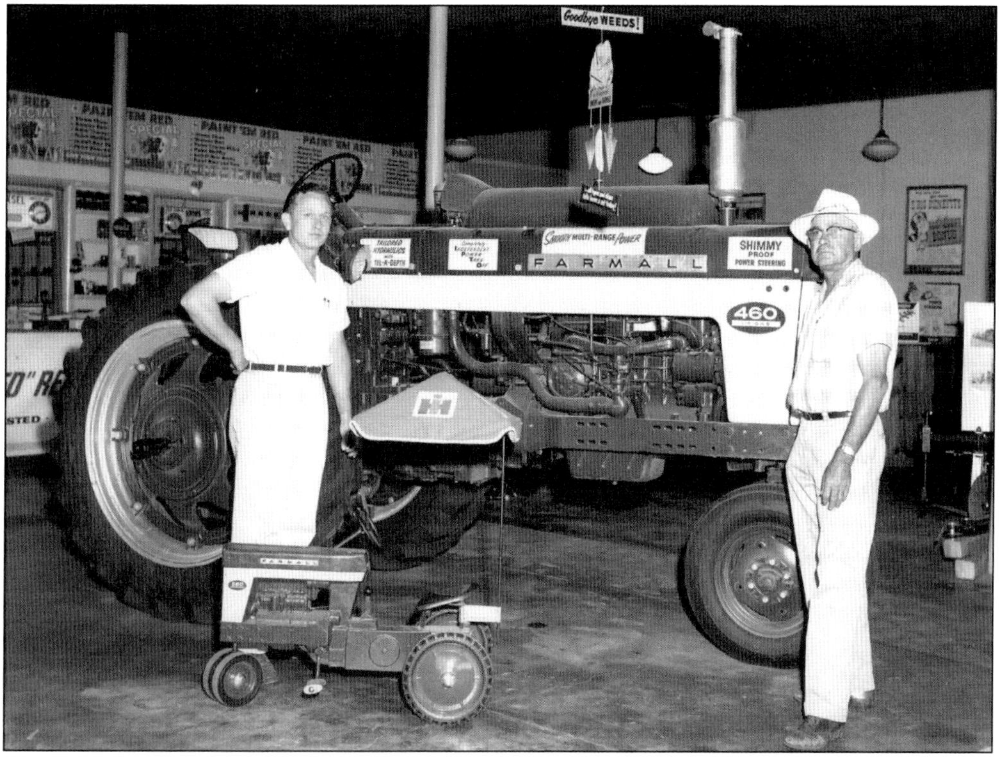

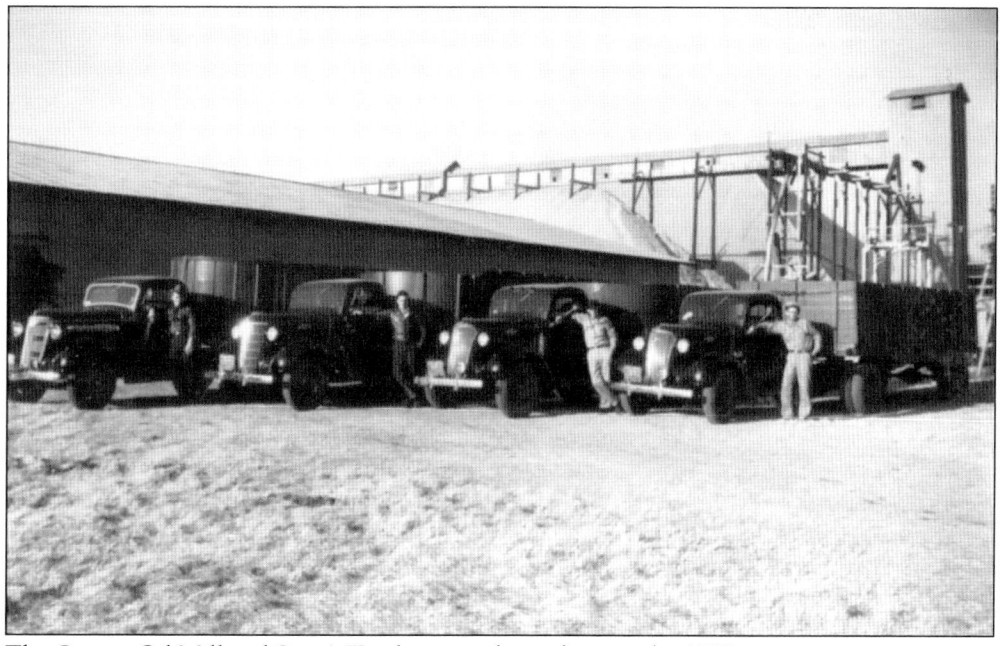

Slaton Implement, the IHC tractor dealer, was located on Slaton Highway (US Route 84). The railroad fueled the economy when it arrived, but agriculture and farming have always been crucial in the area. Pictured here are Marvin Harris (left) and Ed Childress.

The Cotton Oil Mill and Stott's Trucking are shown here in the 1930s.

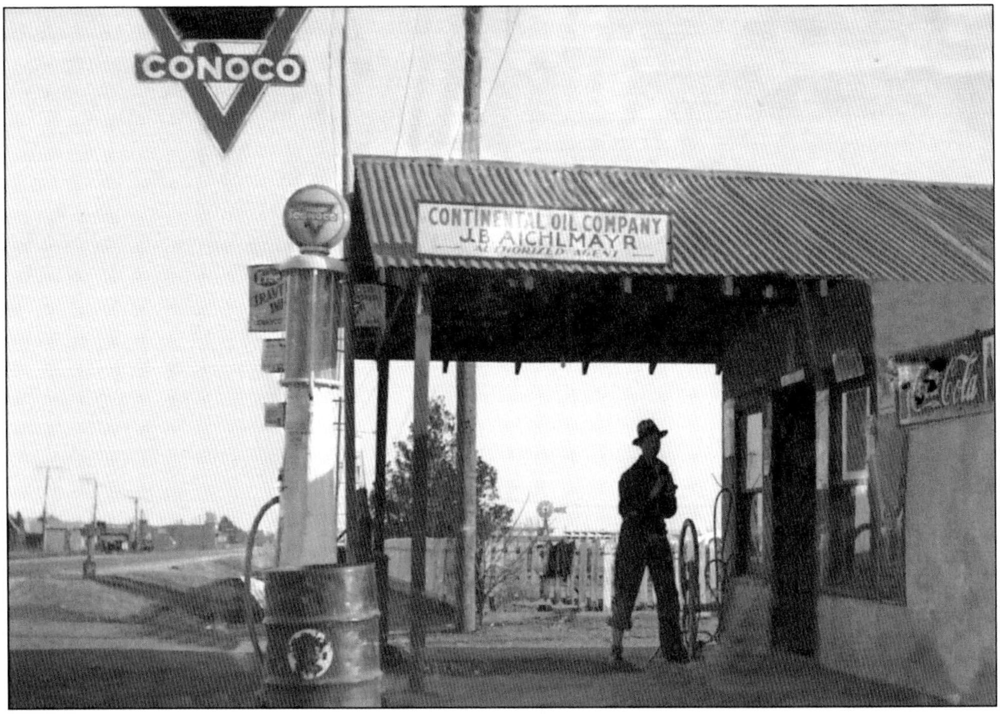

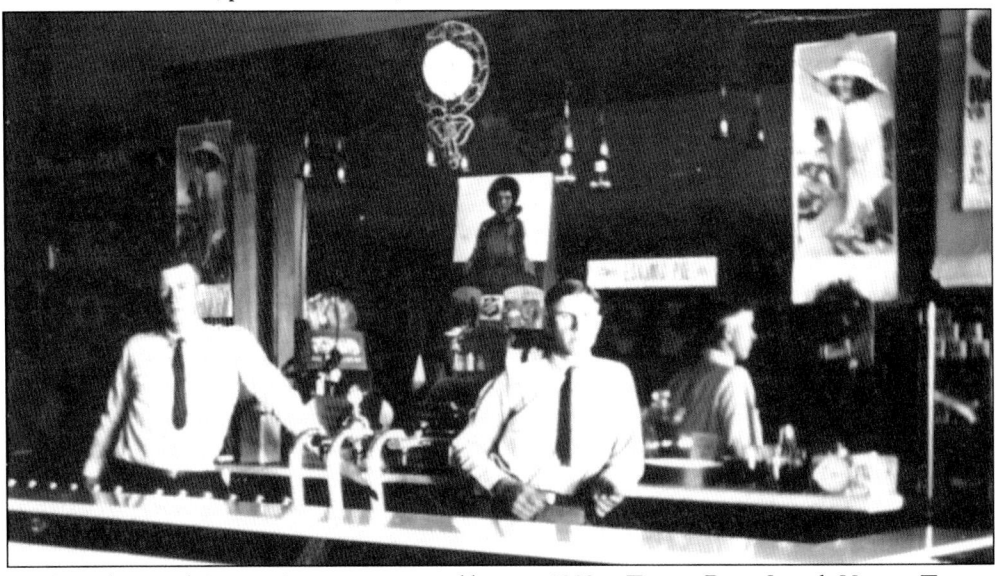

This Conoco station, pictured in 1929, was located at 425 Industrial Drive.

Grady Wilson and George Green are pictured here in 1922 at Teague Drug. Joseph Hinton Teague Sr. and his only son, Joe Jr., decided to go into business for themselves and opened a store in the lobby of the local theater in 1916. It was a smart plan, because moviegoers had to go through the confectionery to get to the theater. The business, originally called Joe H. Teague and Son, Confectionery, moved to its own location in 1918, and in 1923, changed the sign to read "J.H. Teague and Son, Confections, Drug Sundries." It became a popular hangout. Joe Jr. took a course so he could operate a prescription department. Joe Sr. became the first city marshal of Slaton, served as a city commissioner, and was mayor from 1939 until his death in 1945.

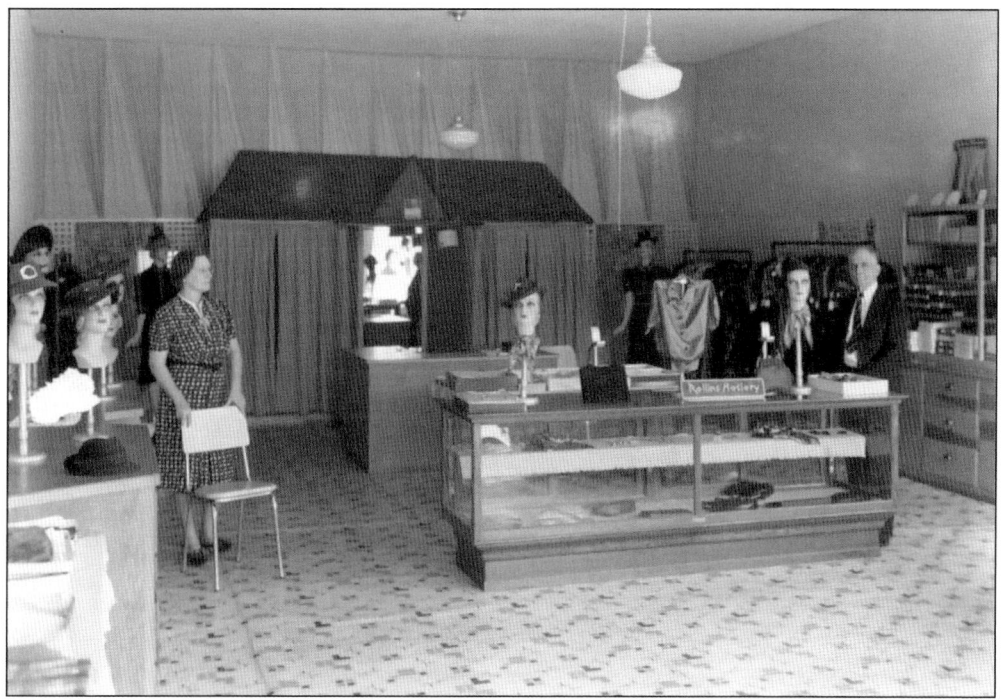

Payne's Dry Goods Company operated in Slaton, advertising in the local newspaper in 1922: "For quality goods at live and let live prices, come to Payne Dry Goods Co., Successor to Robertson D.G. Co."

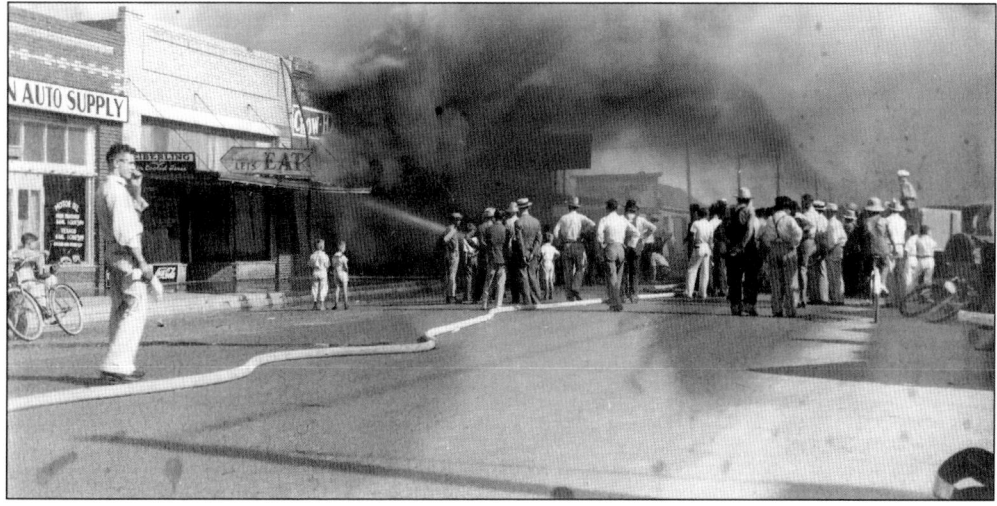

O.O. "Doc" Crow moved from Abernathy in 1937 to partner with Leonard Harral, who was also from Abernathy and moved to Slaton to begin the partnership of Crow-Harral Chevrolet at 145 North Ninth Street. In 1939, they had a bad fire, as pictured here, and moved across the street to 120 North Ninth Street.

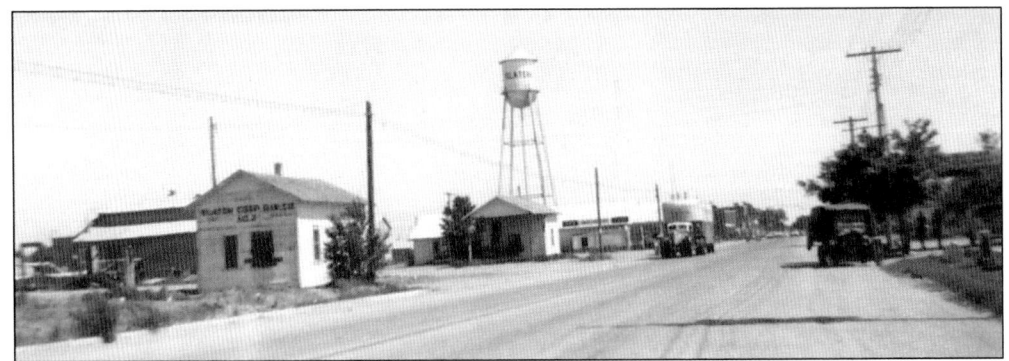

This image shows the Slaton Cooperative Gin in the 500 block of North Ninth Street and the Thornton Davis Gin in the 400 block. The Slaton Cooperative Gin was organized on April 1, 1935. The directors at the time were J.W. Nesbitt (president), C.Z. Fine (vice president), H.M. Cade (secretary), L.B. Kitten, and C.E. Lilly. They had an authorized capital stock of $50,000, $22,300 of which belonged to the patrons and stockholders (132 individuals at the time). The previous year, 2,646 bales of cotton had been ginned and paid eight percent dividend on the stock besides distributing $7,467 as a patronage dividend credit to members and non-member patrons. The Slaton Coop Gin is still in operation today.

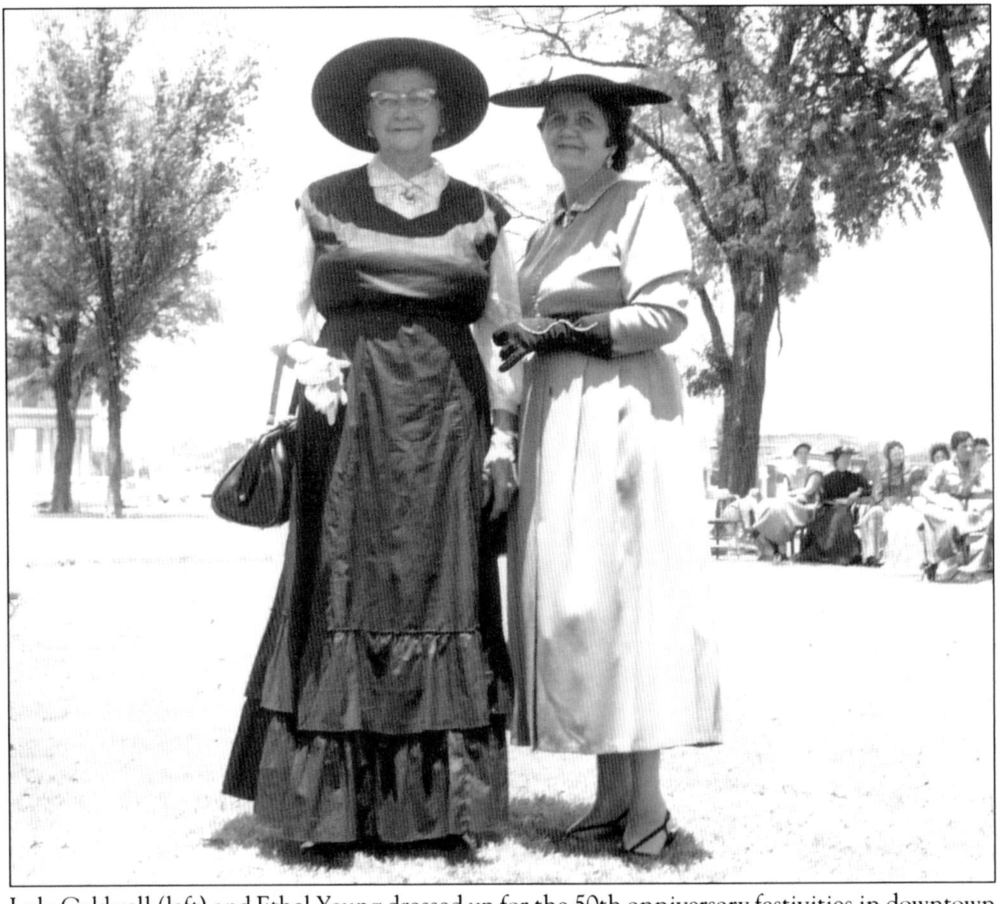

Lula Caldwell (left) and Ethel Young dressed up for the 50th anniversary festivities in downtown Slaton in 1961.

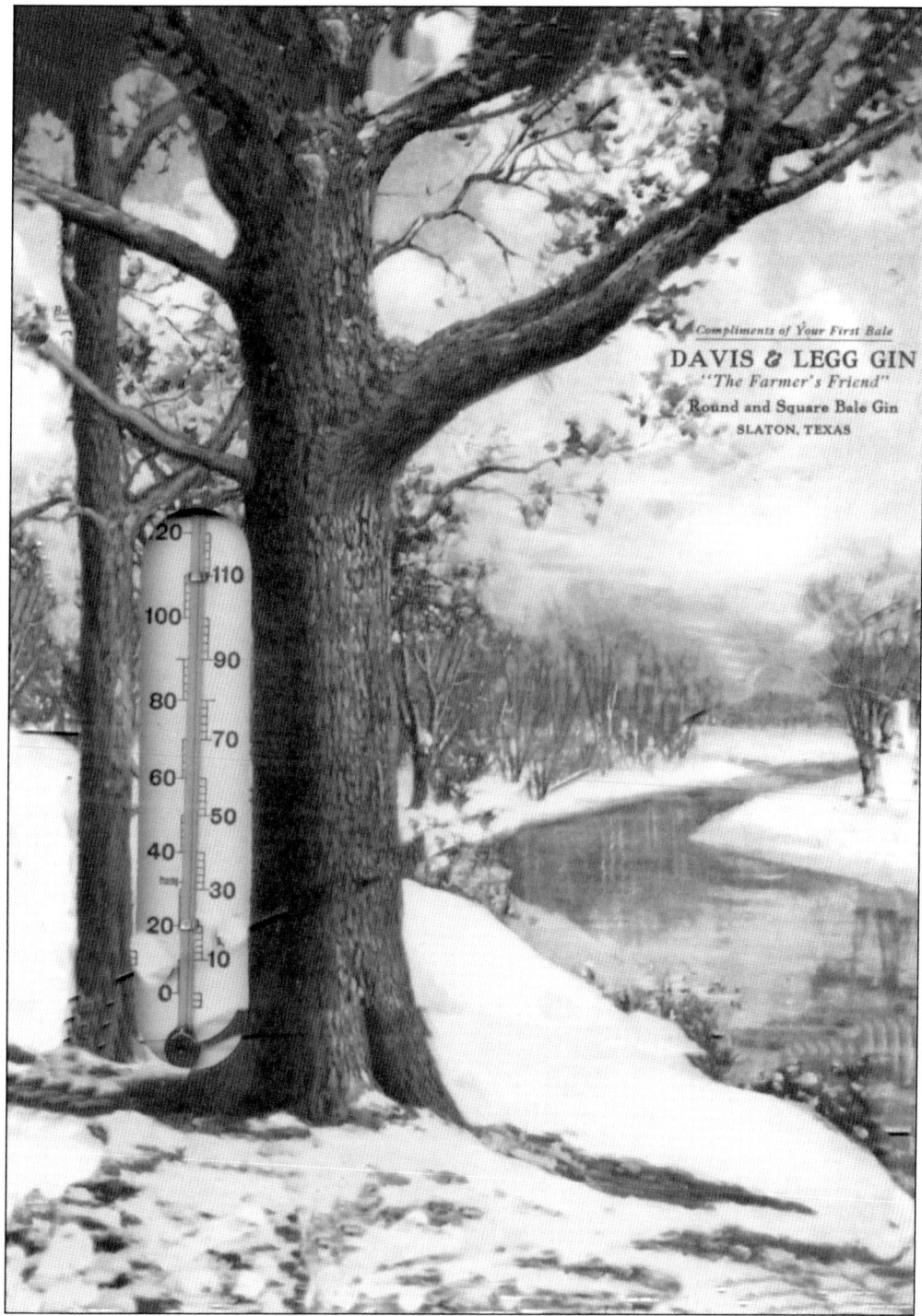
This picture and thermometer was given to customers of Davis and Legg Gin in the 1930s; their slogan described them as "The Farmer's Friend."

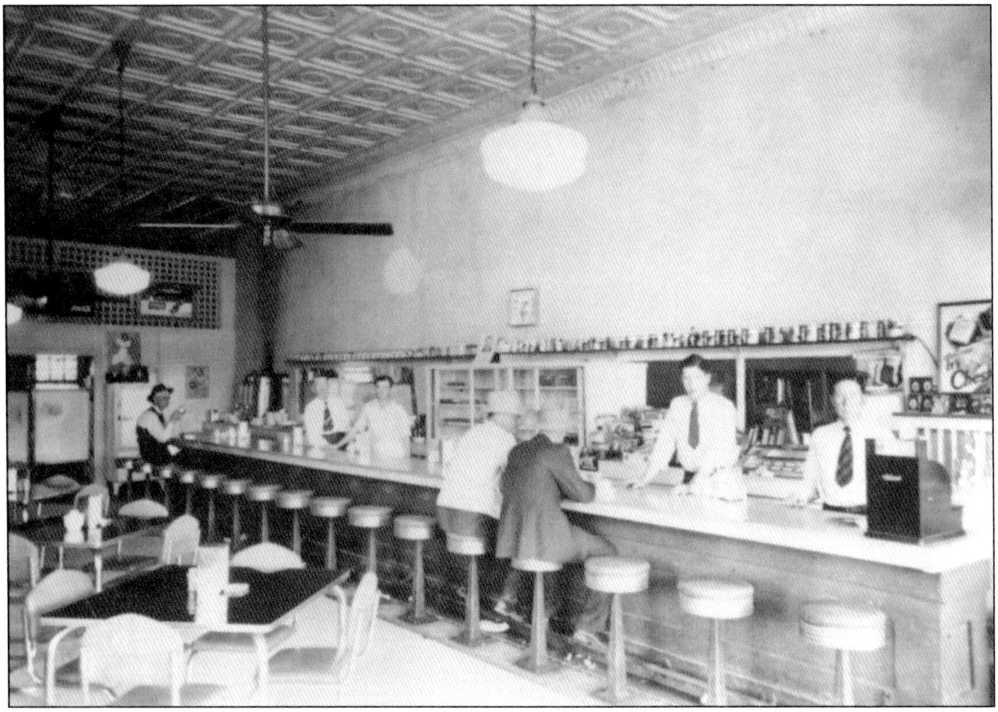

Vasker Browning established The Palace of Fine Eats in Slaton in 1923. After several remodels and updates, it was considered one of the nicest cafés in the area. Browning was an experienced restaurant owner who understood what the public expected of a first-class café. It had a homey atmosphere that made people feel welcome. H.C. Maxey bought the business in 1943.

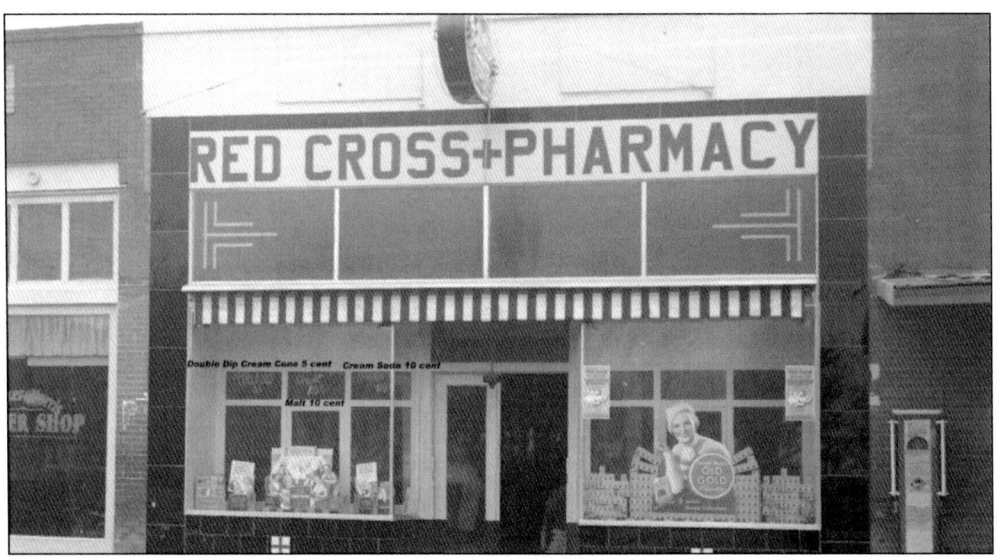

The Red Cross Pharmacy is seen here in 1937. Believed to be the first pharmacy in Slaton, it was located at 109 South Ninth Street (the current location of the Slaton Bakery). It was originally owned by Groner Drug Company, and L.P. Loomis sold it to R.L. Blanton in 1913. C.F. Anderson bought half of the interest in 1915.

This Gulf station operated in Slaton from 1937 until 1977. Elbert (left) and T.D. Custer are shown in the bottom image.

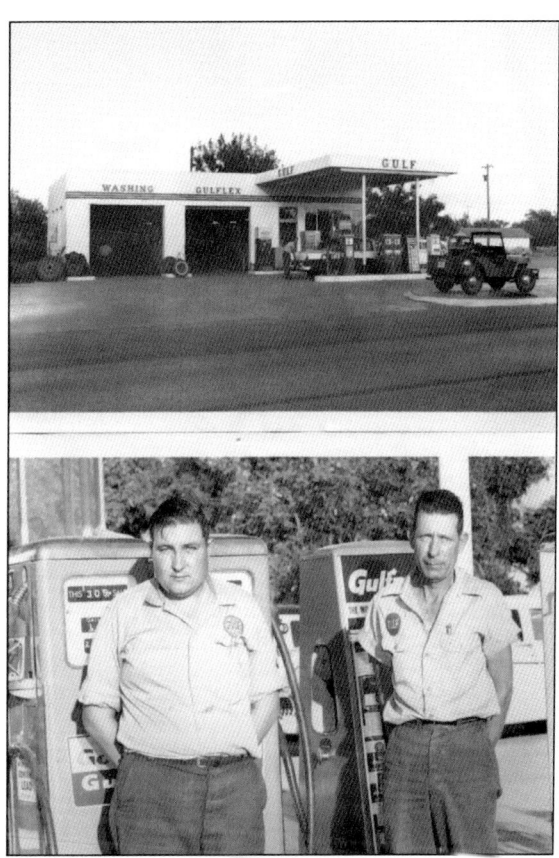

The Slaton Bakery is seen here in 1946. It was first owned by ? Brooks until it burned down in 1927. The Star brothers operated the bakery for the last half of 1927. Smith and Caldwell owned it from December 1927 to December 1928. They sold to C.C. Carr, who had the bakery for one year before selling to R.D. Hickman in 1929. Hickman owned the bakery until 1943, when he sold it to Barney Wilson. Wilson operated it until 1973, when Sherrell Wilson (Barney's son) took over; Sherrell still runs it today.

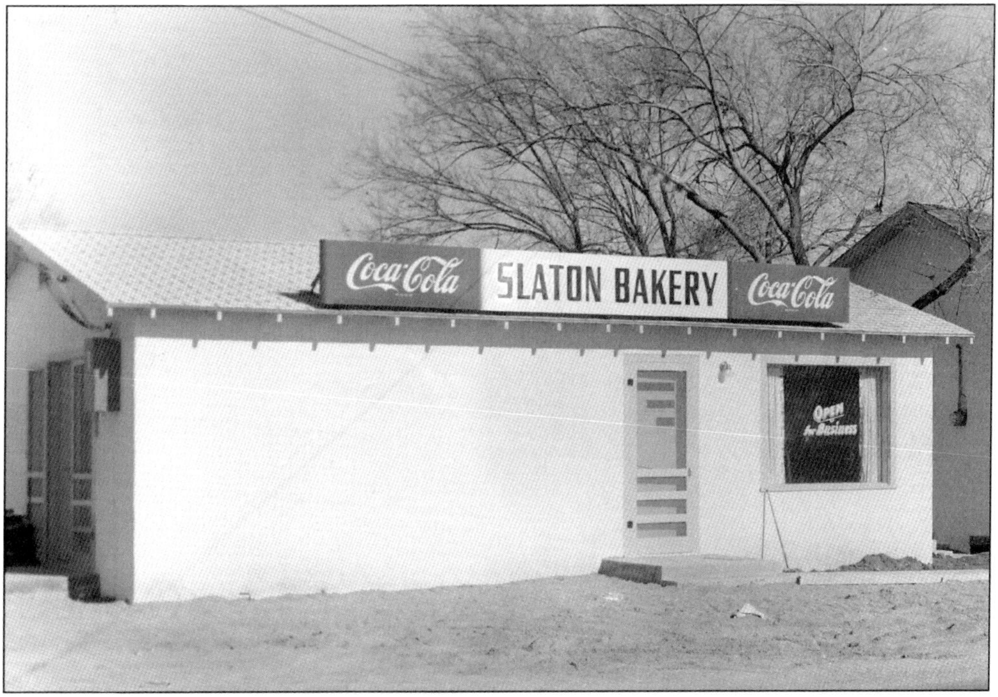

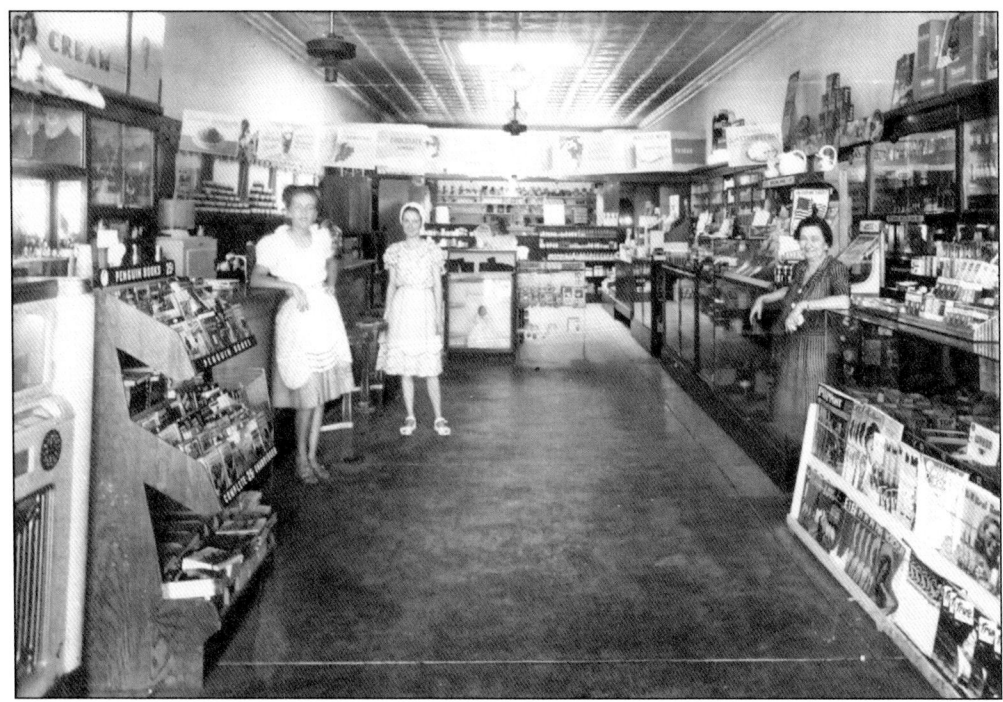
City Drug was located at 112 West Garza Street from 1939 until 1950.

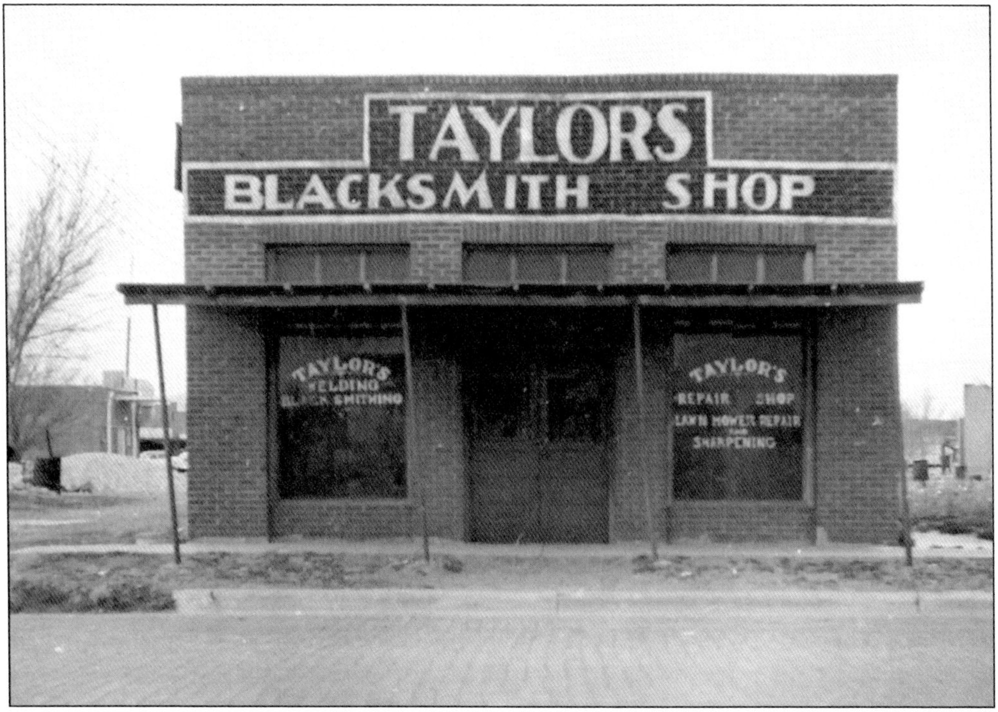

Taylor's Blacksmith Shop is pictured here in the 1940s.

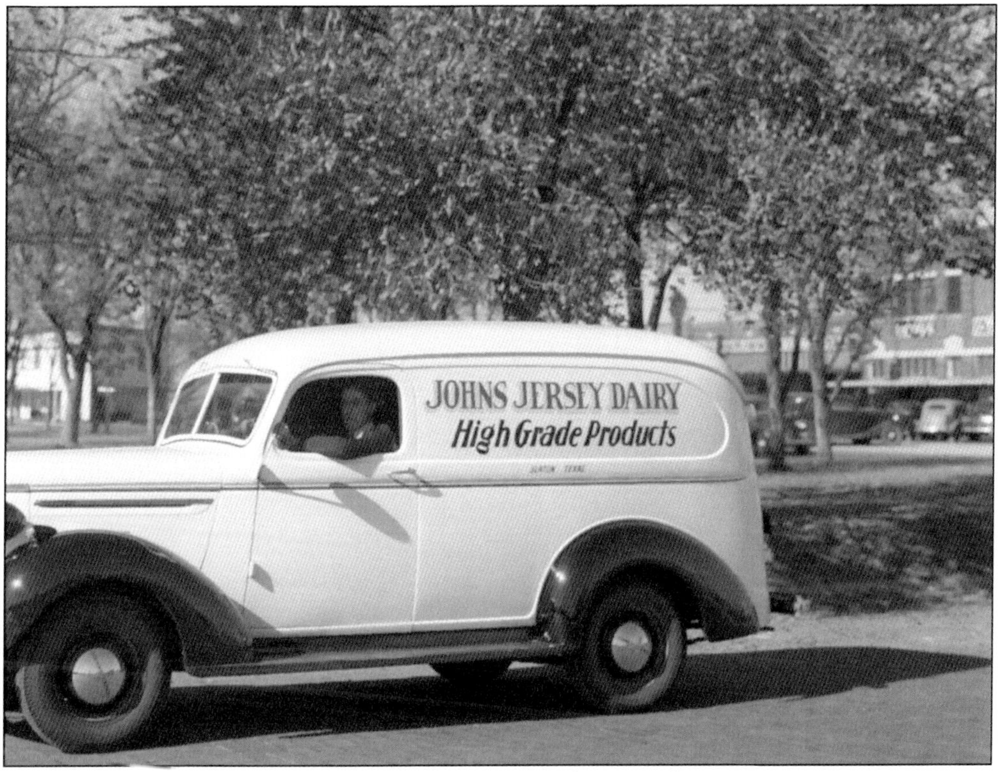

The John's Dairy truck is driving through downtown Slaton in the 1940s.

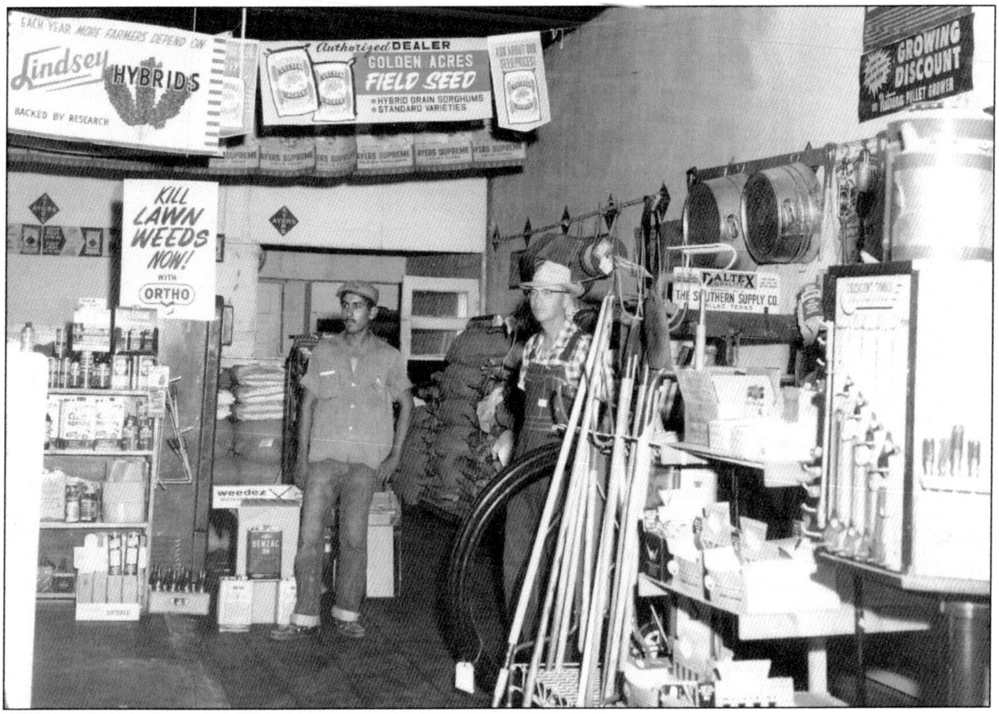

The Slaton Feed Store, which was owned by Joe VanNess, is pictured in the 1940s.

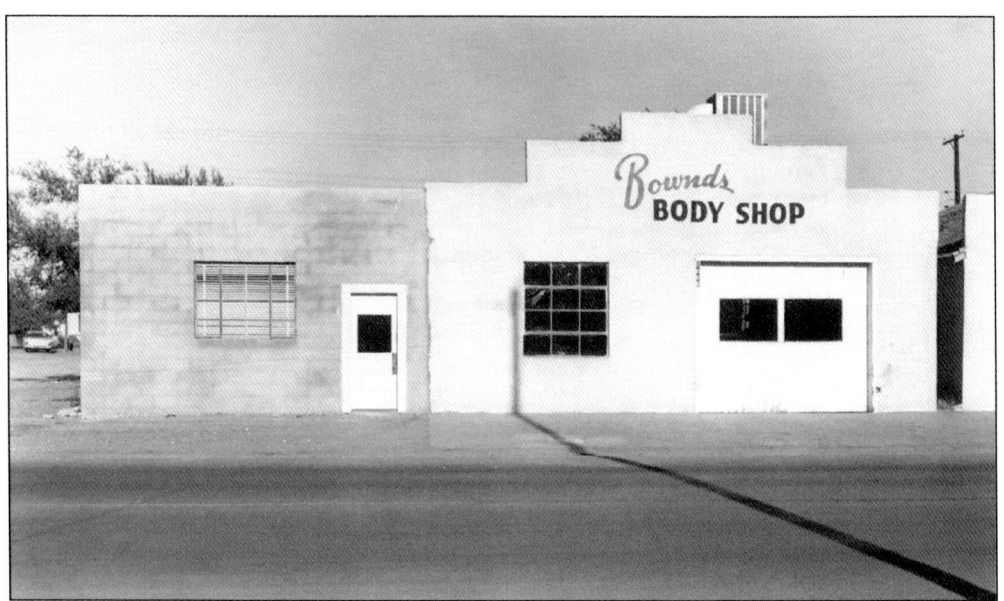

Bownds Body Shop was originally run by Truly A. Bownds, then Truett Bownds; Lance Bownds now owns it. It has been owned by the Bownds family since 1943, and is still going strong today.

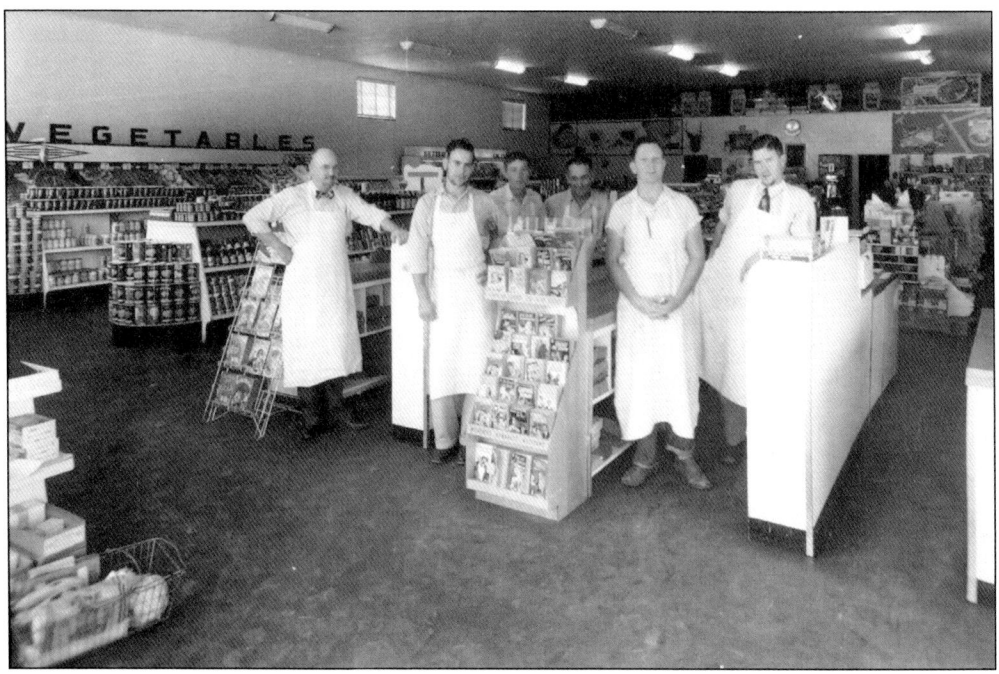

This photograph of the Red and White Grocery is from 1946. Originally called Chick's Market & Grocery, it became the Red and White Grocery in 1928. Pictured are John Berkley, Billy Goldman, Robert Woodfin, Roy Parks, Gene Berkley, and Calvin Lamb.

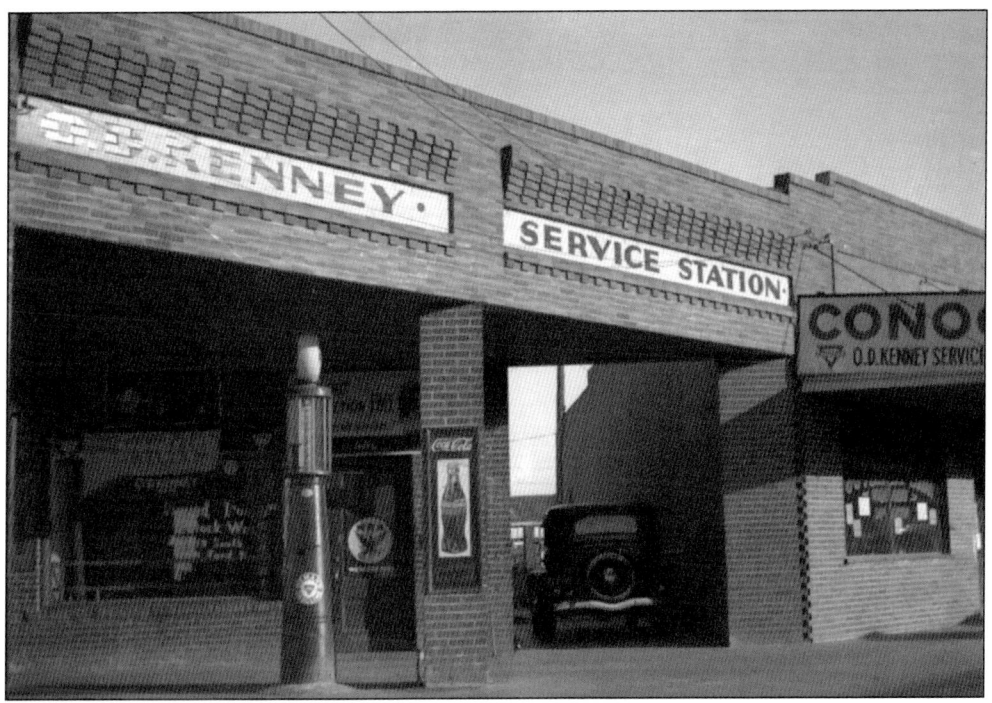

This is the O.D. Kenney Conoco, which was located at 750 South Eighth Street.

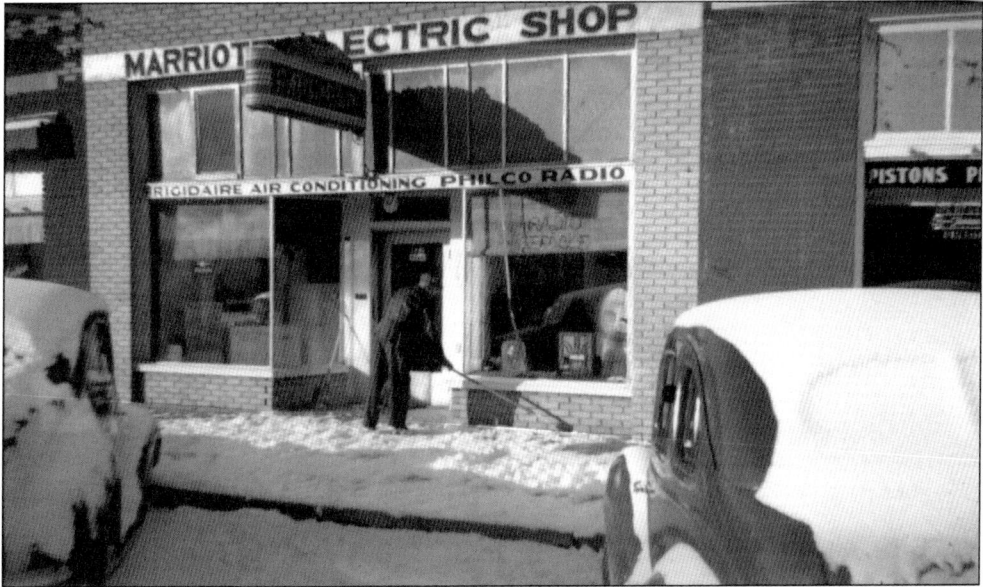

This picture of Charlie Marriot Electric Shop was taken on a snow-covered day. Marriot was interested in radio and made the first radio set in Slaton. He also became a ham shortwave radio operator with the call letters W5ILA; his slogan was "I Love America." Marriot's shop sold Frigidaires and Philco radios in addition to other appliances.

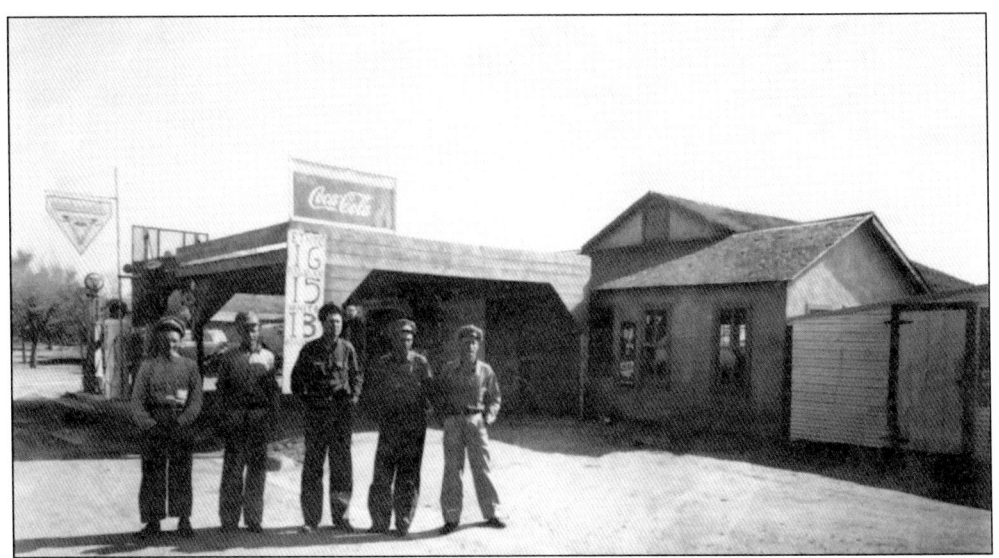

In 1919, David Sidney Biggs came to Slaton by wagon from Mesa, New Mexico. His grandfather worked for the Santa Fe Railway. The Biggs family moved to Slaton to farm. In 1932, David opened a garage and wrecking yard at 1140 South Ninth Street; it later became a welding and machine shop. David's son, Coy, became a partner in the business in 1953.

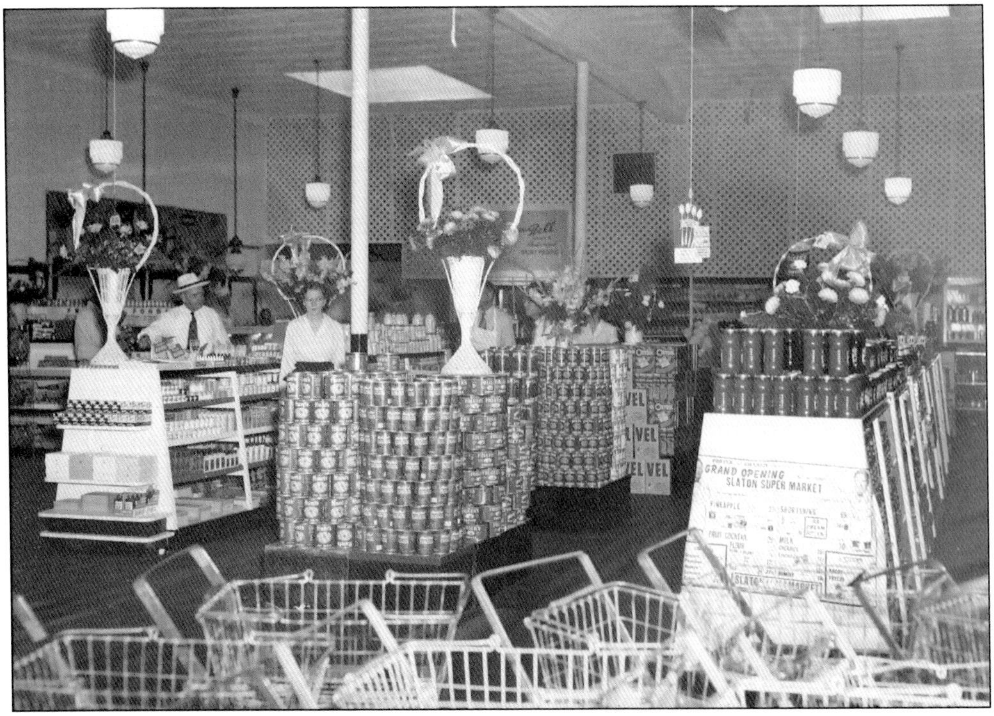

Here is a 1949 picture from the archives of the Slaton Supermarket, which was located at 155 North Eighth Street.

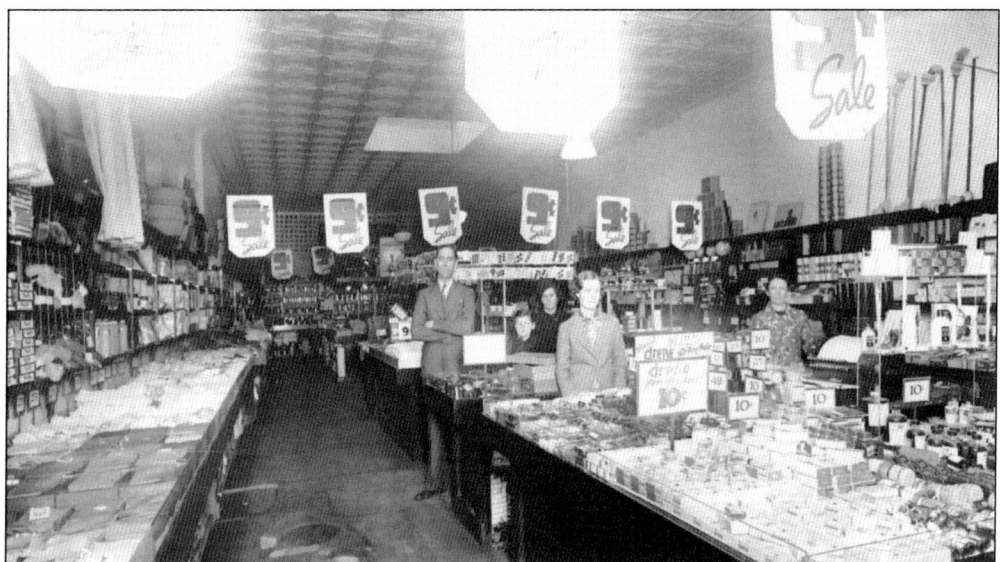

The Abe Kessel Variety Store is seen here in the 1930s. Kessel was born in Kupisik, Lithuania, on September 14, 1889, and it took him 32 years to make the journey to Slaton, Texas. In 1908, he was an uneducated immigrant unable to speak English and living in New York. He made many stops before he finally made it to Slaton, including opening a dry goods store in nearby Post, Texas. In 1923, he built two modern stores on Texas Avenue in Slaton and even expanded to other towns, including Levelland, Texas, and Roswell, New Mexico.

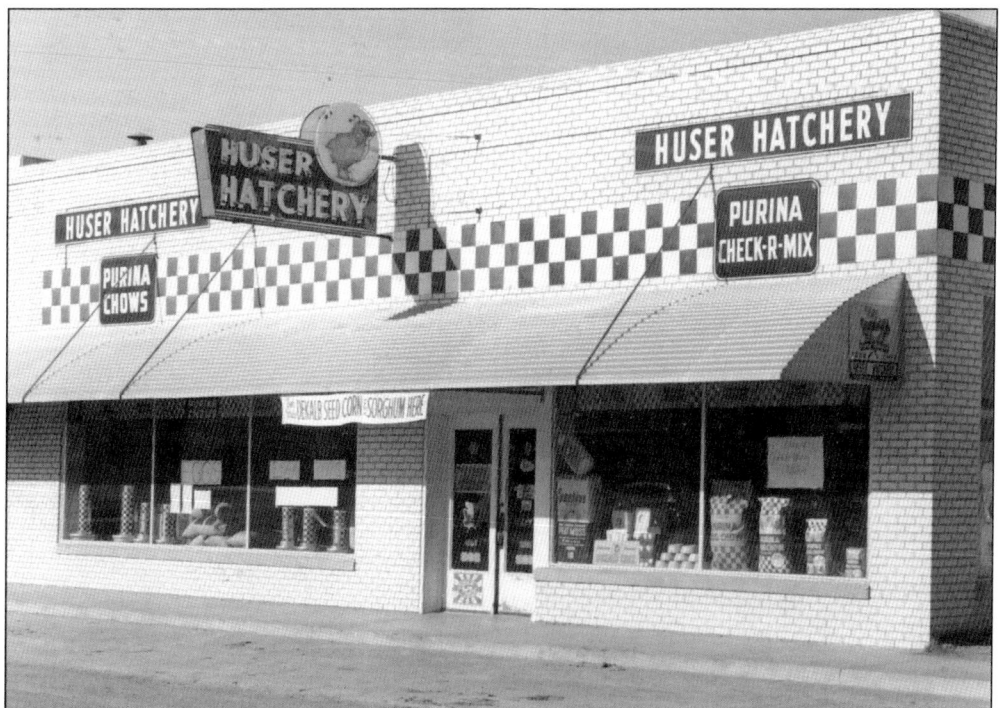

Bob Huser owned Huser Hatchery in Slaton. The hatchery offered baby chicks from breeds such as White Rocks, Austria Whites, Red and Leghorn Cross, White Leghorn, and Black Leghorn, as advertised in the classified section of the March 27, 1947, edition of the *Post Dispatch*.

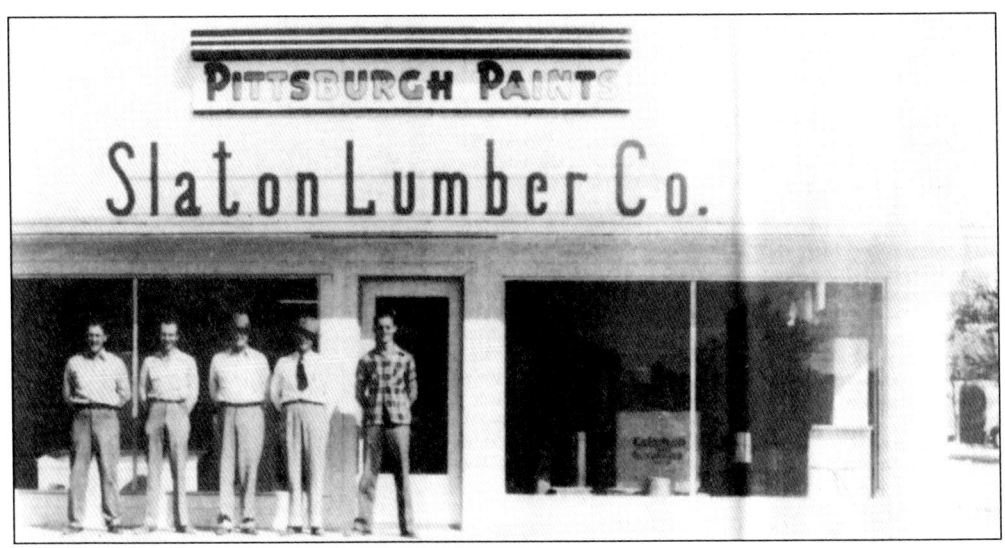

This story about Slaton Lumber Company is from a 1997 edition of *The Slatonite*.

A Half Century Ago

A half century and three generations back, the Davis family and Slaton Lumber Company began their shared existence. Saturday they'll celebrate the birthday with a 10:30 to noon coffee and cake reception at the business at 220 W. Crosby. A half century ago, June 7, 1947, it was (left to right) Arnold Alcorn, Marshall G. Davis, W. T. Davis, B. B. "Doc" Castleberry and William T. "Tommy" Davis opening the doors for the first time. Marshall Davis' father, W. T., and Castleberry were the founding owners, Marshall says. His father bought Castleberry out in 1957 and Marshall, now the sole owner, took over in 1971. He's now been joined by his son, David. Marshall says he'd spent the war years as a torpedo technician in the Navy at Pearl Harbor, Hawaii, before returning home to spend a year in college. After that, he asked his father for a summer job, he says. He was handed a broom, told the work day was 8-6, the work week was six days a week and he'd be making $25 a week, he says. "I've been here ever since. If I didn't like it, I'd do something else."

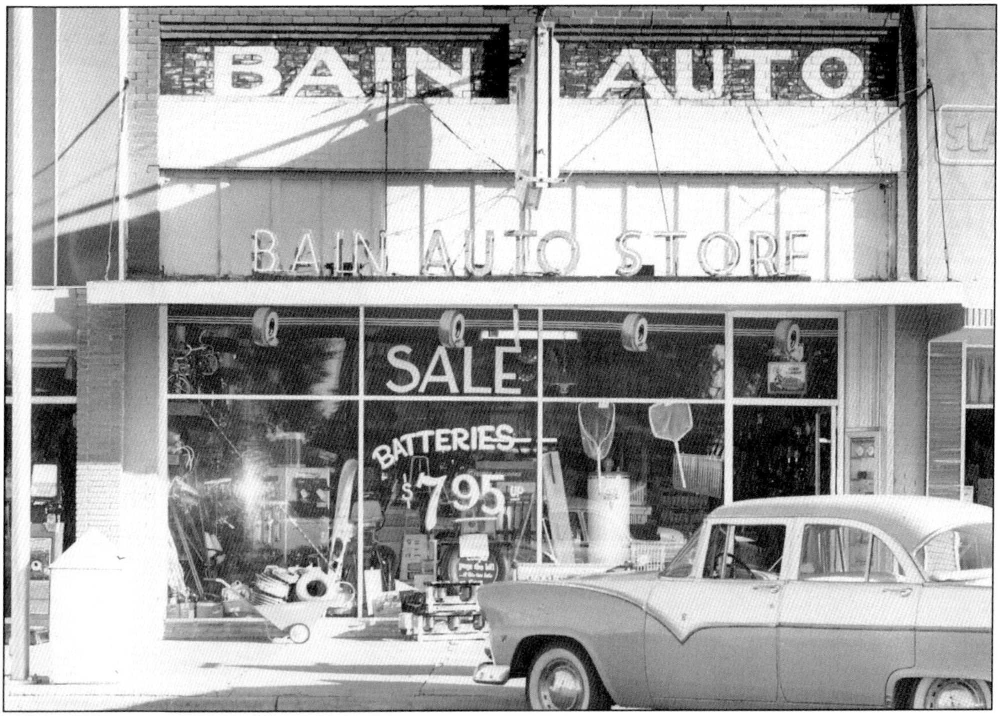

C.R. and Leonard Bain bought a service station on South Ninth Street in Slaton and later turned it into Bain Auto Store, which is pictured here in the 1950s.

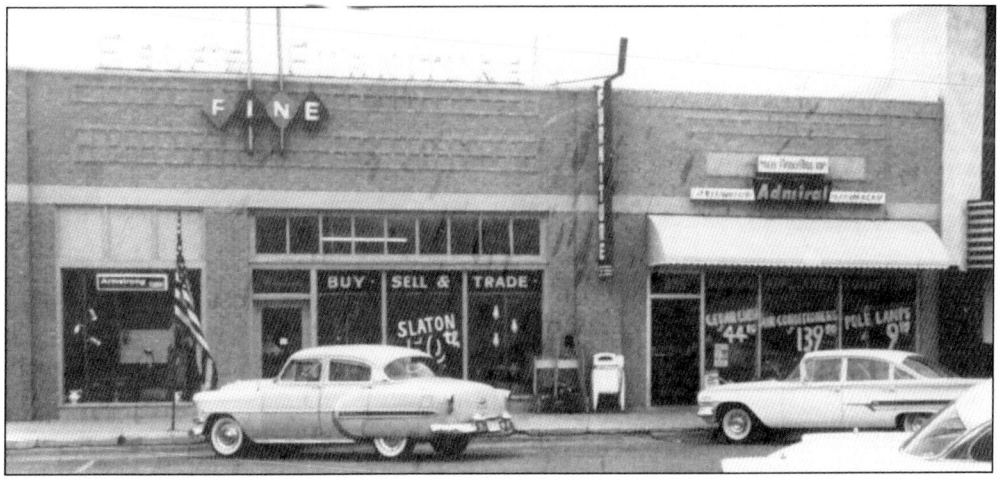

Gilbert and Esther Gentry Self came to Slaton in 1920. They had five children, including Clark Self, who worked at Slaton Pharmacy and eventually opened his own furniture store, Self's Furniture, which he operated for 27 years. He and his wife, Mary Irene, had two children, Clark Jr. and Sharon. Clark Jr. operated Self's Furniture till 1996. Clark Sr. was very involved in the Slaton community, serving on the school board, as president of Slaton Savings and Loan Association, and on the board of the Slaton Development Foundation. Clark Sr. was named Outstanding Citizen of the Year by the Slaton Chamber of Commerce in 1960. Clark Jr. was also very involved in the community, serving on the school board, as a member of the Slaton Lions Club, and as vice president of Citizens State Bank. Clark Jr. was also the developer of the housing project known as New Century Heights.

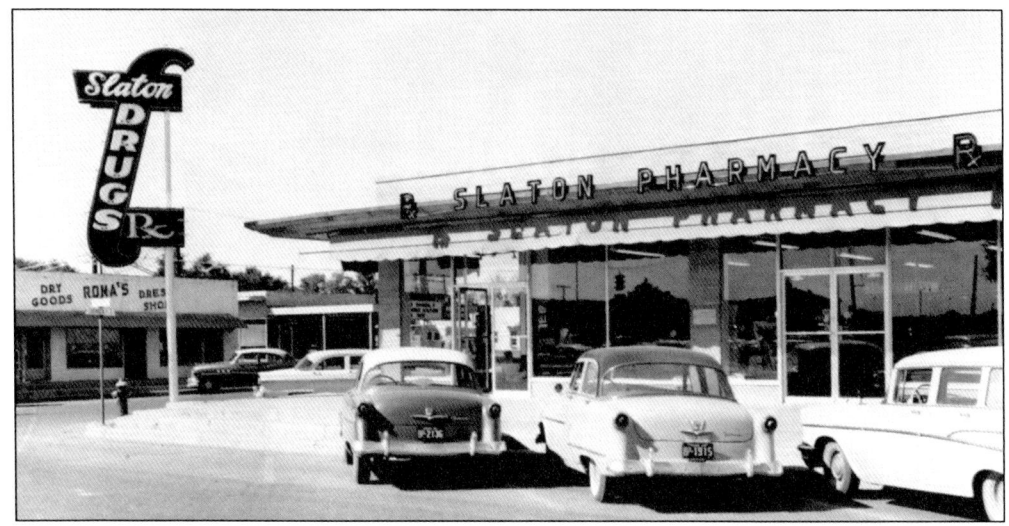

J.D. Holts owned the Slaton Pharmacy from 1948 until 1961. This photograph shows the pharmacy in 1953. Holts worked for Claude Anderson for several years at the Red Cross Pharmacy before opening his own drugstore.

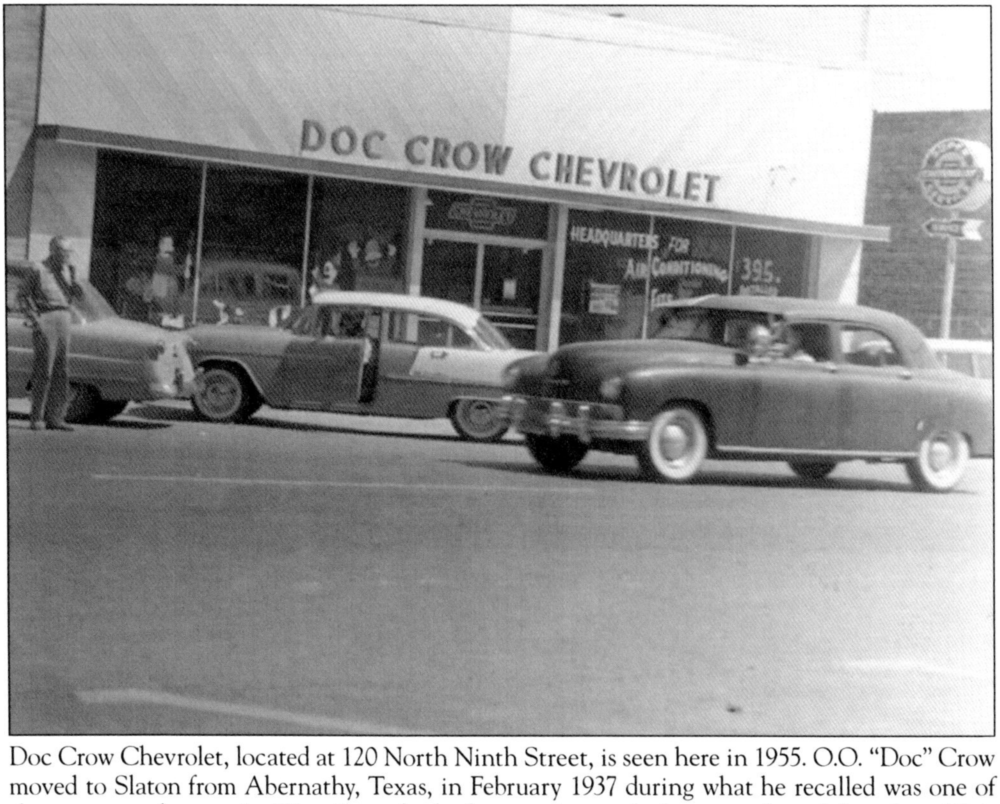

Doc Crow Chevrolet, located at 120 North Ninth Street, is seen here in 1955. O.O. "Doc" Crow moved to Slaton from Abernathy, Texas, in February 1937 during what he recalled was one of the worst sandstorms in West Texas he had ever witnessed; the storm lasted four days. This business was originally called Crow-Harral Chevrolet, but in 1953, Crow bought out his partner and changed the name of the business to Doc Crow Chevrolet.

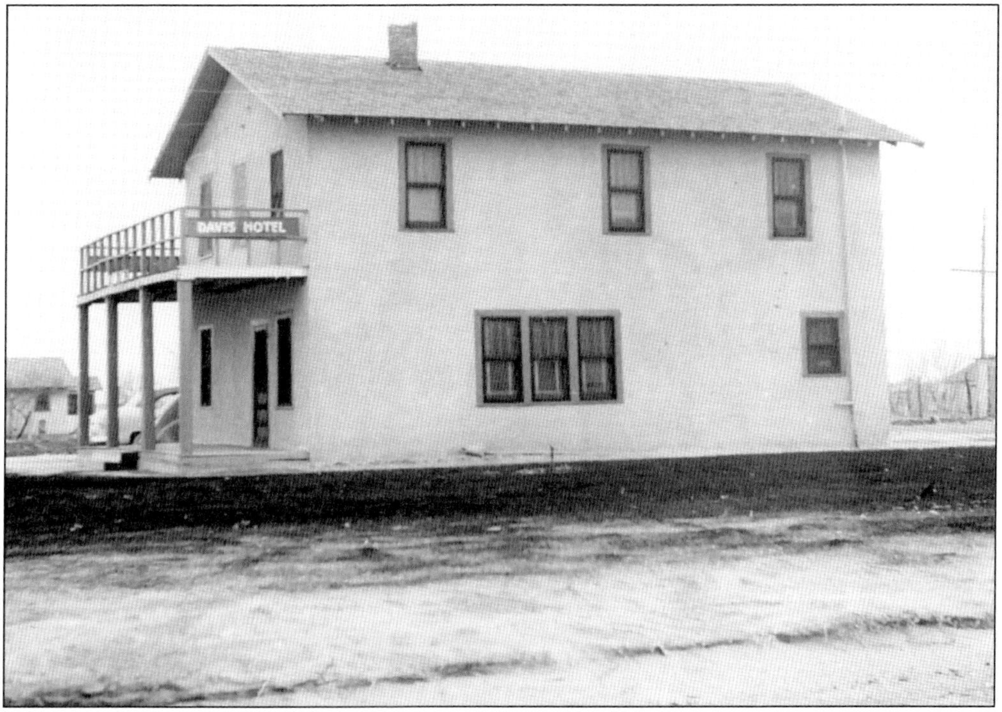

A 1955 edition of *The Slatonite* referred to The Davis Hotel as the "Negro Hotel." At that time, in segregated Slaton, black people were only allowed in certain stores. On July 7, 1924, ten thousand people gathered in Slaton to witness a Ku Klux Klan parade; an estimated 3,000 Klan members participated in the parade.

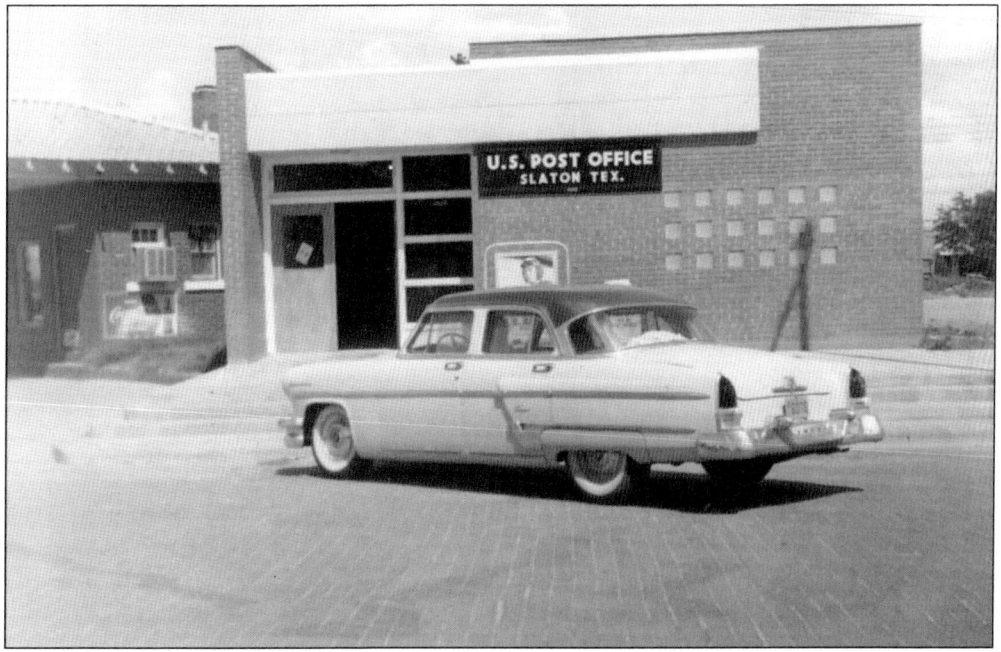

The Slaton post office is pictured in 1955. T.E. McClanahan served as postmaster from 1954 until 1958. Barry Ford was postmaster from 1959 until 1962, followed by Rush Wheeler in 1963.

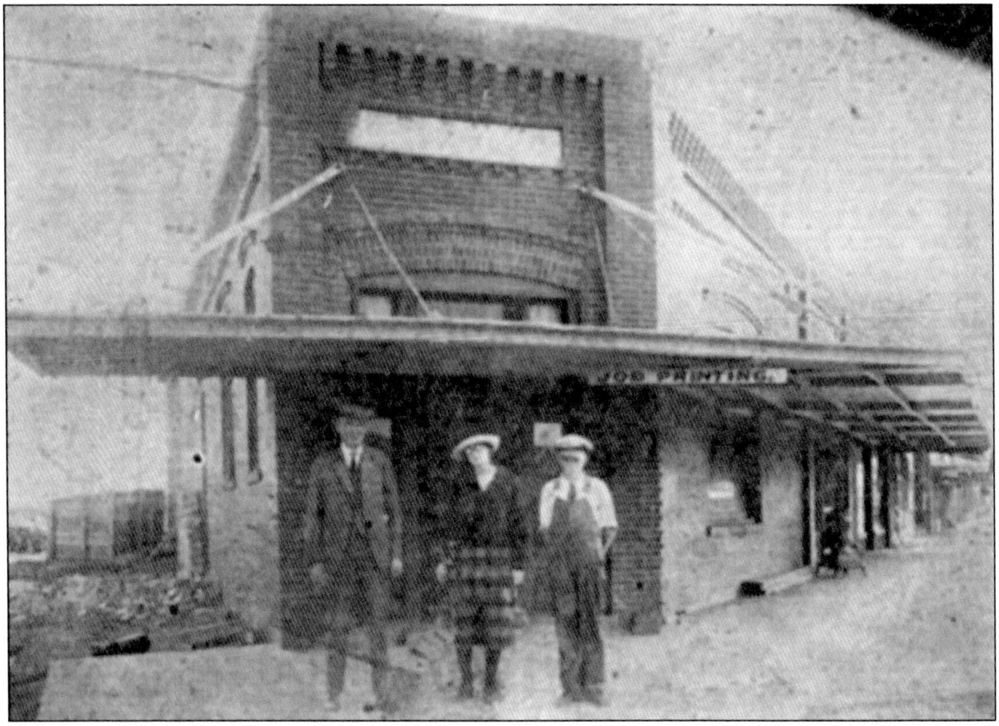

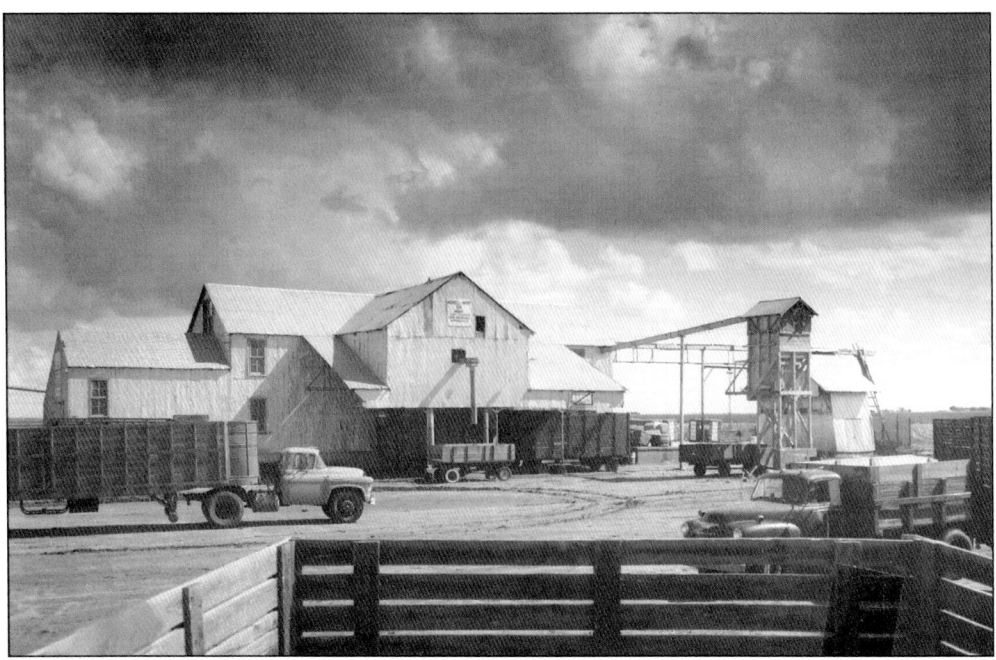

The Slaton Journal, the area's first weekly newspaper, started on June 15, 1911. On October 19, 1911, *The Slatonite* took over as Slaton's weekly newspaper. This photograph from the August 25, 1950, edition shows the *Slatonite* staff from 25 years before.

There have been many gins in Slaton over the years. This is the Nowell-Avery Gin. Agriculture and farming are a very important part of the local economy.

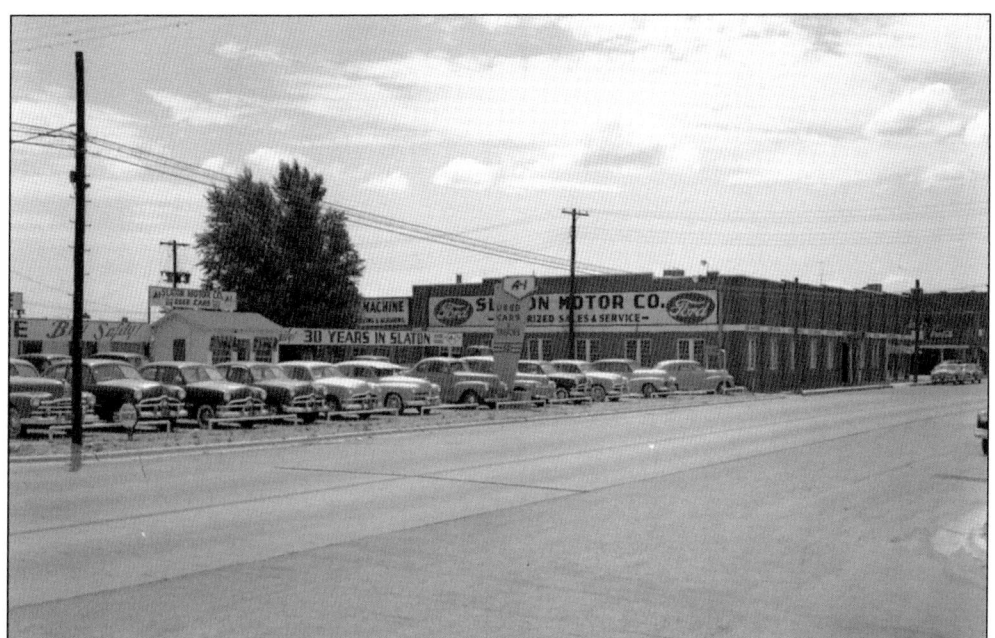

In December 1951, Bill Smith came to Slaton from Dallas, where he had worked for Ford Motor Company as assistant sales manager. The Forrest Hotel was his first home in Slaton. He built a home at 950 West Lubbock Street in June 1953. Smith had bought 49 percent in the Ford dealership, Slaton Motor Company, and signed an agreement to buy out stock owned by Harry Stokes over a 10-year period. In 1954, Smith purchased controlling interest, and by 1962, he was the sole owner and changed the name to Smith Ford Inc. His son, Steve, came into the business in May 1965. Smith South Plains is still in business in Slaton and Levelland, Texas, and is owned and operated by Steve's daughter, Annette Smith Sykora, and her husband, Pat.

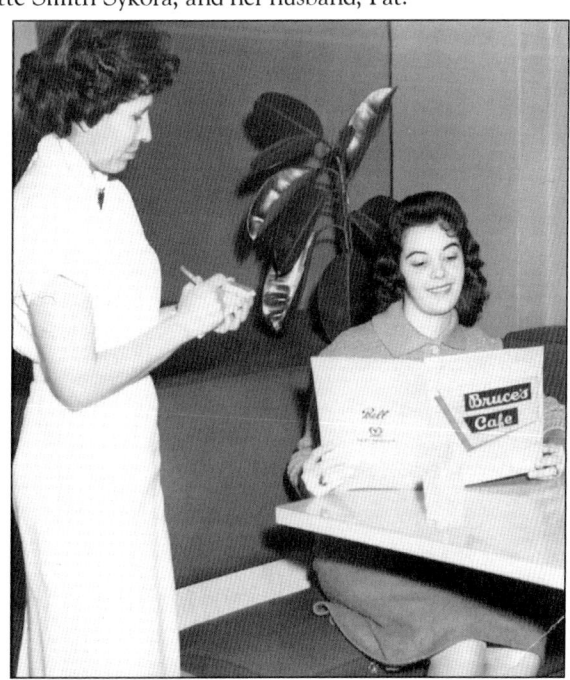

In 1963, Slaton had an eating place called Bruce's Café. It was owned by Bruce Blair, who was a restaurant entrepreneur. He and his mother, Gert, ran Bruce's Café, which was the hot spot in town for lunch. They served breakfast, lunch, and dinner.

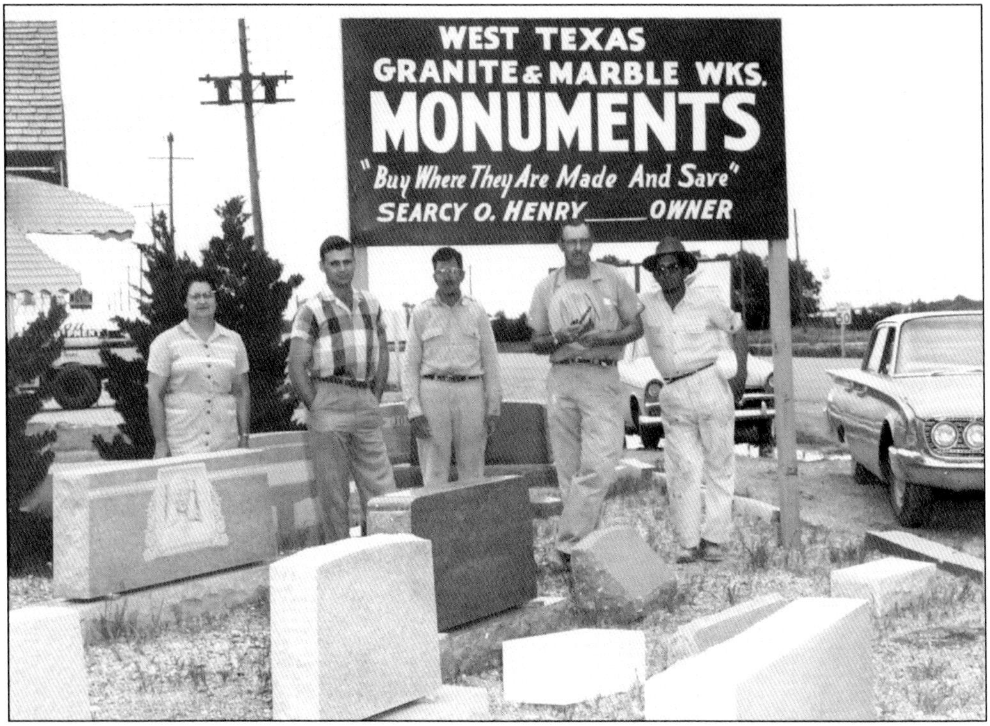

This photograph of the West Texas Granite and Marble Works is from the 1960s. The business was owned by Searcy Henry.

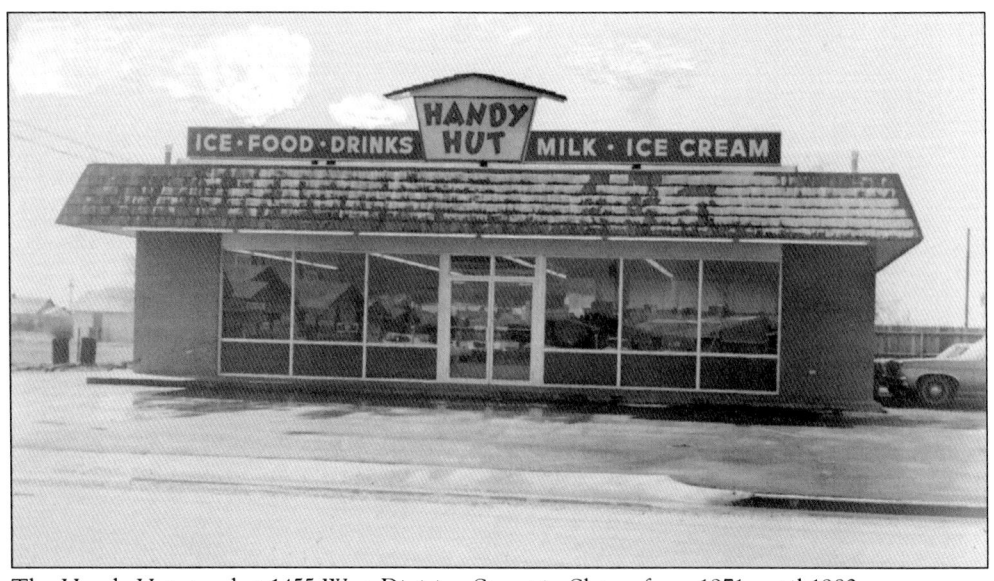

The Handy Hut stood at 1455 West Division Street in Slaton from 1971 until 1983.

This 1965 wooden nickel is from Slaton Lumber Company, the local Pittsburgh Paints dealer.

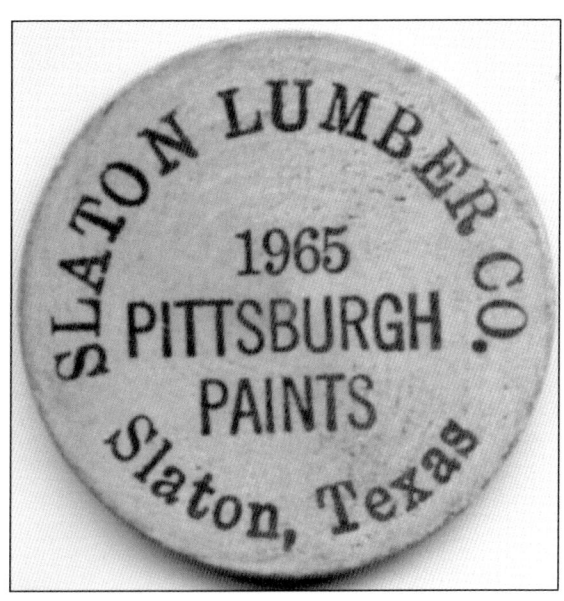

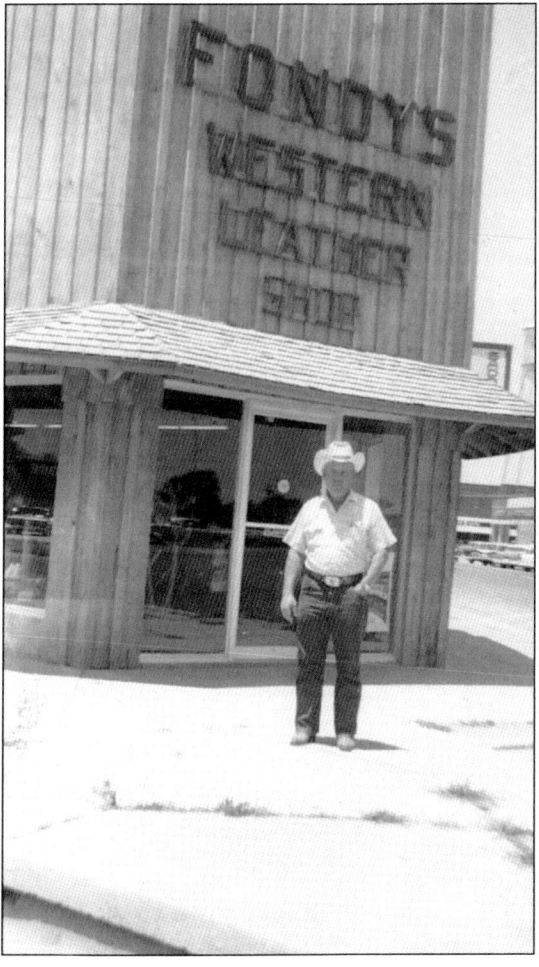

Pictured here is John M. Fondy Jr in front of his Slaton business, Fondy's Leather Shop, which was located at 109 North Ninth Street. It opened in 1944. John married Jolene Tate of Slaton. Her mother was a Harvey Girl. They have two children, Marvin Tate, born in 1951, and Judy Louise, born in 1953. John had a distinguished service record with the Army during World War II. His cousin, Dee Fondy, was from Slaton as well and became a professional baseball player who played in the Major Leagues from 1951 to 1958 with the Pittsburgh Pirates, Cincinnati Reds, and Chicago Cubs. (Courtesy of Jolene Fondy.)

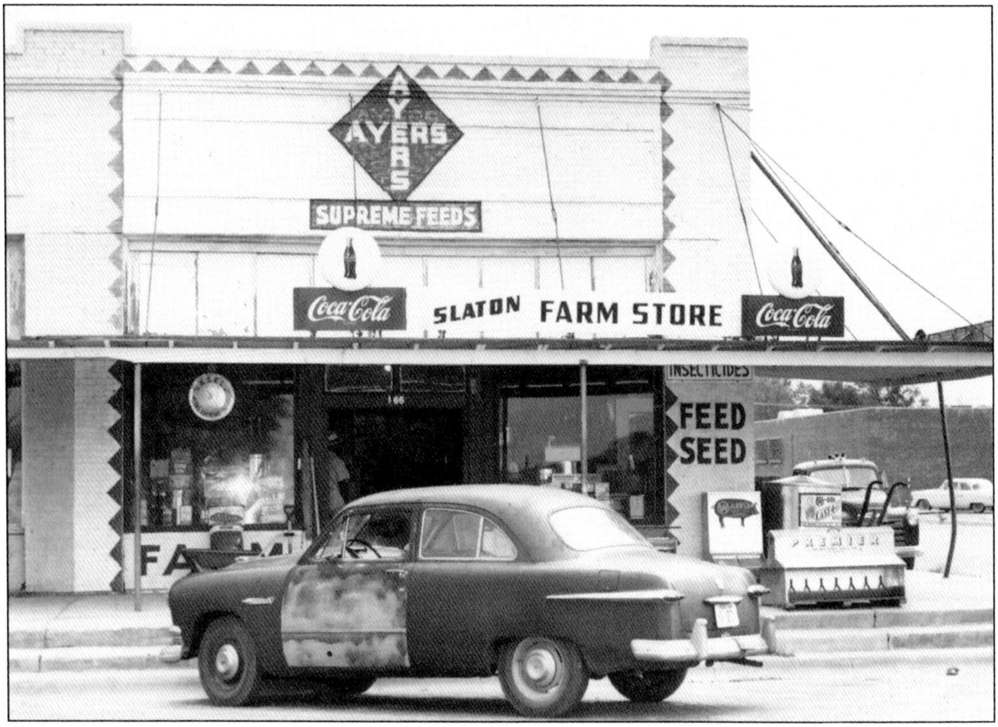

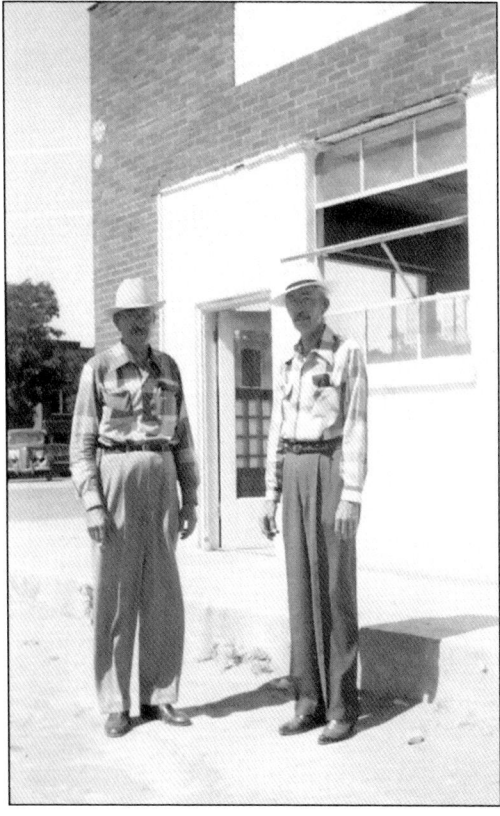

Slaton Farm Store, located on the Slaton Town Square, is pictured here in the 1950s. It was one of Slaton's successful businesses at the time.

This 1961 picture shows M.L. (left) and M.W. Abernathy, owners of Slaton Steam Laundry, which was in business from 1928 to 1971.

Five
CELEBRATING SUCCESS

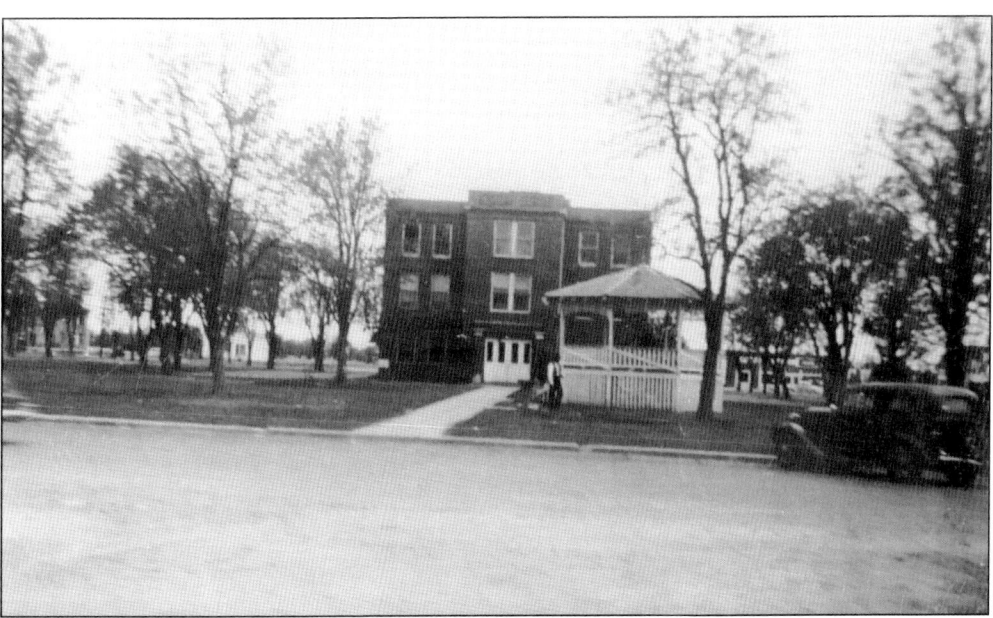

Slaton's city hall is pictured in the spring of 1943. The first city hall was built in 1922 in the middle of the square as the "hub" of the wagon-wheel design of the town. (Courtesy of Slaton Museum.)

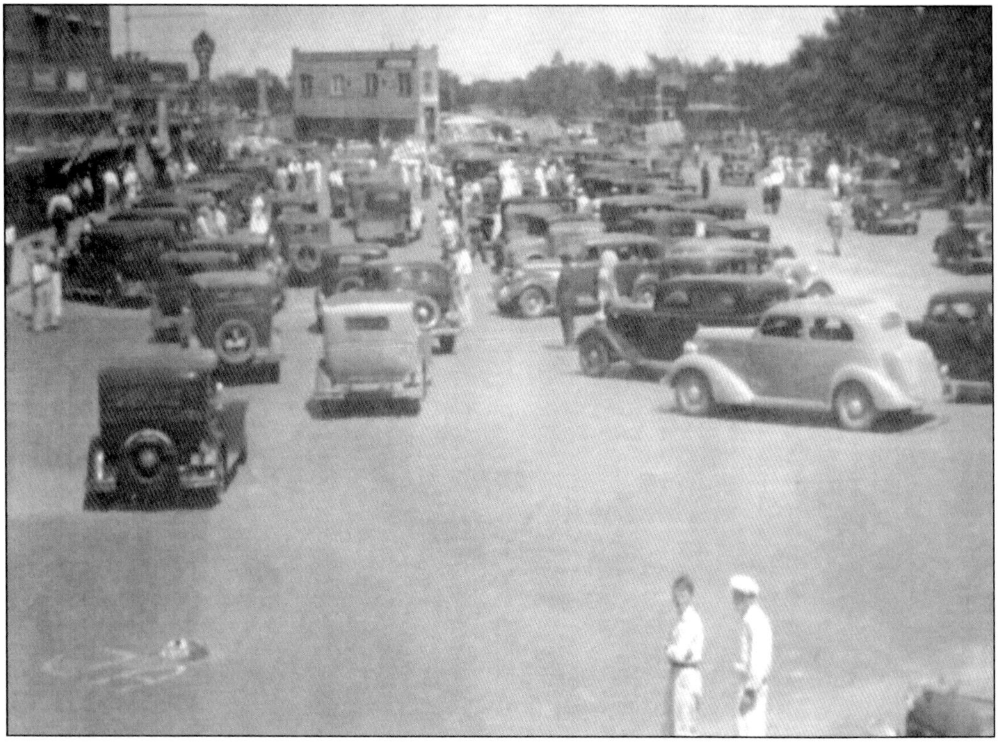

These 1936 photographs show a parade during Slaton's 25th anniversary celebration. Above is the 100 block of West Garza Street, and below is Railroad Avenue.

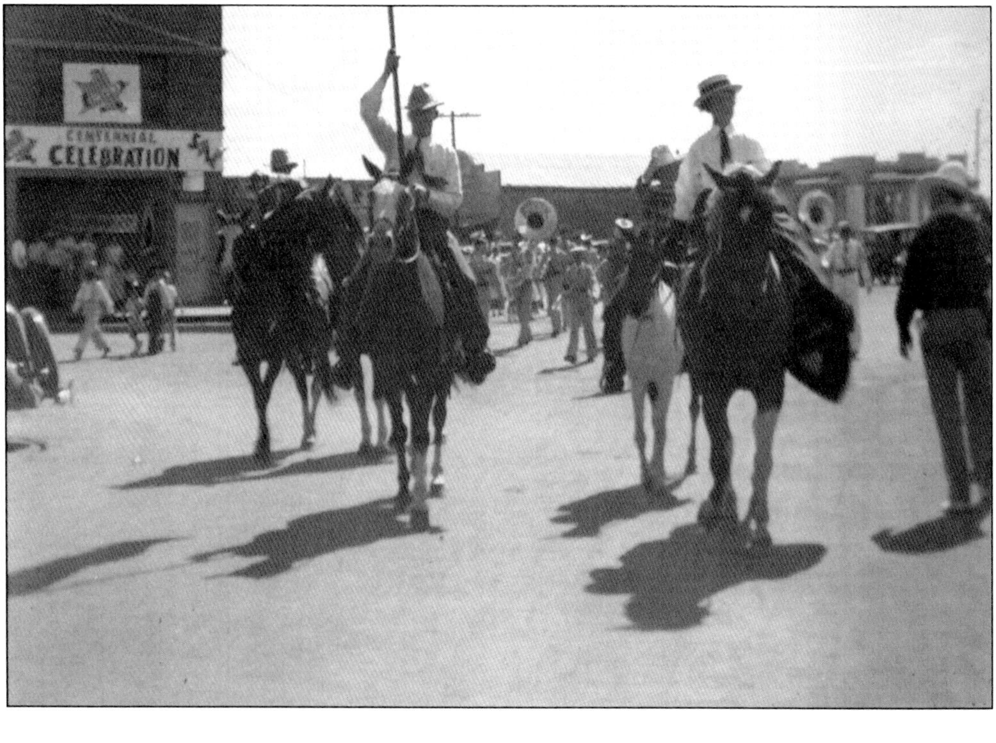

96

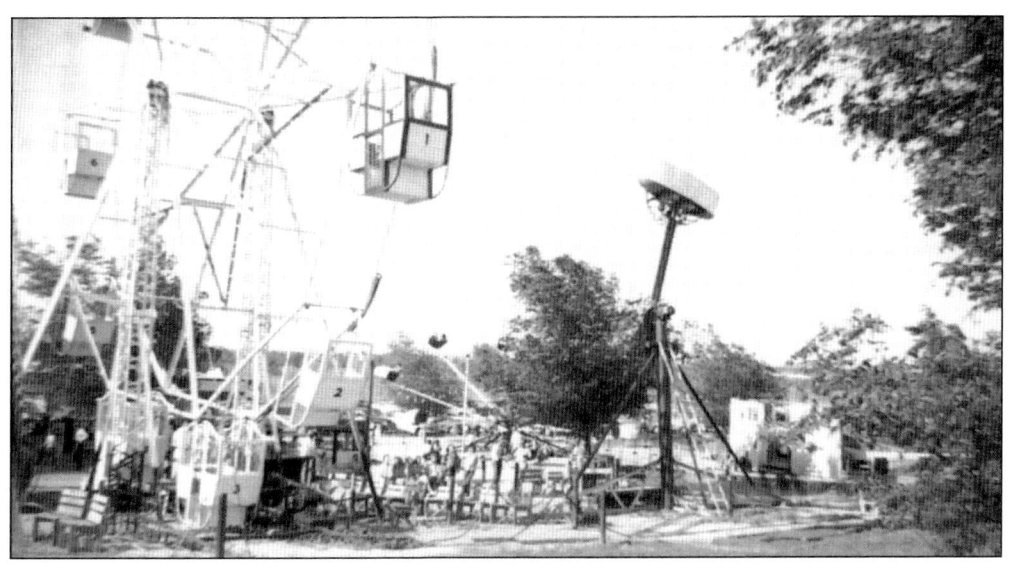
In the 1940s, this carnival came through Slaton and set up on South Eighth Street.

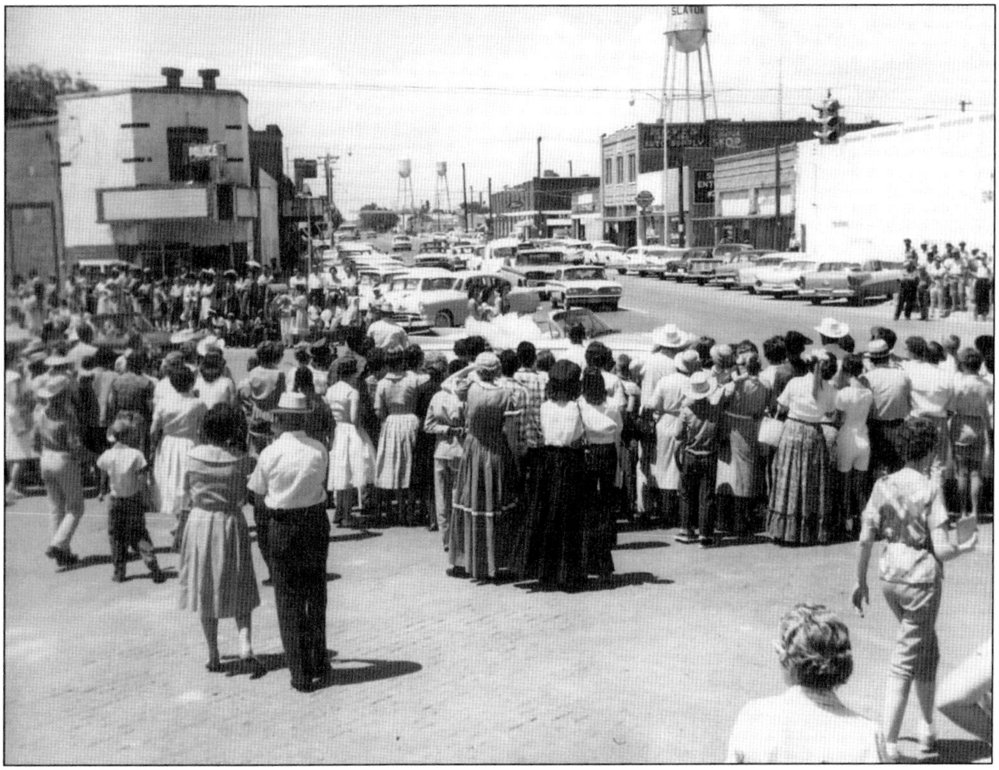

Another parade was held in downtown Slaton in 1953.

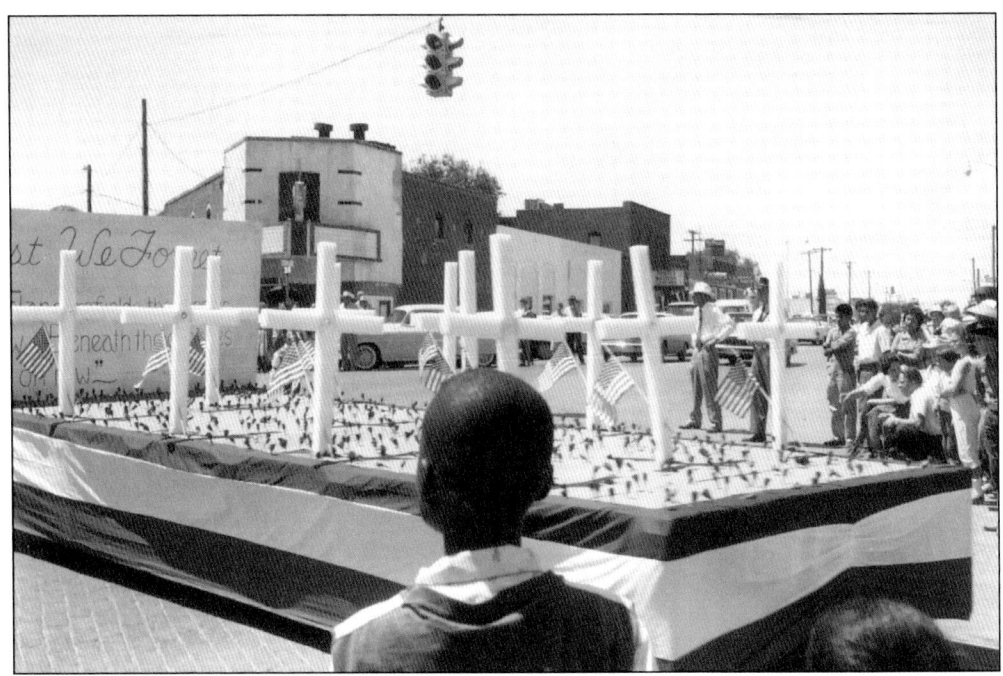

Slaton residents celebrated the town's 50th anniversary in 1961. Pictured above is a parade float, and below is the original bandstand in downtown Slaton.

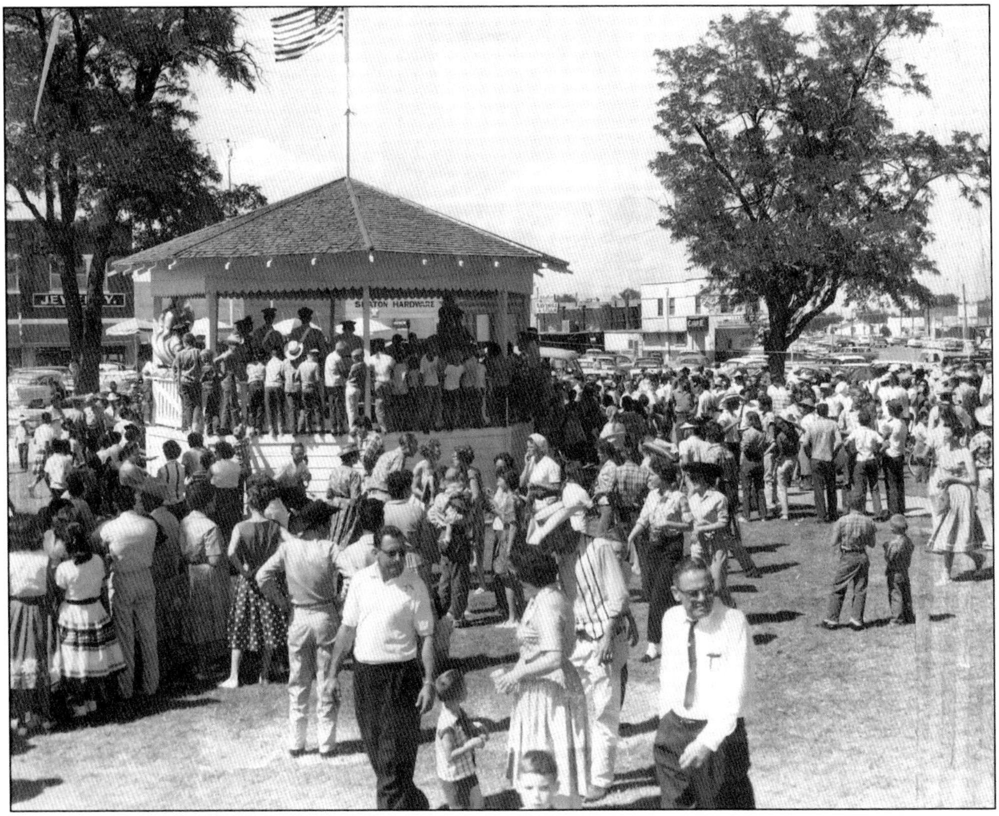

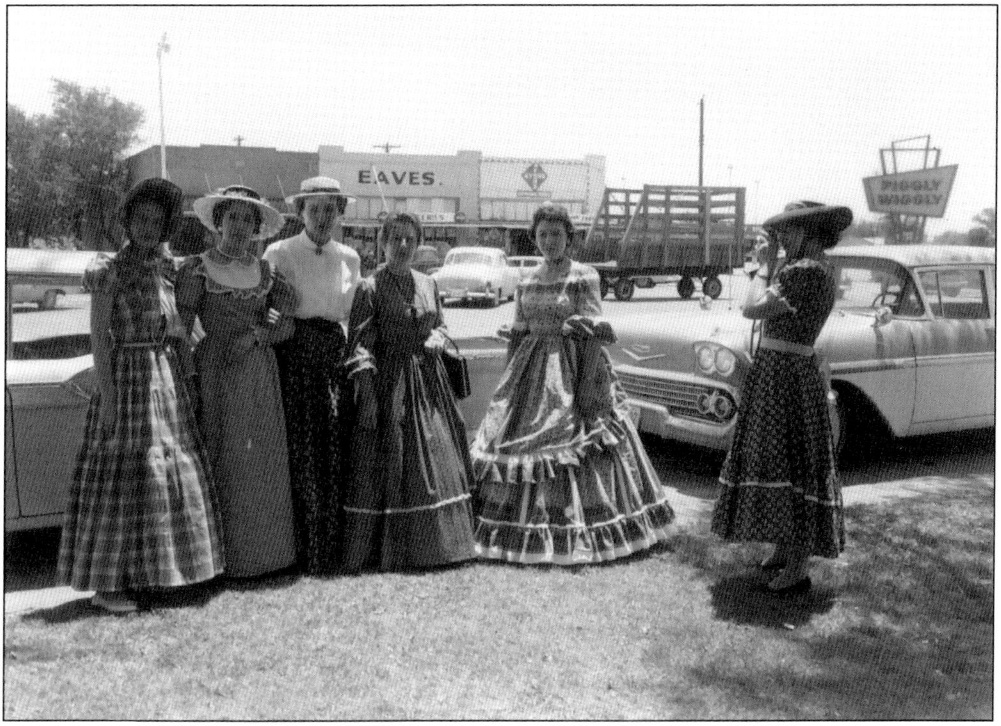

Above, well-dressed ladies are posing during Slaton's 50th anniversary celebration in 1961. Below is the 50th anniversary parade at Ninth and Garza Streets.

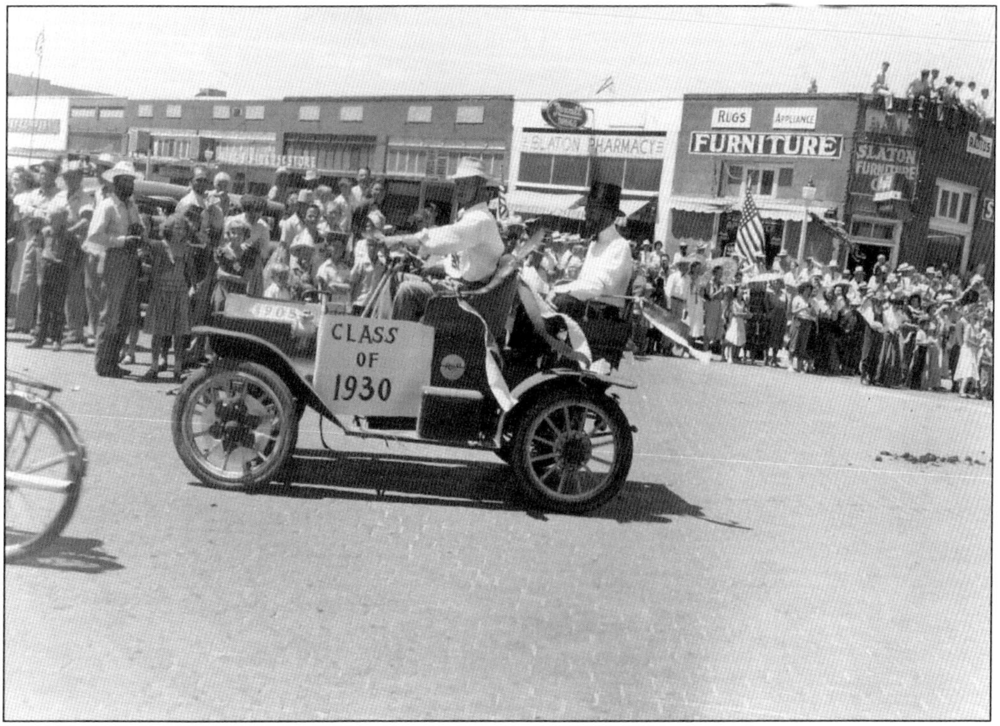

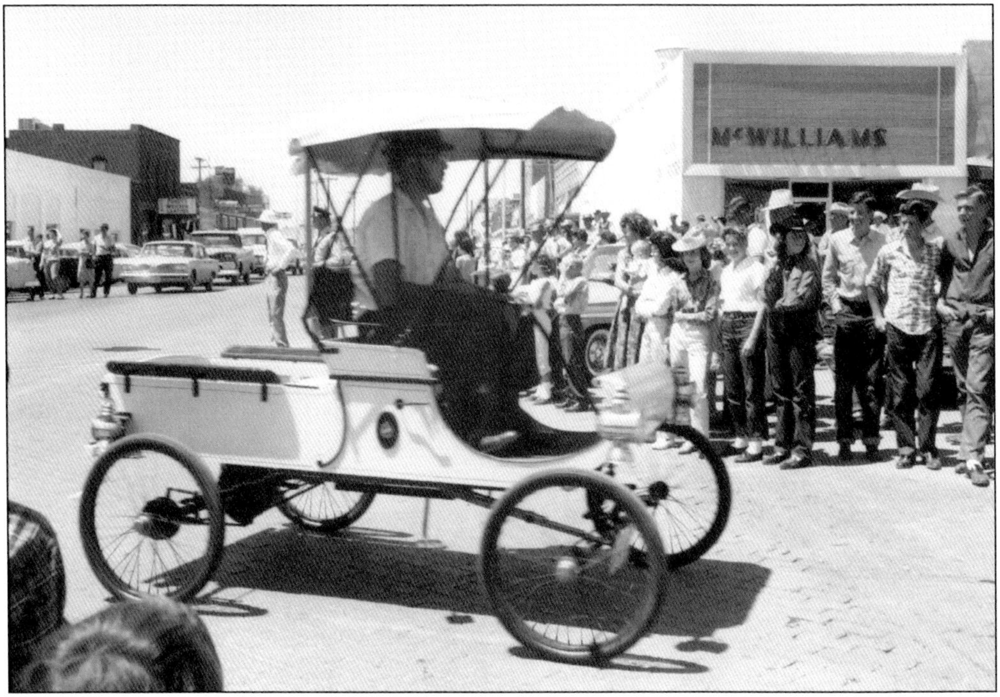

Community members celebrated the 50th anniversary of Slaton with a parade, good food, and the company of friends and family.

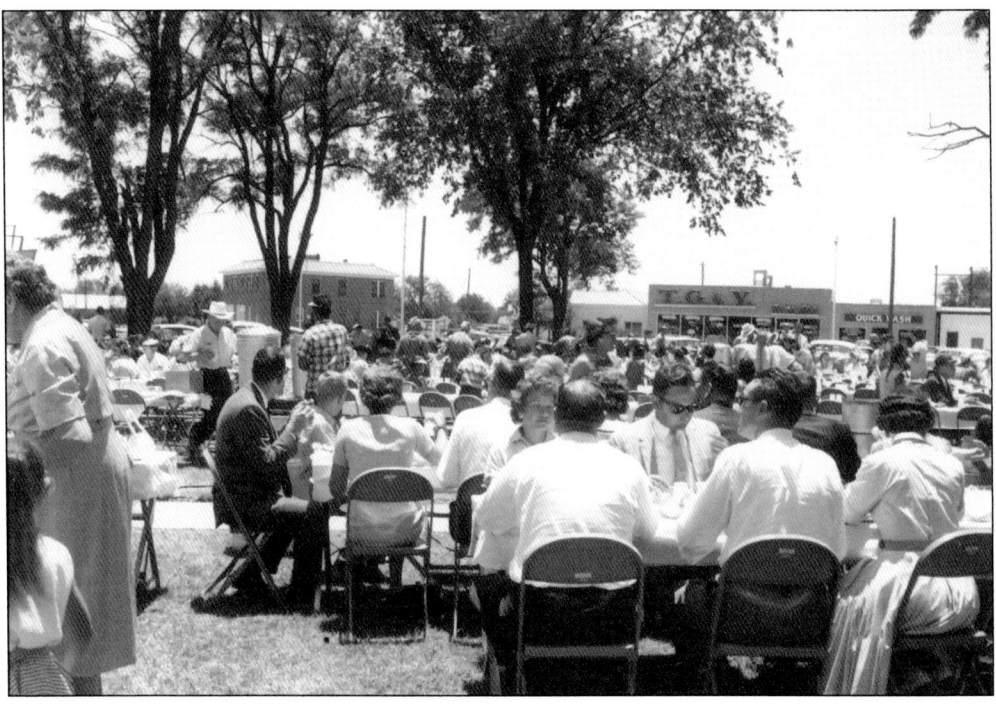

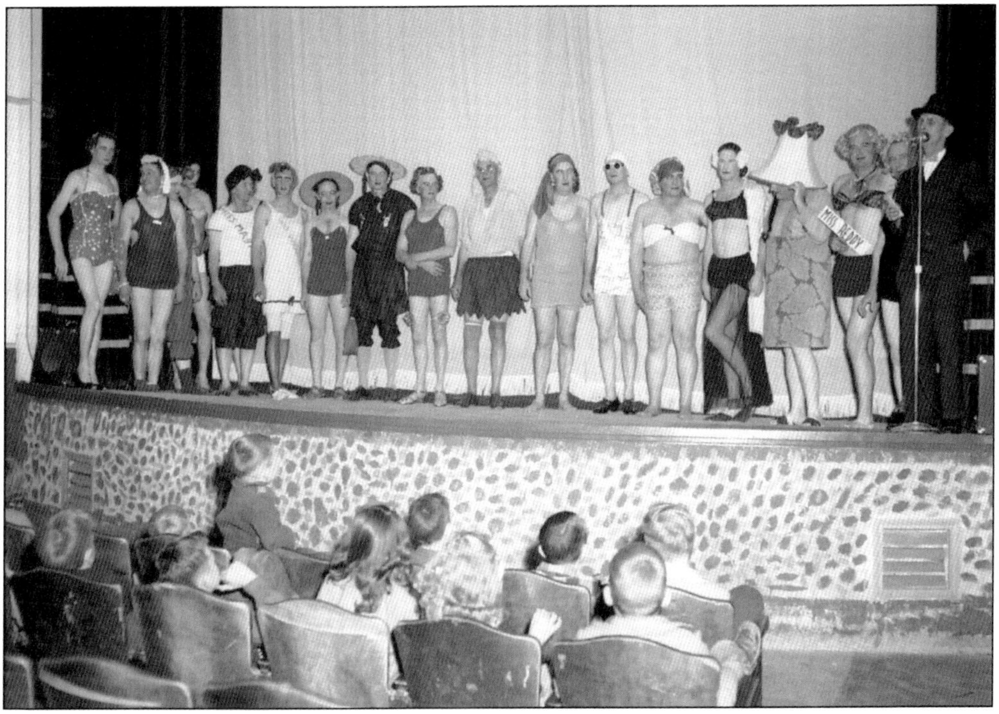

In this "beauty pageant" held in 1949 at the Slaton Theatre, it looks like everyone is having fun. Brother Burns, a preacher from the First Christian Church, was the emcee. Businessmen in the Slaton community performed as the pageant contestants.

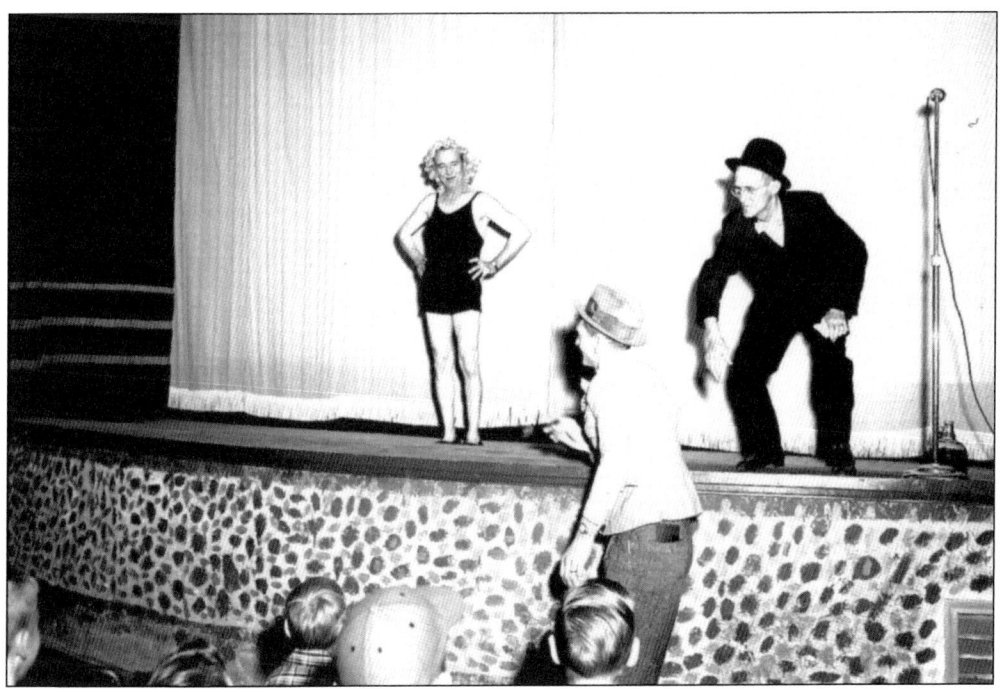

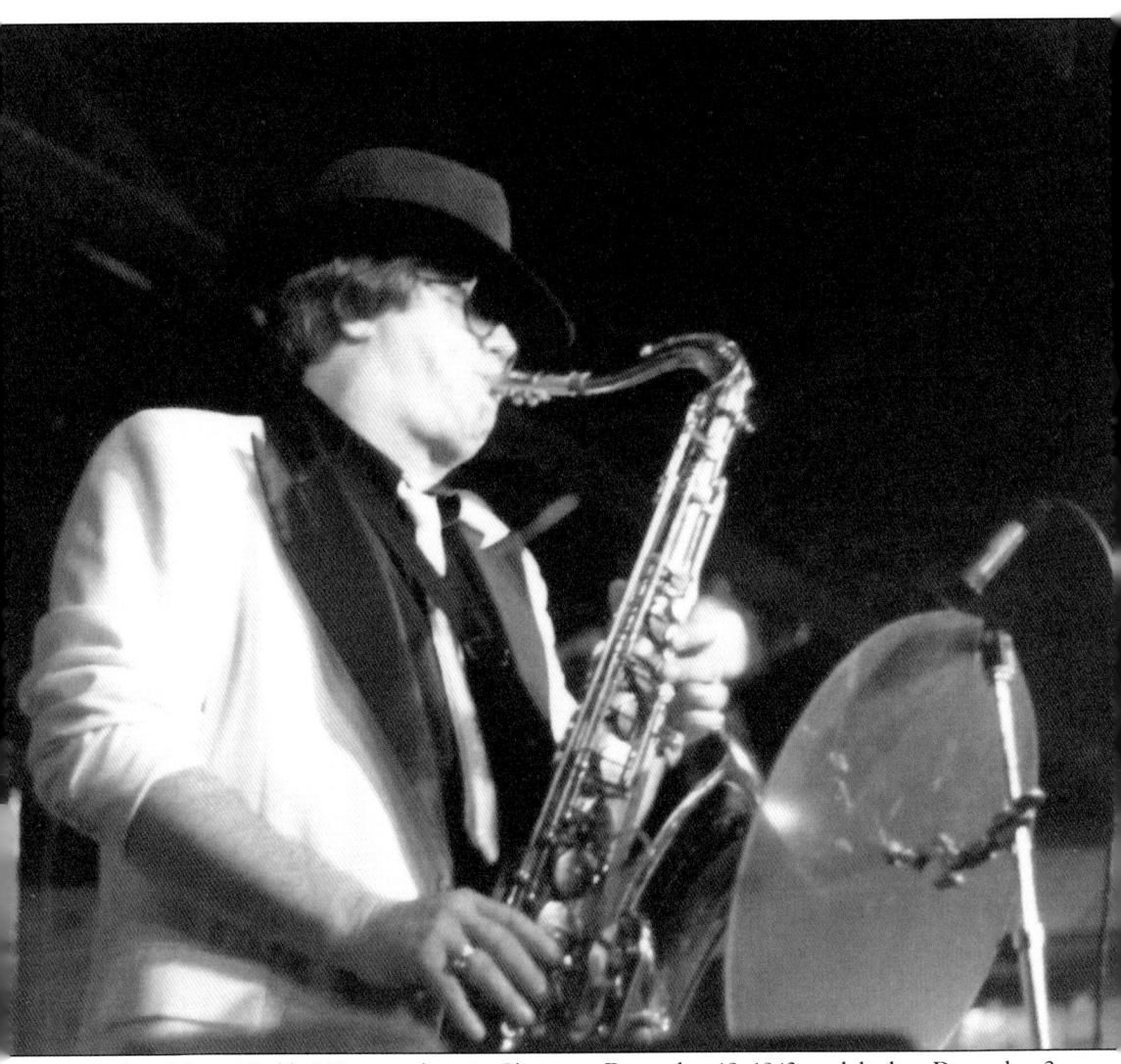

Robert Henry "Bobby" Keys was born in Slaton on December 18, 1943, and died on December 2, 2014. He was a saxophonist who played with prominent musicians from Elvis to Lynyrd Skynyrd, Eric Clapton, Joe Cocker, and George Harrison. When Keys was six years old, his father, Bill Keys, got a job with the Santa Fe Railway in Belen, New Mexico, but young Bobby stayed with his grandparents in Slaton. At age 15, Bobby began touring with acts such as Bobby Vee and Buddy Holly. He is best known for playing with the Rolling Stones. (Courtesy of T.G. Caraway Collection, Crossroads of Music Archive, Southwest Collection/Special Collections Library, Texas Tech.)

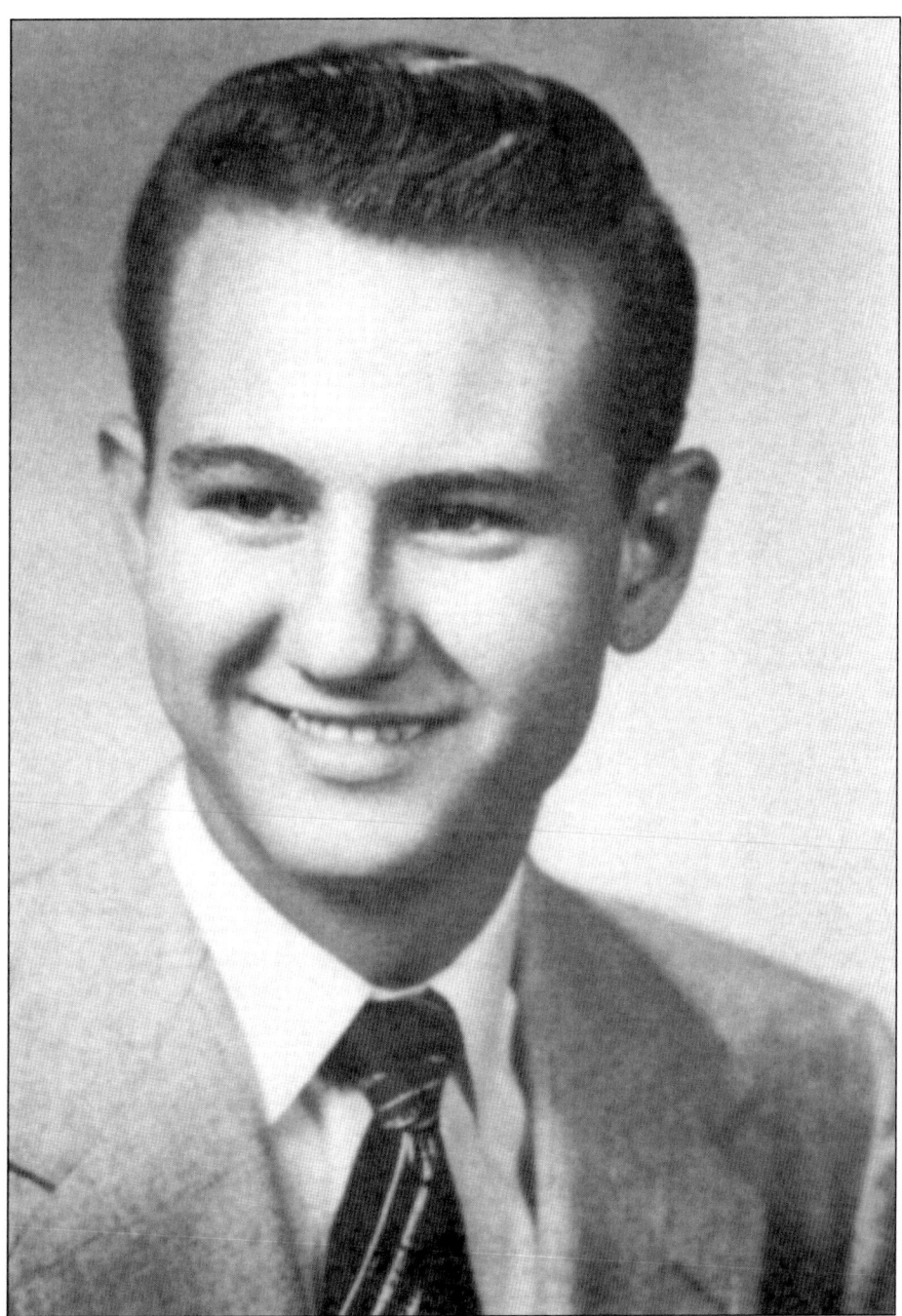

Sonny Curtis graduated from Slaton High School in 1955; this is his senior picture. He was born in Meadow, Texas, on May 9, 1937. Sonny was friends with Buddy Holly and became the guitarist for the Crickets. Curtis is known for writing such songs as "I Fought the Law" and "Love is all Around," which was the theme song for the *Mary Tyler Moore Show*. He cowrote the 1989 hit song "I'm No Stranger to the Rain," performed by Keith Whitley. Curtis was inducted into the Musicians Hall of Fame and Museum and the Rock and Roll Hall of Fame as a member of the Crickets. (Courtesy of Slaton Museum.)

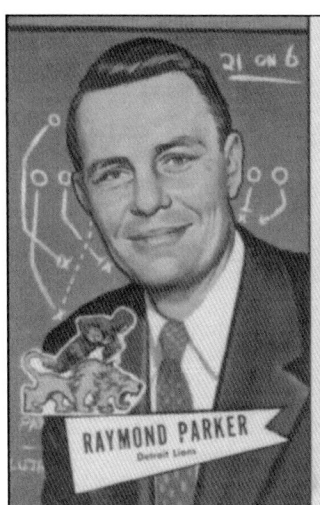 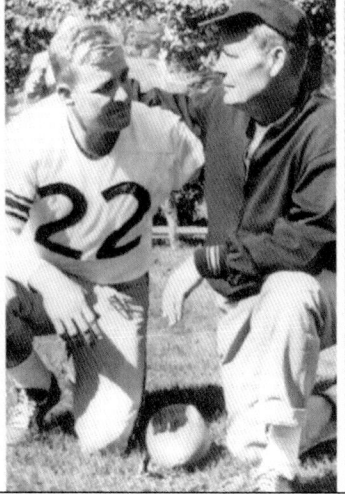 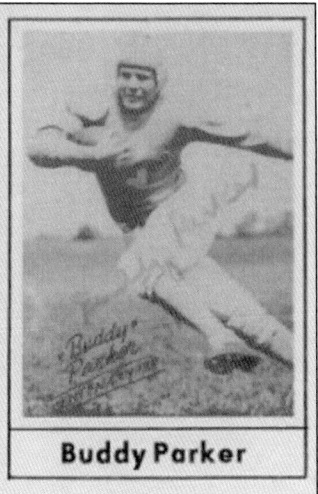

Raymond "Buddy" Parker, a football player and coach, was born in Slaton on December 16, 1913, and passed away on March 22, 1982. He signed with the Detroit Lions as a fullback in 1935, and during his first season, helped the team obtain an NFL championship. Later, he was traded to the Cardinals, where he also played linebacker and defensive back, and was with them for seven seasons. He served as head football coach for the Chicago Cardinals, Detroit Lions, and Pittsburgh Steelers. A highlight of Buddy Parker's career came when he and Bobby Layne popularized what would become known as the two-minute offense, which allowed a team to quickly move down the field late in the game. Parker was superstitious and would not let any of his players wear the number 13.

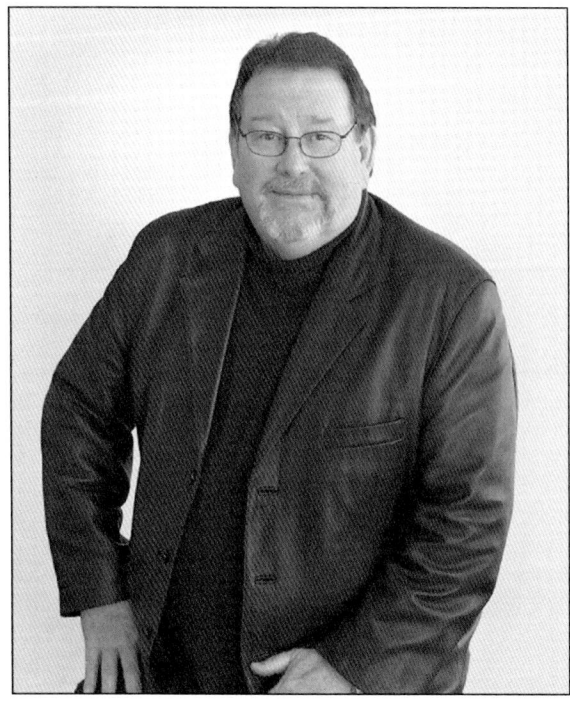

Don Caldwell graduated from Slaton High School in 1963. He played saxophone at Bruce's Café in Slaton with The Kados in the summer before his senior year, and was hooked on music from that moment. Caldwell has a recording studio that has been in operation since 1971. He married Terri Sue Newman in 1977, and she operates the Cactus Theatre mentor program and has trained hundreds of singers and musicians. Caldwell is one of the founders of Lubbock's Fourth On Broadway Celebration; in 1993, he and some of his friends renovated the old Cactus Theater, which is now a legendary performance space in Texas. His life's work has been to heighten public awareness and promote the cutting-edge music and performers of West Texas. (Courtesy of Don Caldwell.)

Six
A Picture Paints a Thousand Words

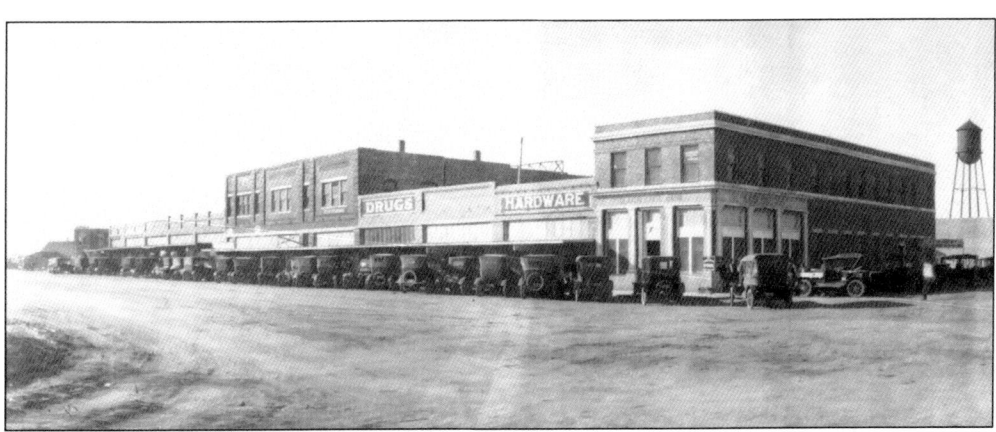

The downtown area of the frontier town of Slaton is shown in the 1920s. Banking was big business at the time, and Slaton State Bank, owned by the Paul family, is seen here on the corner. Officers were J.C. Paul, president; and J.H. Paul, cashier. The bank did well until the Depression, when it went out of business. The Paul family had previously been in the banking business in Amarillo.

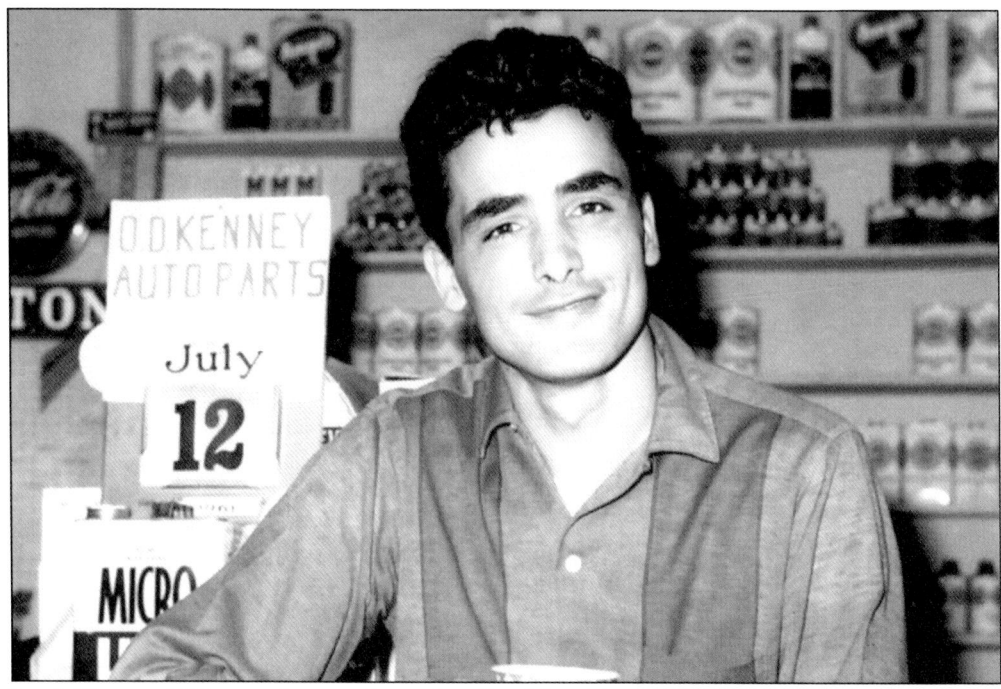

Lewis Thomas D'Elia was born and raised in Brooklyn, New York. "Lew Dee," as he was known on the radio, worked for Slaton radio station KCAS in the early 1960s. He began his career with Texas broadcast pioneer R.B. "Mr. Mac" McAlister. Lew Dee worked for many stations in the area, including KSEL Radio and TV, KZZN, KEND, KKCL, KUKO, KUCO, KKIK, 98Kool, and Stars 104.3. He and his wife, Diana Dee, had popular morning shows.

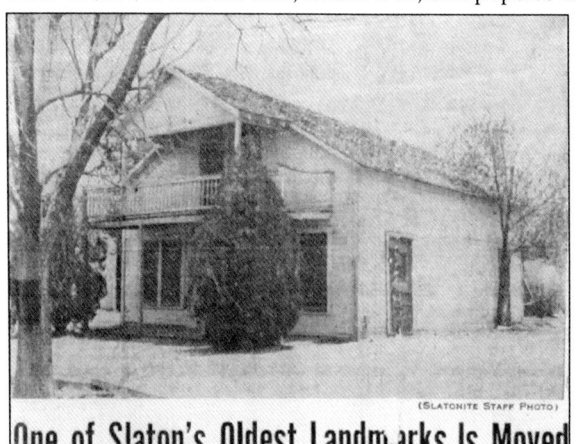

This story from *The Slatonite* is about the relocation of the historic 1912 Higbee House and post office, which was moved to make room for new business development.

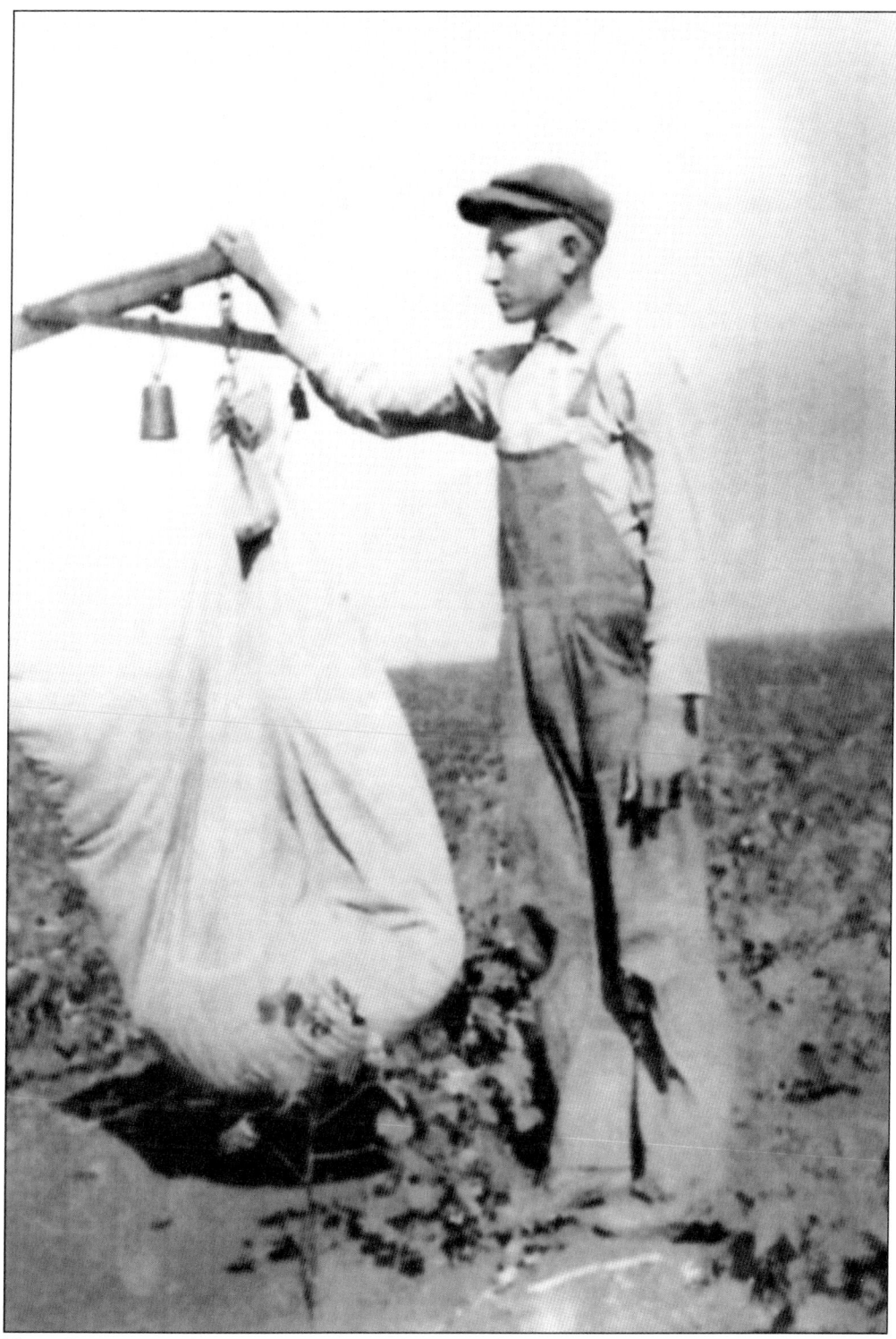
Elmer Kenney is picking cotton in 1924. Elmer was the brother of O.D. Kenney and the son of J.W. and Leta Kenney. The Kenney family lived south of town.

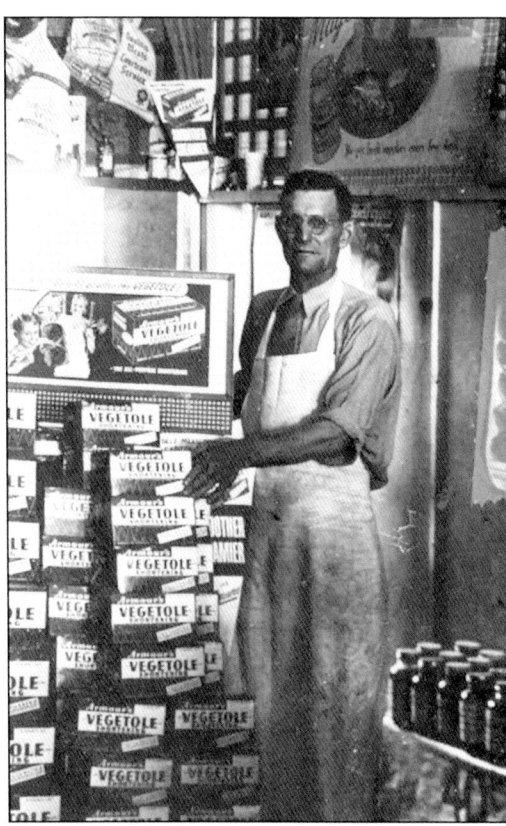

H.G. Sanders is pictured at his Slaton store, Sanders Grocery & Market, at 705 South Ninth Street.

In 1922, the men of the area went to Joe Walker Sr.'s barber shop when they needed a haircut and shave.

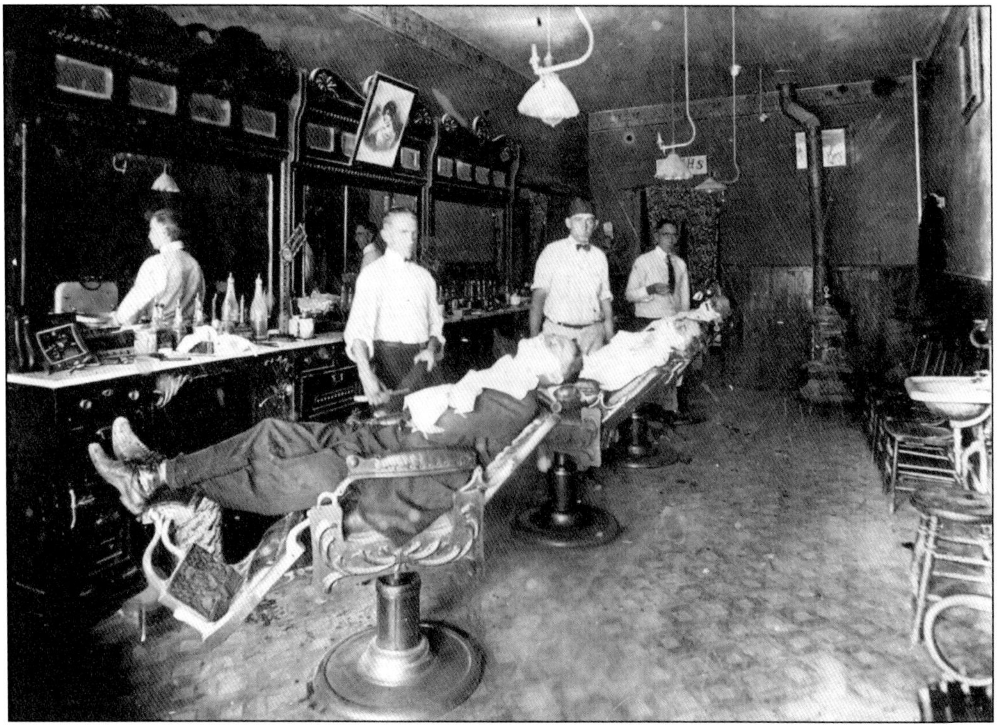

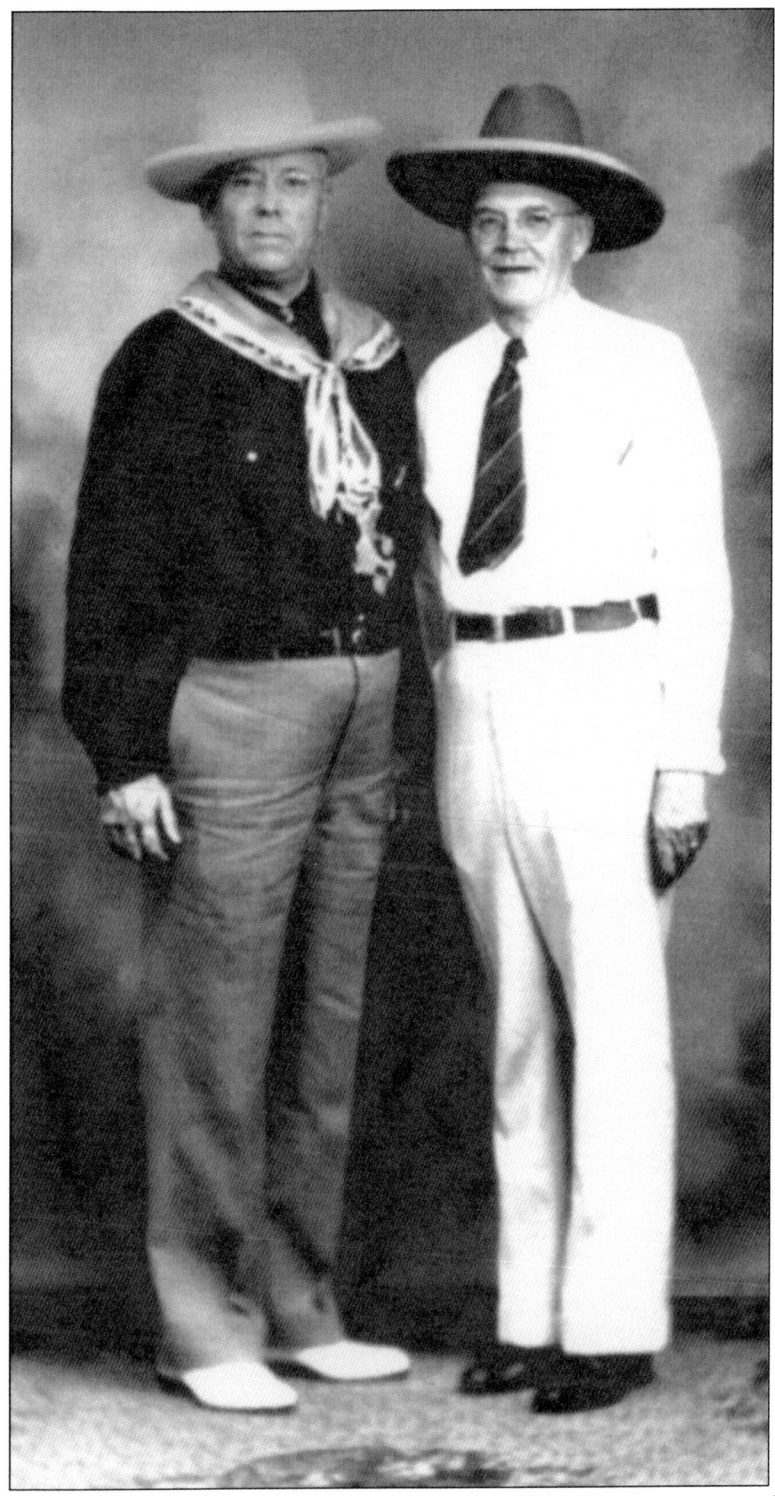

Tom "T.J." Abel (left), who served as Lubbock County sheriff for 17 years, is pictured here with Sam Staggs.

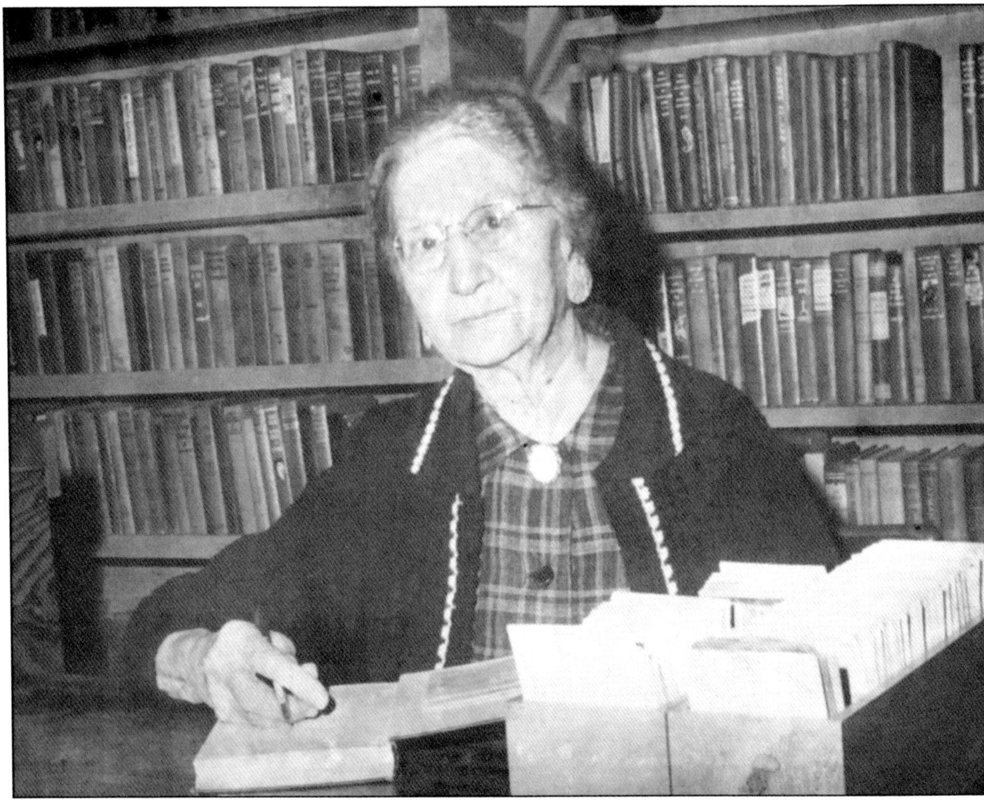

Mrs. Lillian Merrill was the librarian at "the Clubhouse," the library at Slaton City Park.

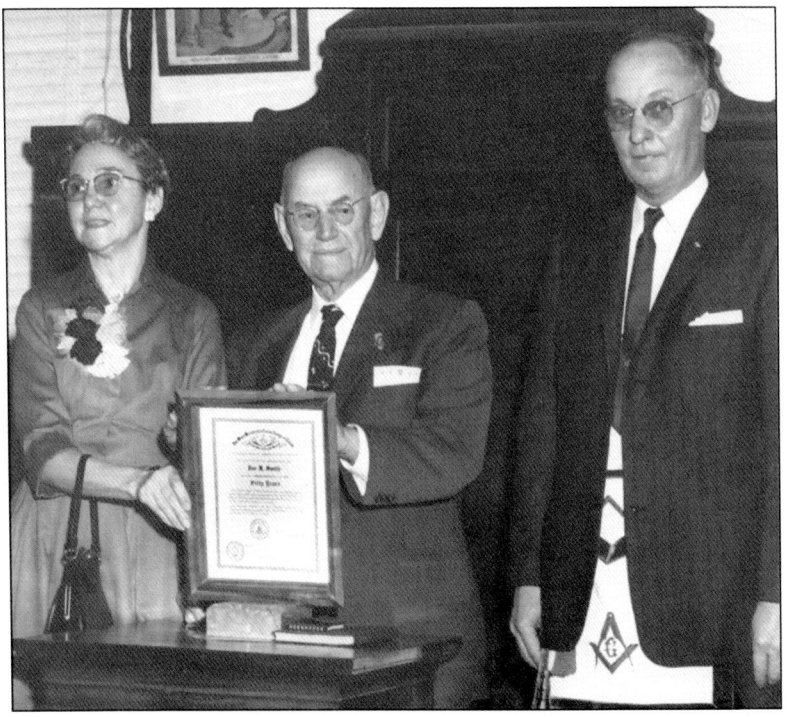

Joe H. Smith (center), a pioneer of Slaton, is being honored for 50 years of service with the Masons.

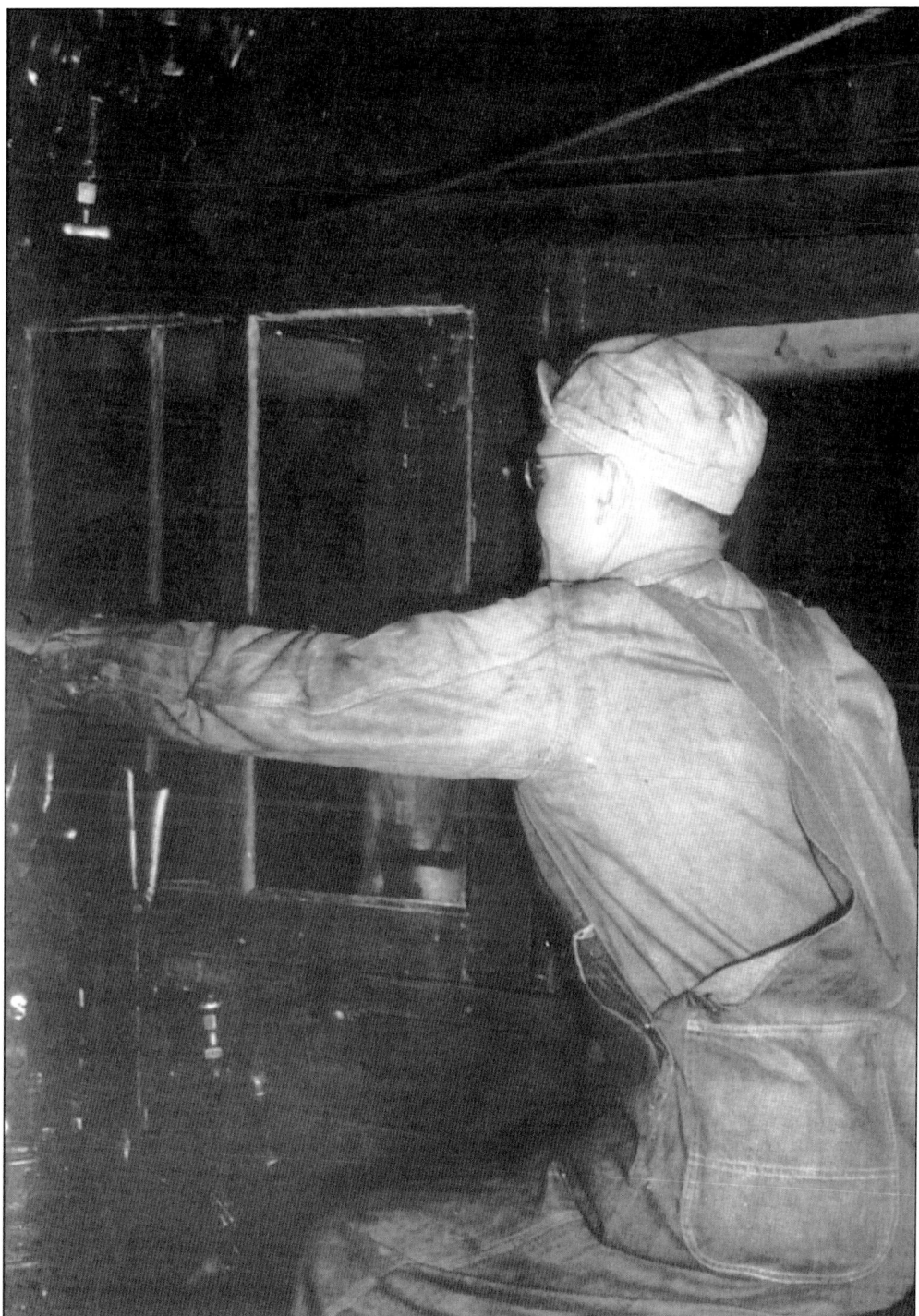

Joe V. Bickerstaff is working on a train. Slaton was the division point of the Santa Fe Railway. Four daily trains linked Slaton with the outside world, and a northbound and southbound train ran between Amarillo and Sweetwater. (Courtesy of the Harvey House and Slaton Railroad Heritage Association.)

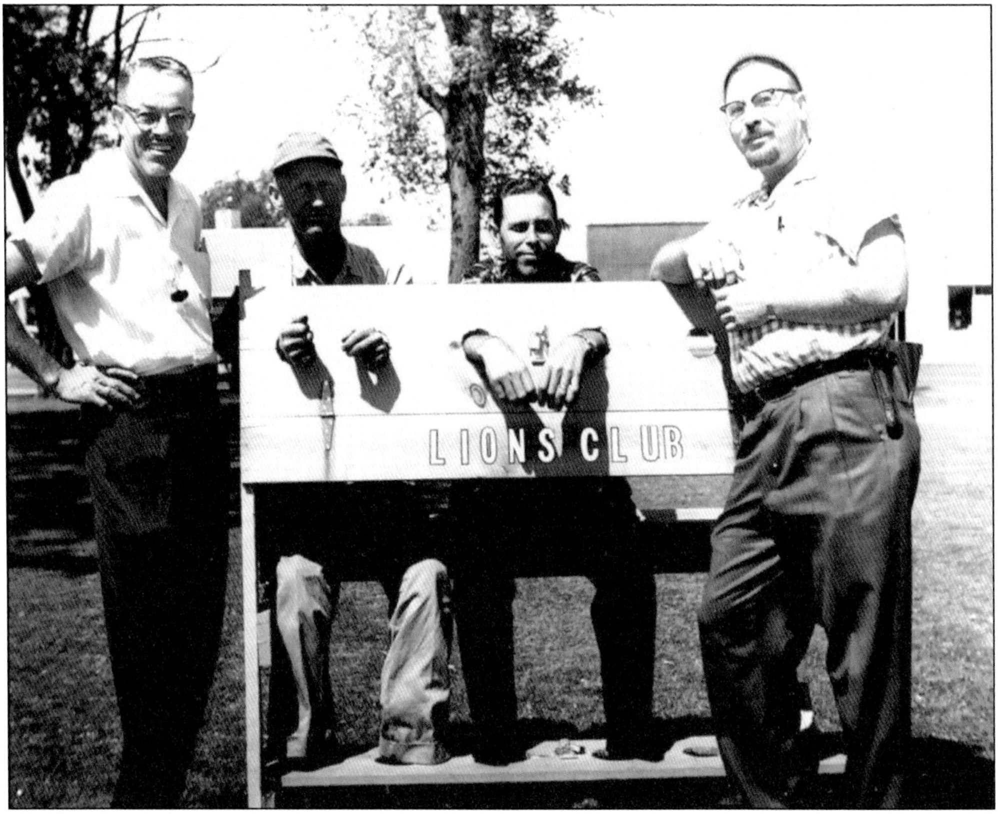

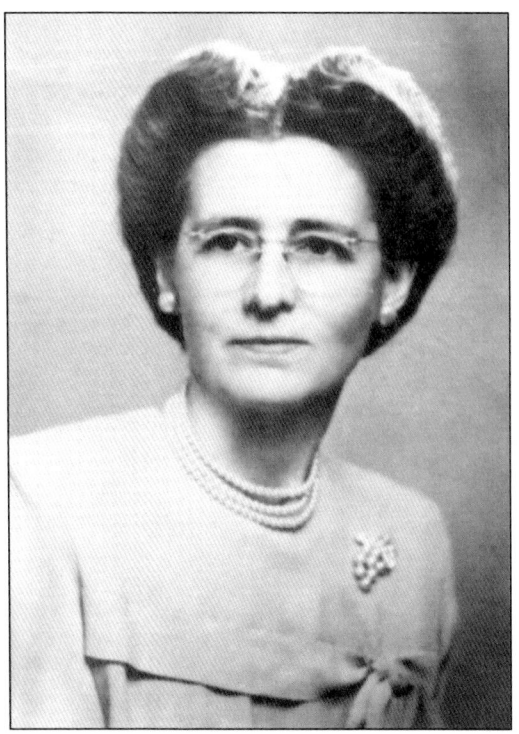

Lions Club members (left to right) H. Lasater, Norbert Kitten, Edd Williams, and Barney Green are pictured here.

Mary Neill worked as an English teacher in Slaton from the 1930s through the 1950s. She and Alma Caldwell were responsible for rewriting the course of study for high school English classes, and they influenced many students.

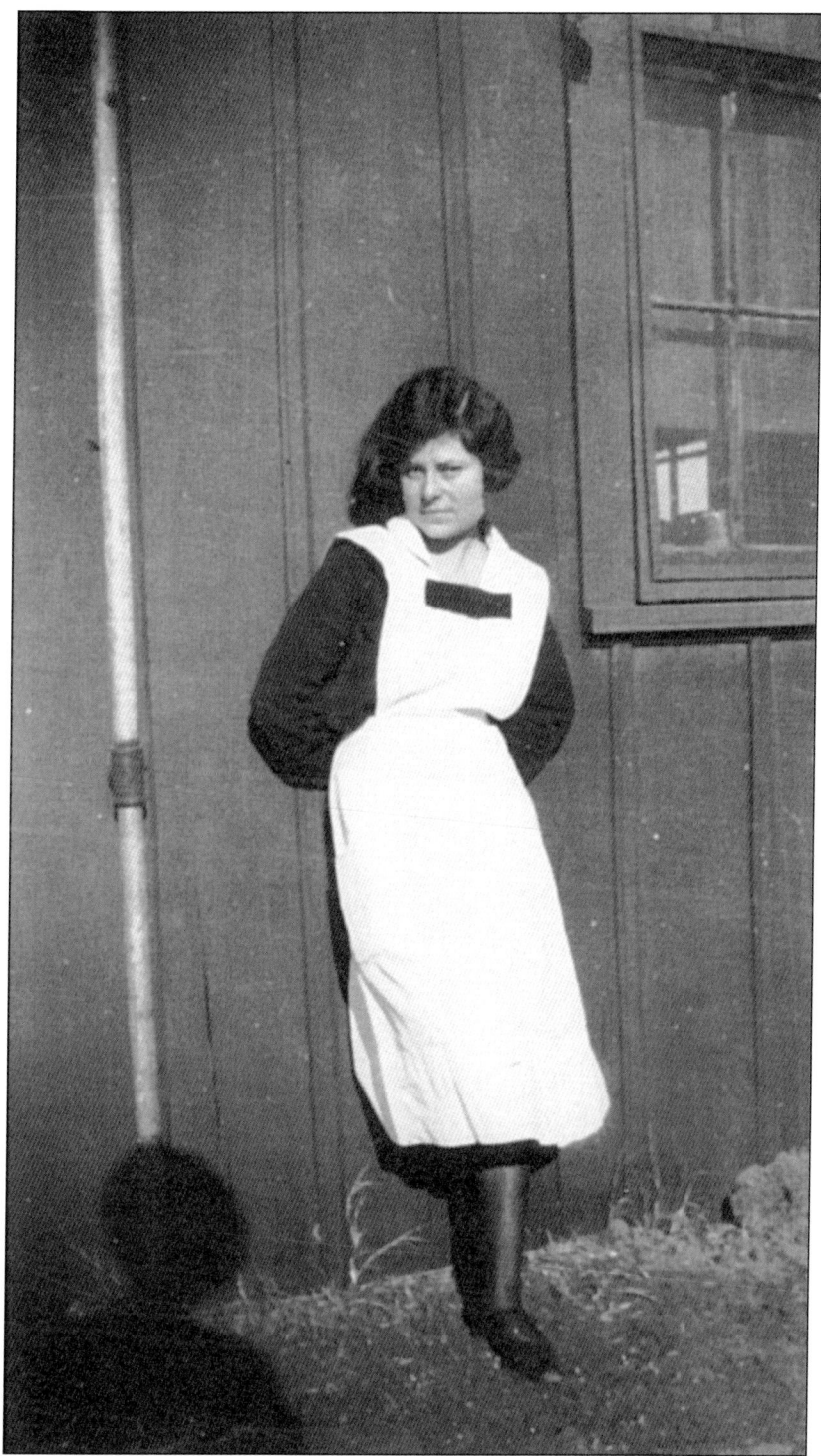

Ethel Reeves Tate was a Harvey Girl at the Sweetwater Harvey House. This picture was taken when she was 21 years old. Ethel met her husband, Joseph Warren Tate, at the Harvey House in Sweetwater. He worked for the Santa Fe. They later moved to Slaton. (Courtesy of Jolene Fondy.)

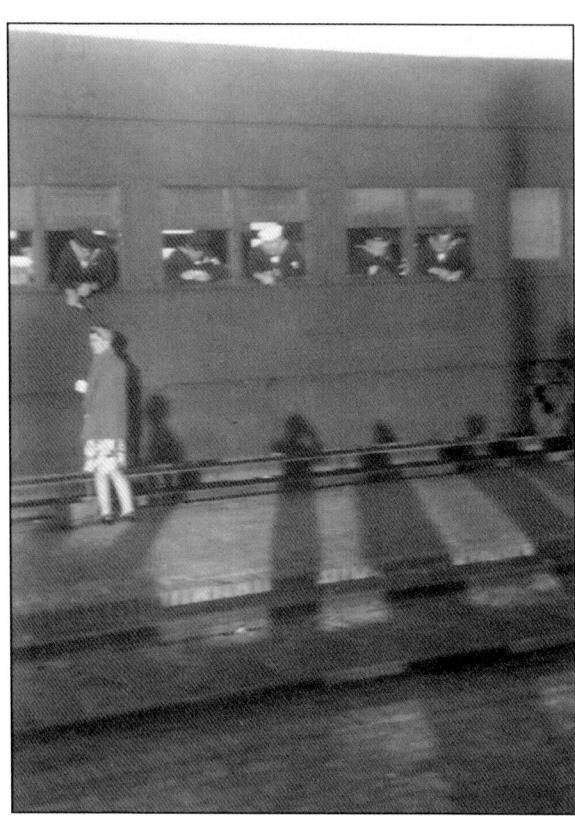

World War II troops are seen here traveling through Slaton on the Santa Fe Railway.

Pictured here are Self, Green, Englund, and an unidentified man at a baseball game.

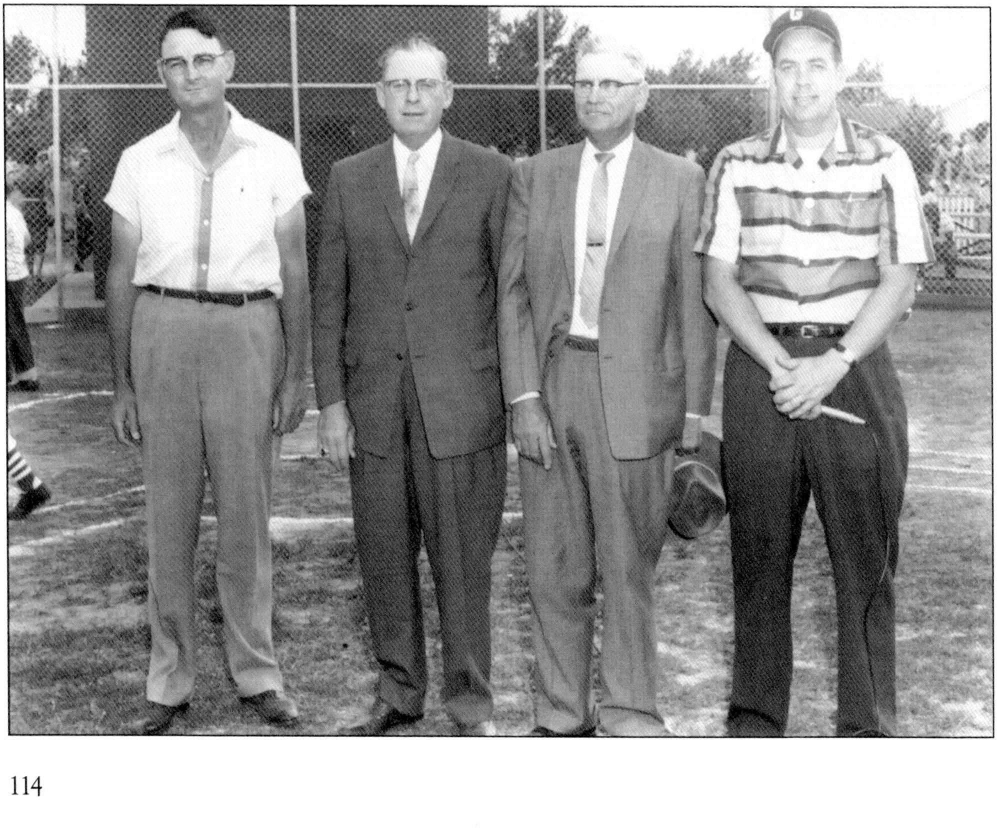

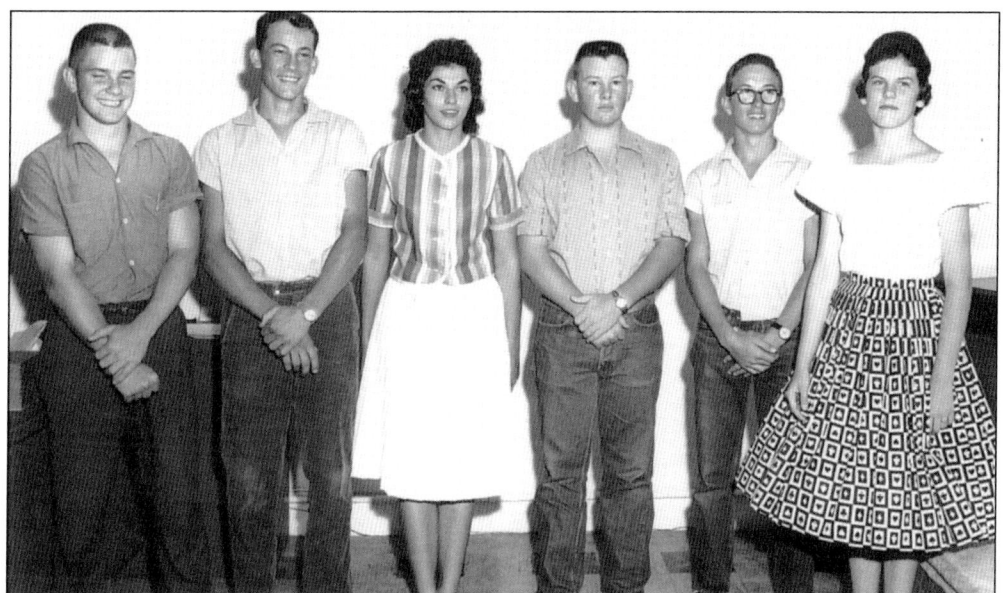

These are the Slaton Tiger Town officers from 1962. From left to right are Steve Ball, Greg Nowlin, Janet Adamek, Don Caldwell, Noel Lee Dickson, and Robin Davis.

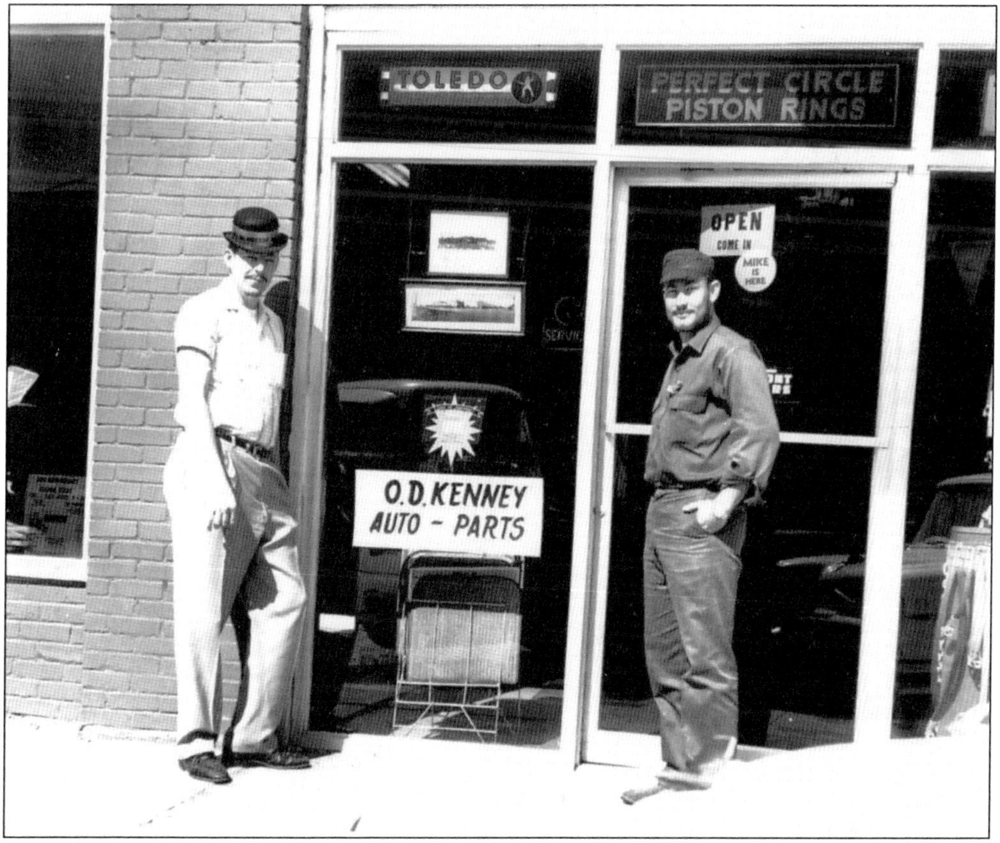

Alton Kenney (left) and Henry Adamer are standing in front of O.D. Kenney Auto Parts.

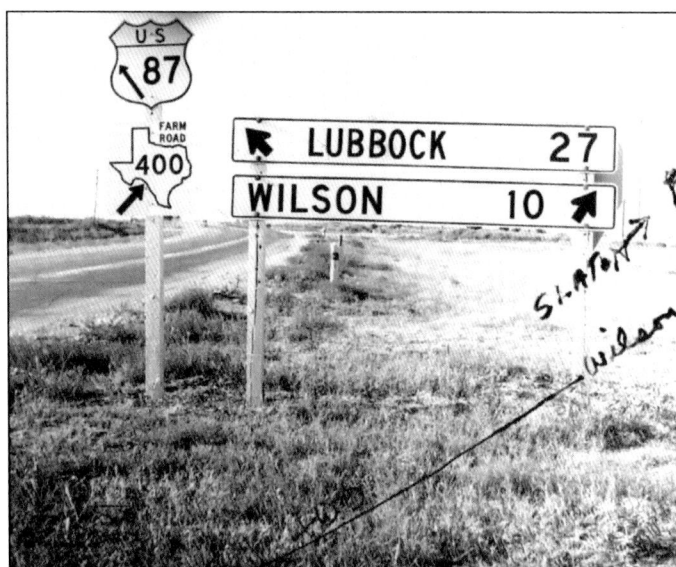

This sign was once located on FM 400 south of Wilson, Texas.

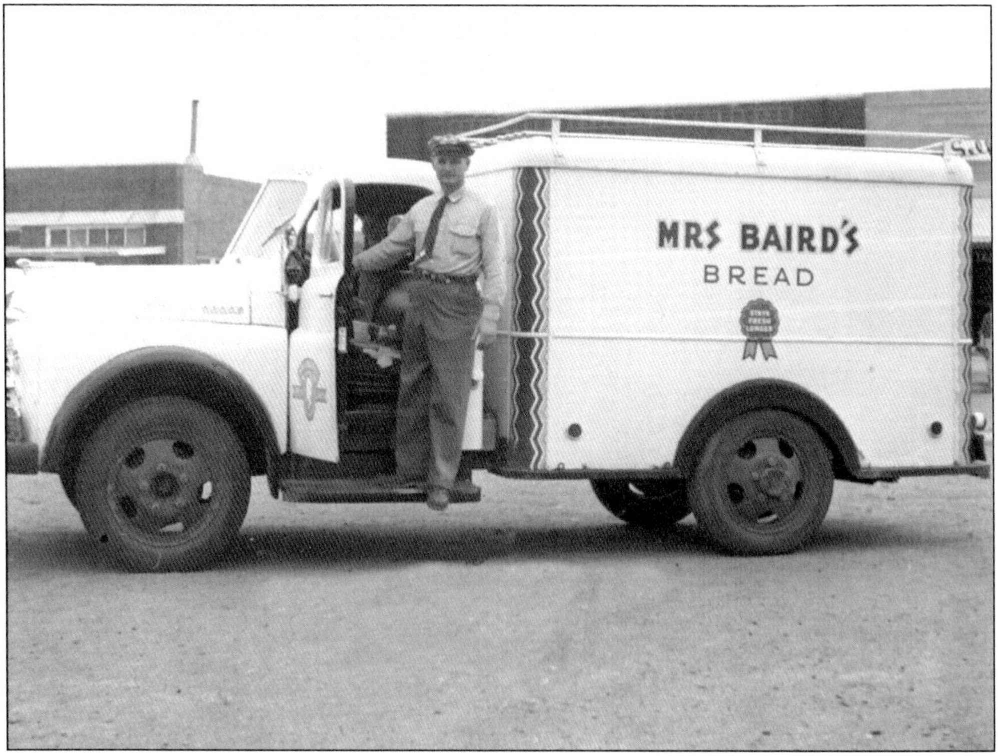

Barney Wilson and the Mrs. Baird's Bread truck are seen here in 1955. Wilson worked for Baldridge Bakery in Lubbock for two years after he moved to Lubbock in 1938. He then moved to Slaton and worked for R.D. Hickman, the owner of Slaton Bakery. Wilson worked there for three years before purchasing the bakery from Hickman in February 1943. At the time, the bakery was located at 145 North Eighth Street, and Wilson and his wife, Ollie Mae, worked together to operate the bakery until 1973, when they leased it to their youngest son, Sherrell, who still owns and operates Slaton Bakery at 109 South Ninth Street.

Seven
SLATON, 104 YEARS STRONG

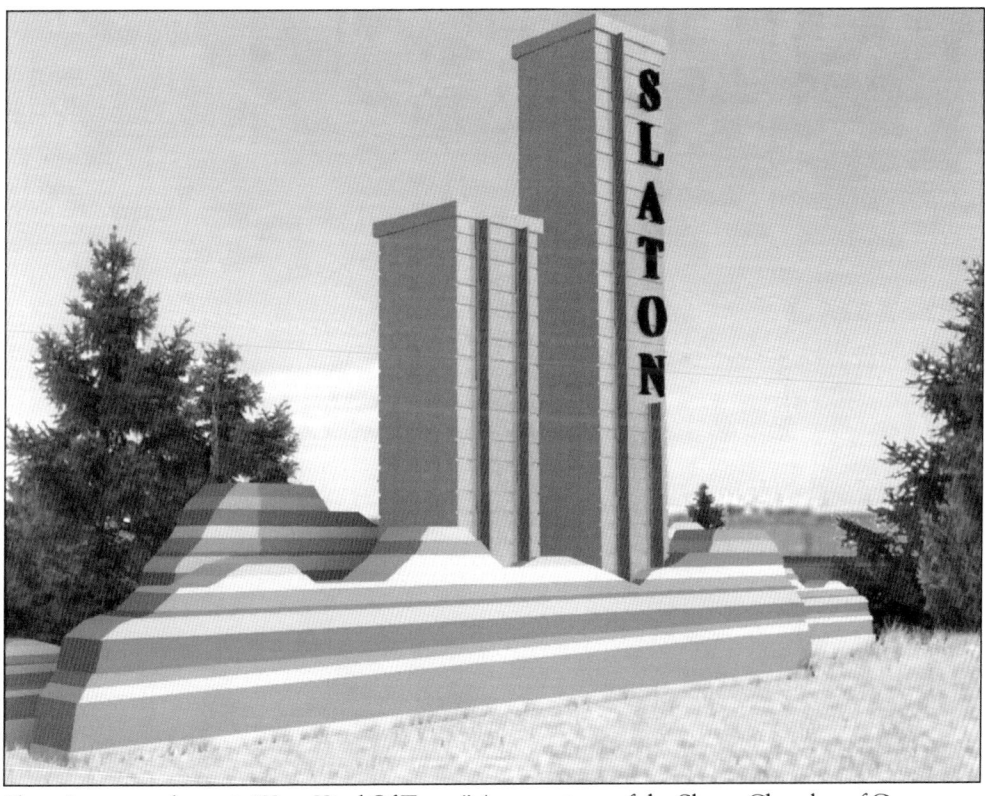

Slaton's current slogan is "Your Kind Of Town." A committee of the Slaton Chamber of Commerce is currently working to erect landmarks to welcome people to the area; an artist's rendering is pictured here. The first one will be located in the triangle between US 84 and US Business 84 at the west entrance of town. The second is planned to be on US 84 at the east entrance of town. Over the years, Slaton has grown thanks to the Santa Fe Railway, agriculture, and local business. With its strong school system, it is a great place to raise a family. Local attractions include the Historic Harvey House Museum and Bed and Breakfast (400 Industrial Drive), Slaton Model Railroad Studio (166 South Eighth Street), Slaton Museum (115 W. Lubbock Street), Steam Engine No. 1809 (located on the town square), and the Texas Air Museum (on FM 400, two miles north of Slaton). (Courtesy of the Slaton Chamber of Commerce.)

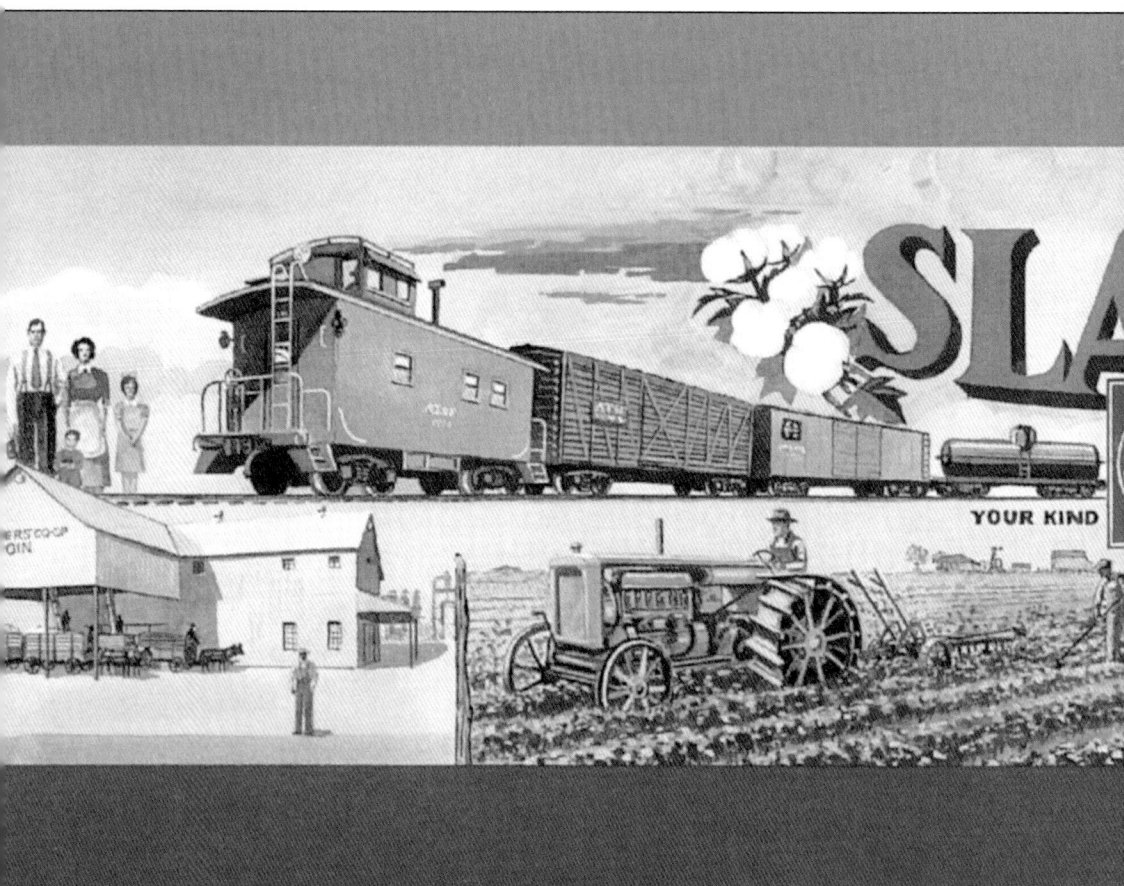

This is the Slaton Heritage Mural, which is located on the corner of Ninth and Garza Streets. The large mural was designed by Bill "Tex" Wilson and captures the heritage of the town. Wilson grew up in Slaton and is a nationally renowned artist. His work features railroaders and cowboys

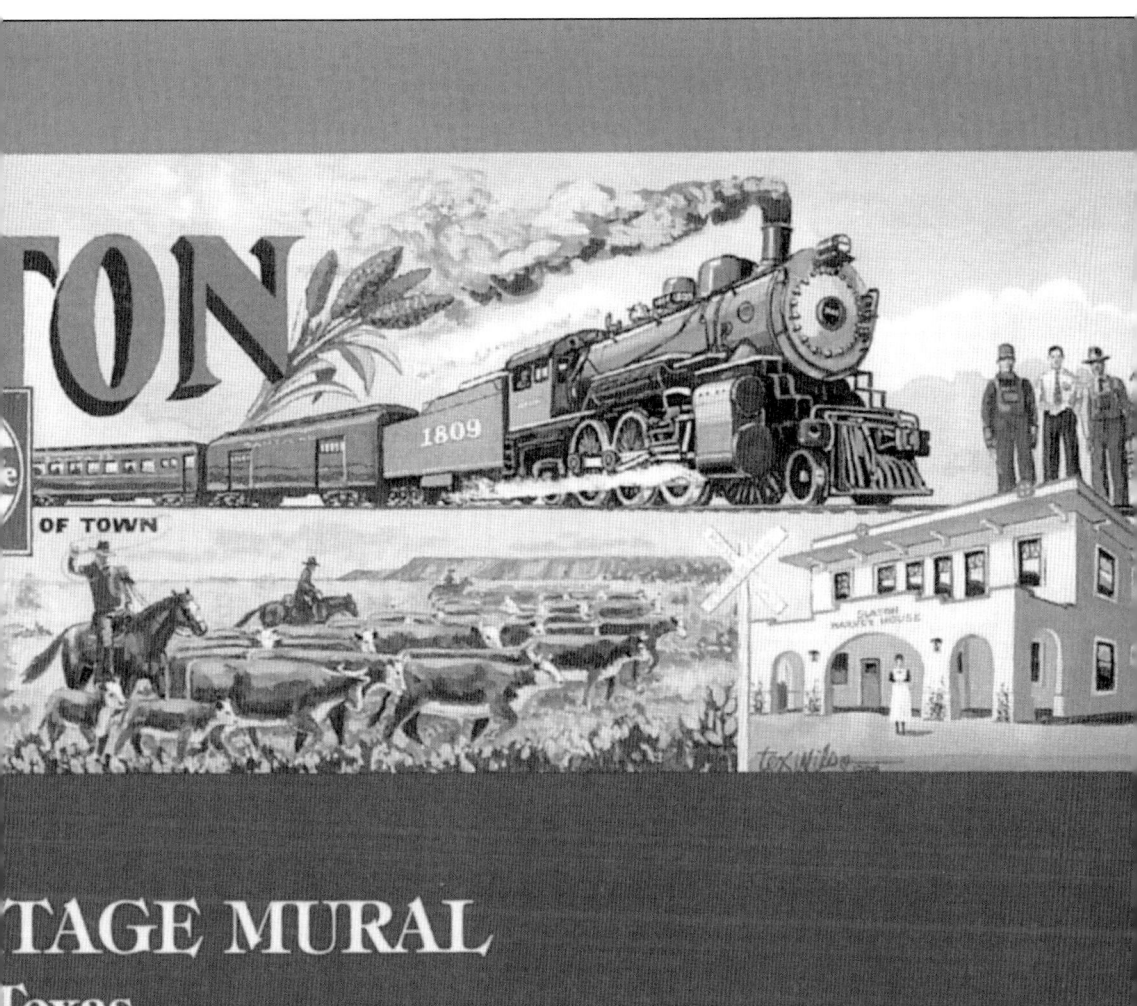

of the Old West. This print is available for purchase at the Slaton Chamber of Commerce or the office of *The Slatonite* newspaper. (Courtesy of the Slaton Museum.)

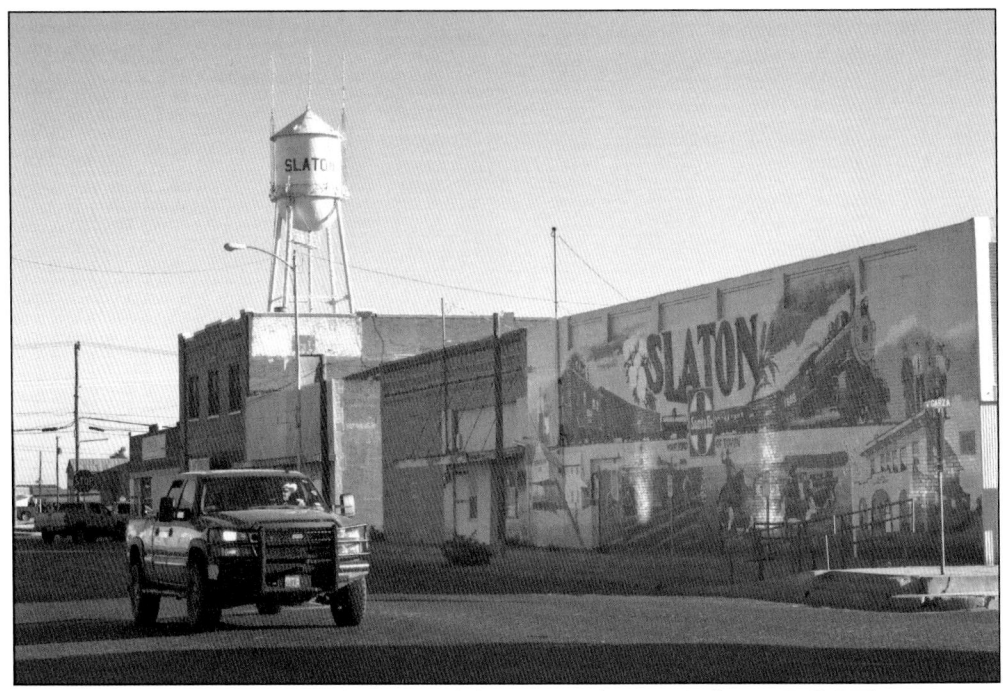

Here is a recent picture of the Slaton mural. (Courtesy of Kevin Stillman, TxDOT.)

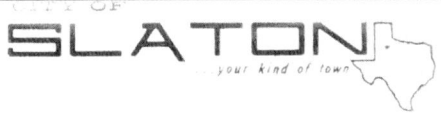

KSSL had a one-year anniversary celebration in 2012, and Mayor D.W. Englund presented this Proclamation of Appreciation to the Slaton radio station. (Courtesy of KSSL Radio.)

The Slatonite is still in print, offering a weekly newspaper that comes out every Thursday. The paper is currently owned by Ken Richardson.

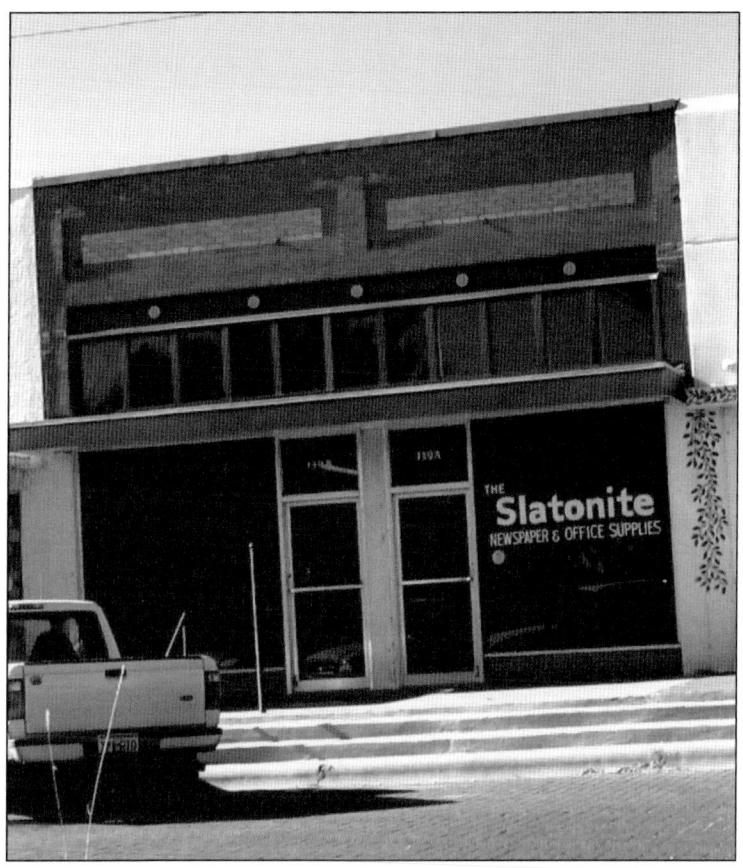

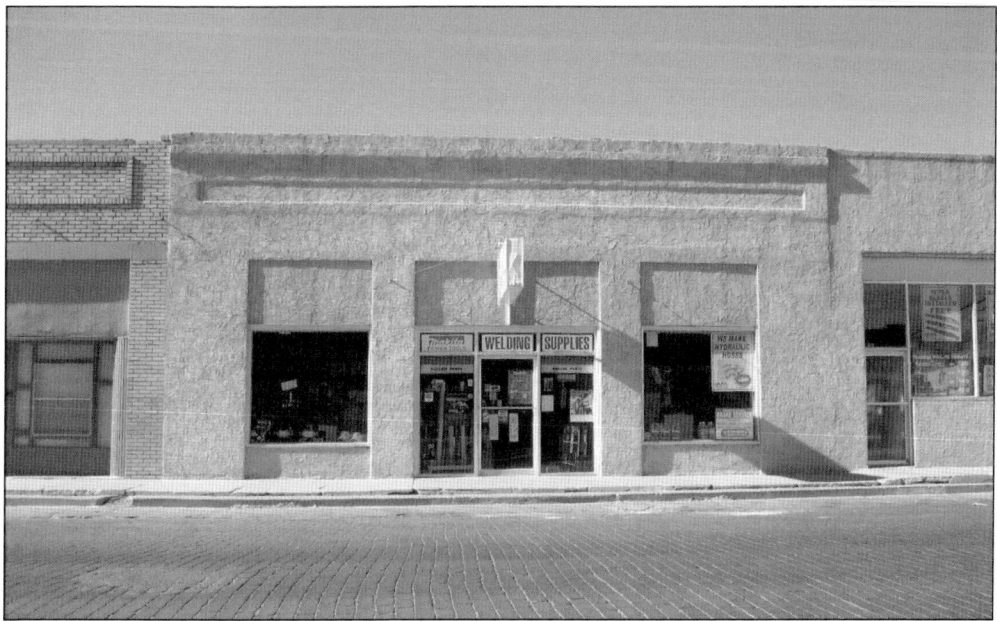

O.D. Kenney Auto Parts has been family- and locally-owned since 1929, and the store is still in business today.

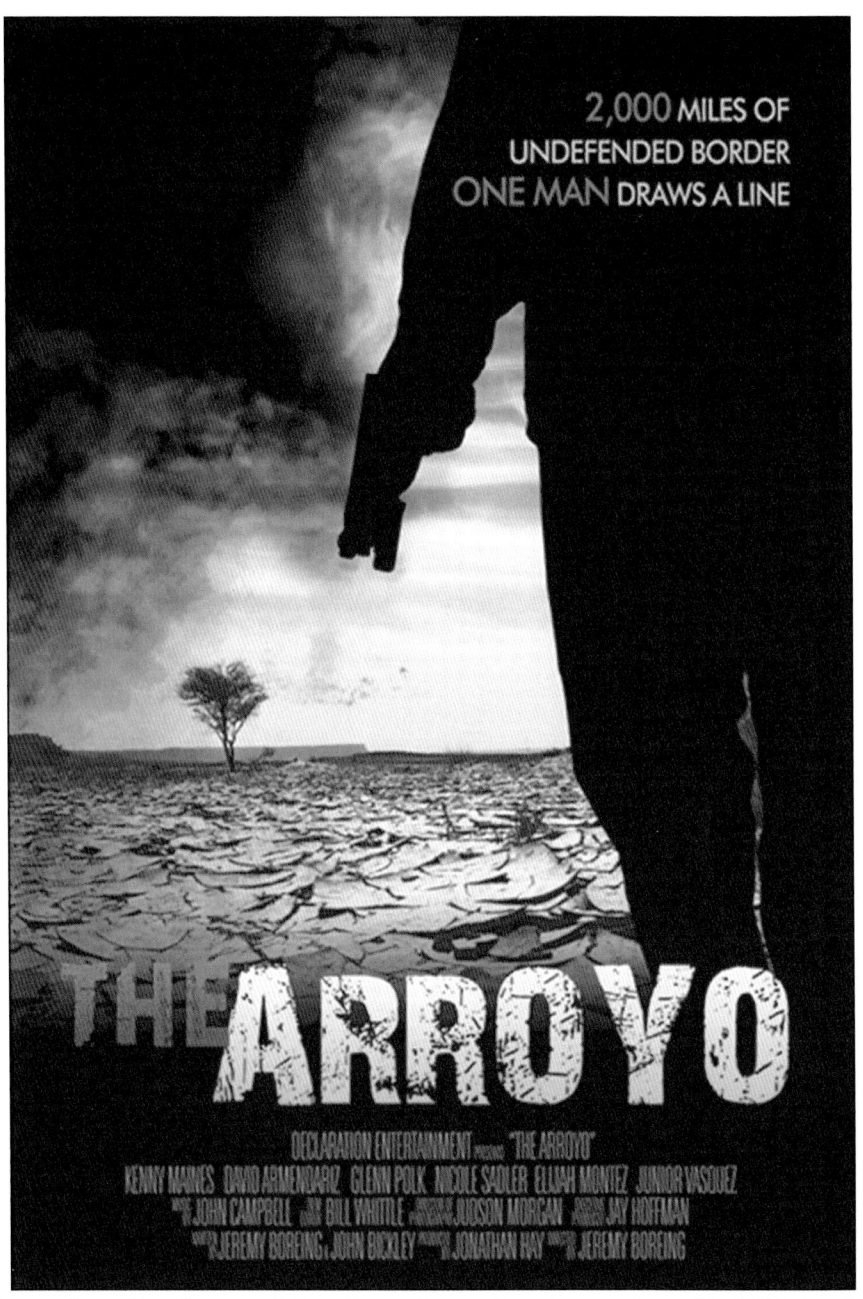

The Arroyo, filmed in Slaton and Post, is a major motion picture released in 2014 that featured many local people. The movie is set 40 miles north of the border on a ranch in the pathway of the drug cartel. Though the ranch owner, Jim Weatherford, has asked for help from the government for protection of his land, he receives none, so he decides to take a stand for his family and freedom. The Arroyo was cowritten and directed by Jeremy Boreing, who was born in Slaton on February 5, 1979, and began his career at the Garza Theatre in Post as a writer and producer. In 2010, he formed an independent film studio, Declaration Entertainment. Some locals cast in the movie include Kenny Maines, Junior Vasquez, Glen Polk, Nicole Sadler, Elijah Montez, Jane Prince Jones, Christy Morris, and Tim Ybarra. (Courtesy of Junior Vasquez and Jeremy Boreing.)

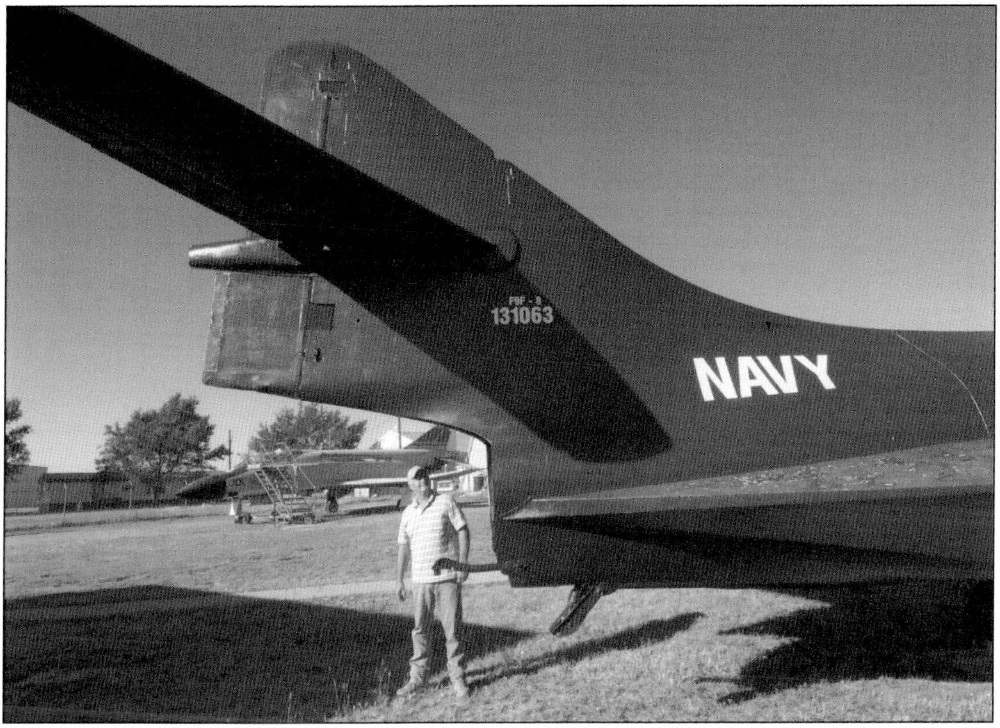

The Texas Air Museum is located on FM 400, two miles north of Slaton. It displays indoor and outdoor exhibits including aircraft, equipment, uniforms, and more from World Wars I and II, the Korean War, and the Vietnam War. (Courtesy of Kevin Stillman, TxDOT.)

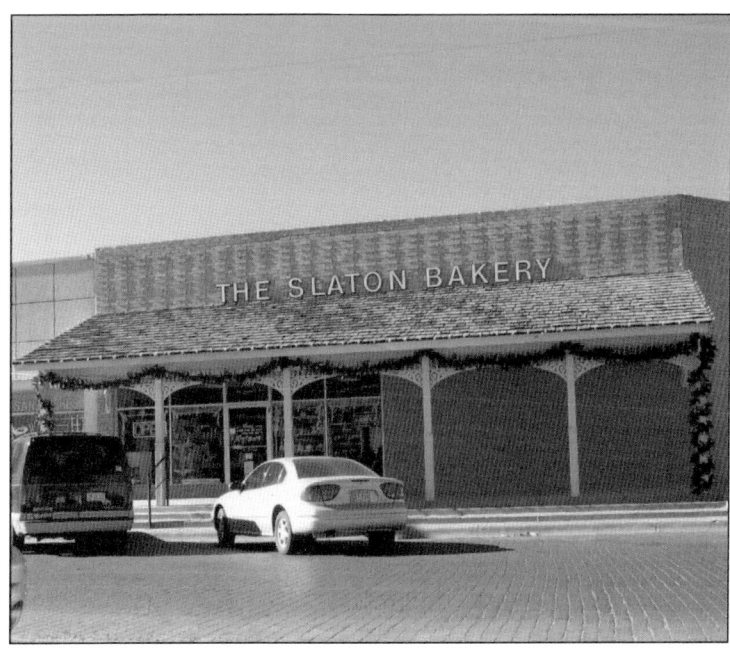

This is a recent photograph of the Slaton Bakery, which has been in business since 1921. The Wilson family has owned it since 1943, and moved the bakery to its current location at 109 S. Ninth Street in 1982. It is now a community institution and one of the oldest operating bakeries in Texas. The bakery even has a historical marker that was erected in 2009. (Courtesy of Kevin Stillman, TxDOT.)

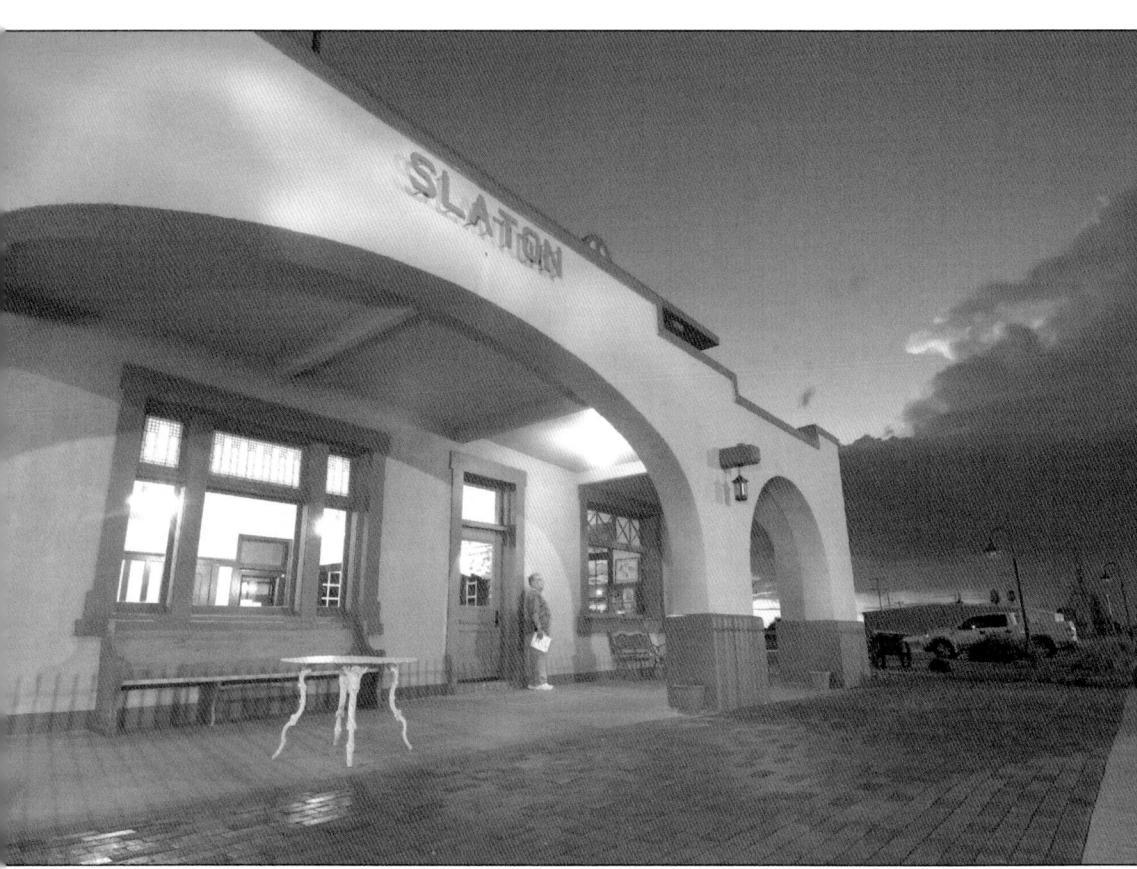

This is a recent photograph of the Harvey House, which received a $40,000 grant from the Helen Jones Foundations and CH Foundation to remodel a Grand Suite on the south side of the building on the first floor. The suite was formerly the baggage and freight room at the depot. The new room will feature a larger area for guests and a full bath with luxurious furnishings. (Courtesy of Kevin Stillman, TxDOT.)

HISTORIC BED & BREAKFAST - EVENT CENTER

Come experience life in the Harvey House as it was in the 1920's.

...joy a beautifully restored building, listen to the trains rumble by, and enjoy sleeping where the Harvey Girls s...

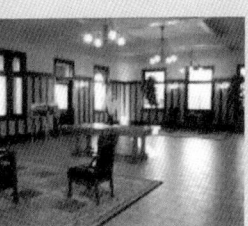

The Harvey House is a "Gem of the South Plains," a place where every event becomes a memorable ...asion. It serves as a historic Bed & Breakfast, ...nt Center, and designated historic landmark ...he State of Texas. Located at the intersection ...ailroad Ave. and Texas Ave., visitors will ...vel at the elegant dining room, and learn the ...ory from ...inal ...tographs ...artifacts ...n the ...den age ...ailroads. ...ouse ...ning, ...catering is available. Book now for reunions, ...ddings, meetings, parties, civic and social ...nts!

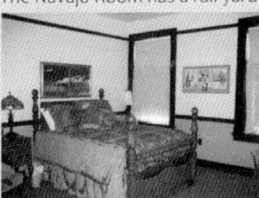

The Navajo Room has a rail-yard view and assigned hallway bathroom. It was furnished and decorated by the Privett Family, in memory of George W. Privett-Slaton Railway Conductor 1942-1976. The furnishings were originally owned by the Garland Family and Eblen Family. This room was Slaton Harvey Girl Rose Farschon's room.

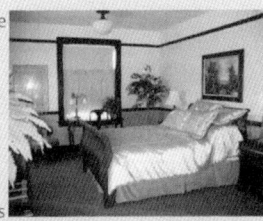

The Apache Room has a queen sleigh bed and an extra large handicap accessible bath. It has a rail yard and downtown Slaton view. It was furnished and decorated by The Consignment Gallery of Lubbock.

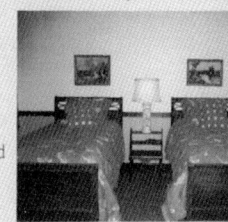

The Hopi Room has a rail-yard view an... assigned hallway bath. It was furnished and decorated by The Pember Family in memory of Slaton Pioneers, Merritt an... Pember and Bruce and Maurine Pembe...

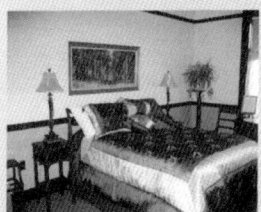

The Z... Room sleep... three... a dou... and t... size b... Two dress... areas, a small refrigerator, and a large handicap equipped bathroom makes it family room. It also has a rail-yard view. furnished and decorated by The Atheni... Study Club and the O.D. McClintock Far...

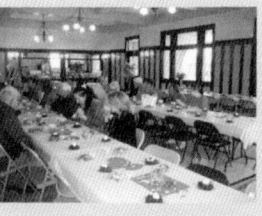

We have accommodations for additional beds for children upon request. Slaton Harvey House guests are treated to a full hot breakfast by gracious hosts who can inform you about the history of Slaton, the Santa Fe Railroad, and places of interest to visit throughout the region. Guests also have access to a comfortable upstairs sitting room with television, and are welcome to browse the downstairs museum or enjoy the afternoons under a covered patio just forty feet from the active train yard.
Our B&B is historically appointed and is suitable for all travelers, including those who need wheelchair accessibility.

This is a Harvey House brochure. Tours of the space are available by appointment. The Harvey House is located at 400 Railroad Avenue. Their brochure states: "Keeping the history of the Santa Fe Railway and the Harvey Girls alive." (Courtesy of the Harvey House and the Slaton Railroad Heritage Association.)

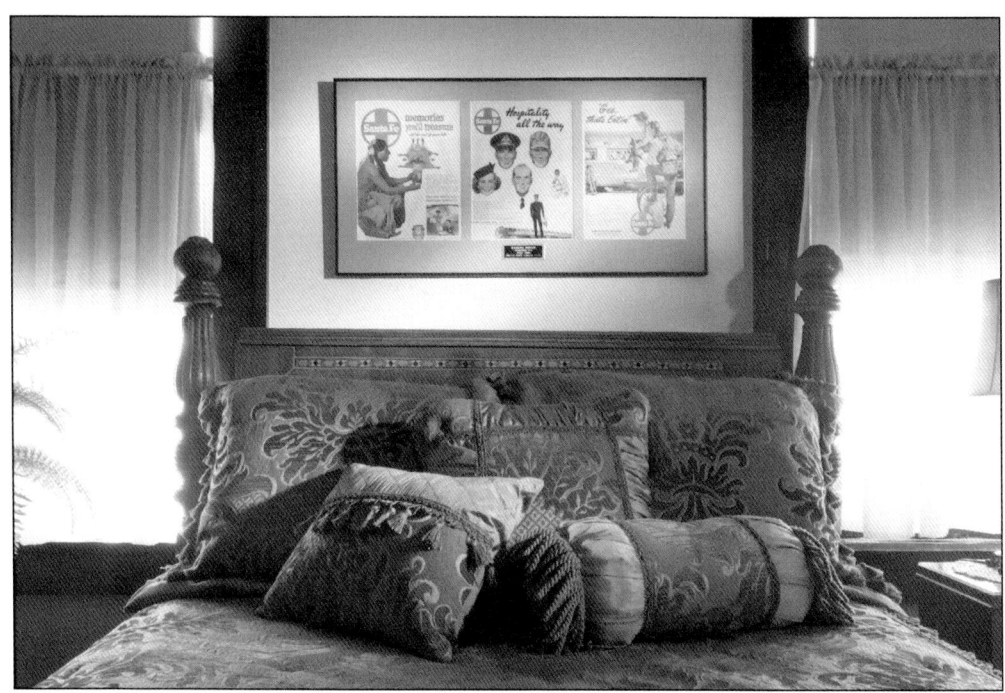

This is the "Navajo Room," one of the current rooms in the Harvey House. It was decorated by the Privett family in memory of George W. Privett, who worked as a Slaton railway conductor from 1942 to 1976. This room was once inhabited by Slaton Harvey Girl Rose Farschon. (Courtesy of Kevin Stillman, TxDOT.)

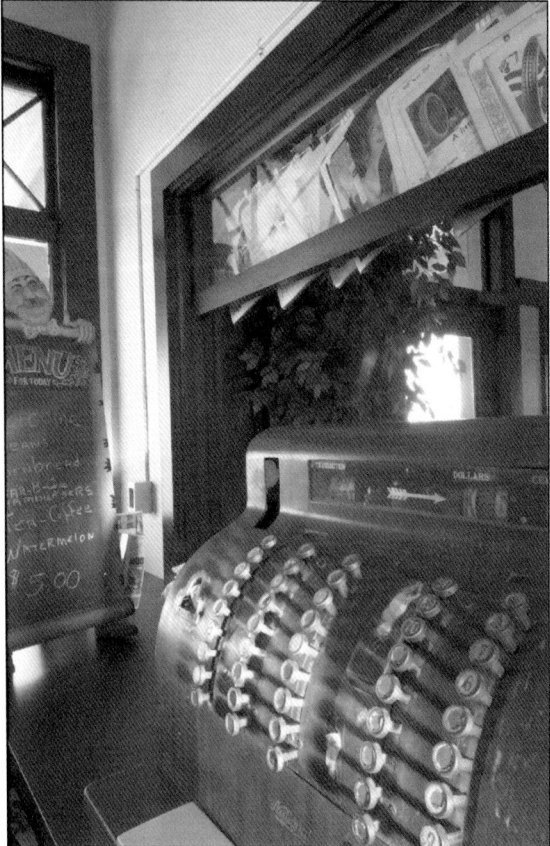

This antique cash register is on display at the Slaton Harvey House. (Courtesy of Kevin Stillman, TxDOT.)

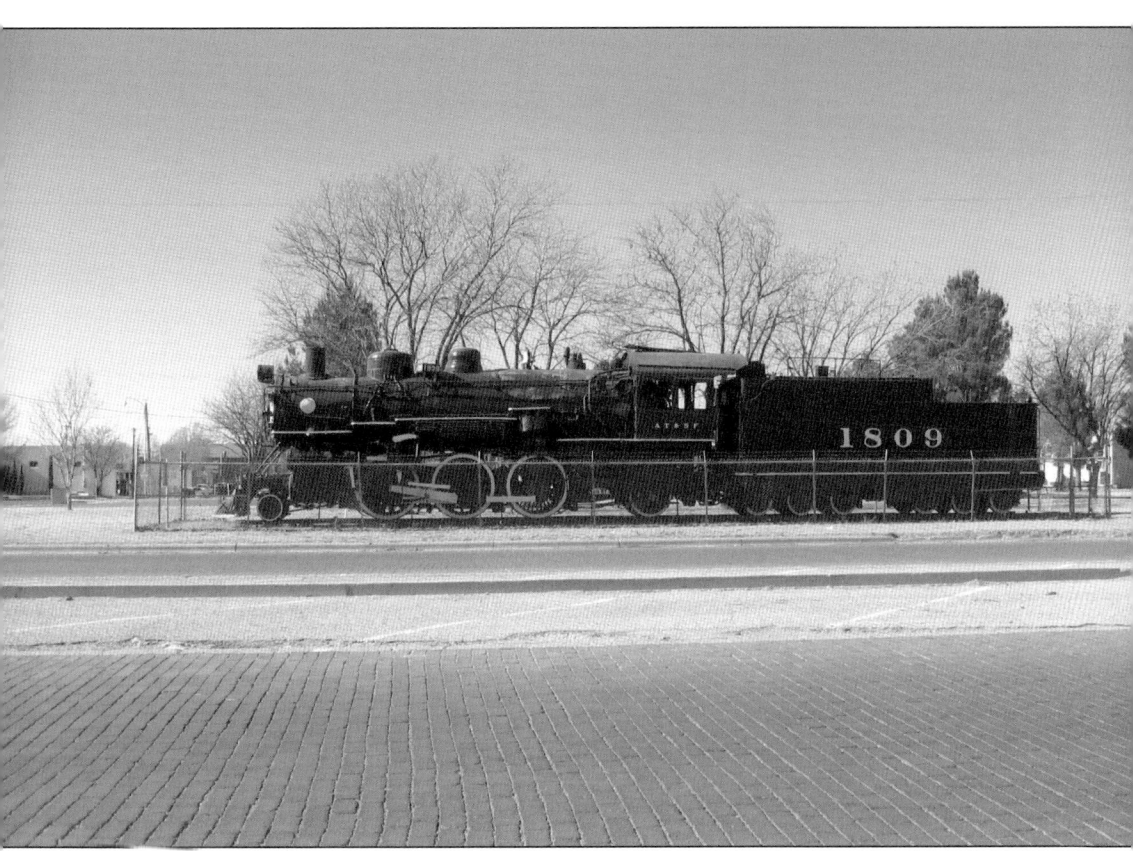

On September 17, 1955, the Santa Fe Railway officially retired the steam-powered Engine No. 1809 and dedicated it to the City of Slaton. At that time, the major was L.B. Wooten, and special recognition was given to retired engineers of Engine No. 1809, including W.R. Lovett, Walter Cannon, Jack Steward, and Louis Smith. Melvin Kunkel, then president of the Slaton Chamber of Commerce, noted the role this engine had on Slaton's agricultural economy, including the run to Houston known as the "Cotton Special" because of cotton deliveries from the Slaton area to Gulf of Mexico ports. Engine No. 1809 was built in 1906 by Baldwin Locomotive Works. Though the State of Texas Historical Society has offered to purchase the engine, Slaton has no intention of ever parting with it, and it remains on display in downtown Slaton. It inspires many fond memories of the town the Santa Fe Railway built.

DISCOVER THOUSANDS OF LOCAL HISTORY BOOKS FEATURING MILLIONS OF VINTAGE IMAGES

Arcadia Publishing, the leading local history publisher in the United States, is committed to making history accessible and meaningful through publishing books that celebrate and preserve the heritage of America's people and places.

Find more books like this at
www.arcadiapublishing.com

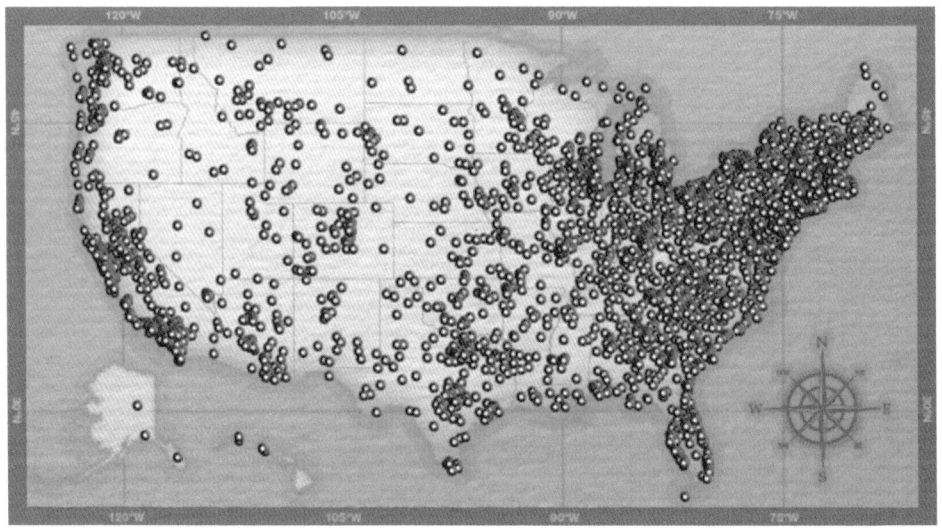

Search for your hometown history, your old stomping grounds, and even your favorite sports team.

Consistent with our mission to preserve history on a local level, this book was printed in South Carolina on American-made paper and manufactured entirely in the United States. Products carrying the accredited Forest Stewardship Council (FSC) label are printed on 100 percent FSC-certified paper.

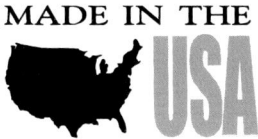